Center for Basque Studies
Basque Originals, no. 1

Robert Laxalt

The Story of a Storyteller

Warren Lerude

Center for Basque Studies
University of Nevada, Reno
Reno, Nevada

This book was published with generous financial support from the Basque Goverment.

Photos: unless another source is given, all photos are from the Laxalt Family Collection, Special Collections, University of Nevada, Reno, Libraries.

Center for Basque Studies
University of Nevada, Reno
Reno, Nevada 89557
http://basque.unr.edu

Cover and series design © 2013 by Jose Luis Agote.
Cover photo: Robert Laxalt by Bill Belknap, photo courtesy of Loie Belknap Evans.

Library of Congress Cataloging-in-Publication Data

Lerude, Warren, 1937-
Robert Laxalt : the story of a storyteller / Warren Lerude.
    pages cm. -- (Basque Originals ; no. 1)
Includes bibliographical references and index.
Summary: "Biography of the Nevada writer Robert Laxalt that focuses on his writing career from journalist to acclaimed author, founder of the University of Nevada Press, and educator"--Provided by publisher.
 ISBN 978-1-935709-36-7 (pbk.) -- ISBN 978-1-935709-37-4 (cloth) 1. Laxalt, Robert, 1923-2001. 2. Authors, American--20th century--Biography. 3. Basque Americans--Biography. I. Title.

PS3562.A9525Z74 2013
813'.54--dc23

[B]
                               2013010245

Contents

6   *Contents*

Foreword

The trifecta of important Nevada literary figures is Mark Twain, Walter Van Tilburg Clark, and Robert Laxalt. None was born in this state, although Laxalt spent most of his life here. The work of all three had regional, national, and international resonance. Twain's *Roughing It* is arguably the most insightful (and certainly the most humorous) treatment of life on the western frontier. Clark's *Ox-Bow Incident* and *Track of the Cat* have been deemed by many critics the two most serious western novels, truly canonical works of the genre. Laxalt's *Sweet Promised Land* made him the beloved literary spokesman of a whole (unheralded) people whose saga is portrayed trenchantly through the life story of a single Basque sheepherder and his family.

I can think of no more appropriate publication for the Center for Basque Studies than the present one—*Robert Laxalt: The Story of a Storyteller* by Warren Lerude. If not the Center's genitor, Laxalt was certainly one of its stepfathers—a key figure in its founding. I sometimes think of Bob, Jon Bilbao, and myself as the three Magi each bearing his offering at the birth of the Center's predecessor—DRI's Basque Studies Program (1967).

It is also true that each of the two contemporaries and intimate friends within the Nevada literary trifecta, Clark and Laxalt, attempted to transcend his narrower stereotype by addressing a universal audience. Both struggled with being labeled (and thereby diminished) as regional (western) writers—their respective replies being *The City of Trembling Leaves* and *A Man in the Wheatfield*. To my mind, each represents an author's attempt to produce the elusive Great American Novel. In Bob's case there was the added weight of being pigeon-holed as an ethnic writer.

Robert Laxalt's literary production speaks for itself and requires no defense. It has earned the plaudits of a whole generation of critics—including a book-length treatment by Basque literary historian David Río. In a very real sense critical treatment of Robert-Laxalt-the-writer has been done. However, there is another dimension to Bob's work and legacy, namely his background in journalism and how that affected his transition to writer of serious fiction and essays. It is less known and appreciated. Laxalt's early years as a reporter, and particularly the types of stories that he covered, clearly did much to configure his subsequent literary interests and persona. While I worked closely with him for many years, even editing his first drafts, I did not realize fully until reading Lerude's book just how important those reporter years were in Bob's formation. I learned much about him, indeed much more than I anticipated.

Given Warren Lerude's own outstanding credentials in journalism, not to mention his close ties with Bob and the Laxalt family, I can imagine no better author to expose us to this side of Robert Laxalt's complex literary persona and extensive oeuvre. It is precisely through the quotes from Bob's press stories and early popular magazine articles that we learn about the reporter and aspiring writer. Lerude's perspective is clearly implicit in his selection and organization of the quotes from a vast corpus of material. Similarly, in constructing Laxalt's biography, Lerude has made extensive masterful use of Bob's own trilogy—but without the detraction and distraction of excessive scholarly trappings and pedantry. In short, Lerude tells the storyteller's story in refreshing fashion and thereby sheds light into the less illumined corners of writer Laxalt's personal and career sagas. Therein lies the originality of the current text.

—William A. Douglass
Reno, Nevada, January 2013

Acknowledgments

The research, writing, editing, and publishing of a book such as *Robert Laxalt: The Story of a Storyteller* is a curious combination of solitary effort by a writer and, conversely, the spirited camaraderie of teams of sources, archival analysts, production specialists, and, most importantly, the family and friends and, sometimes, critics of the subject of the story, in this case those who were closest to Bob Laxalt and the many challenging moments of his complex life.

The odyssey of this book began with an idea in the reflective mind of my long-time friend and colleague Bruce Bledsoe, who has distinguished himself through decades of thoughtful work as both a Reno newspaper and Nevada Humanities writer and editor. It occurred to Bruce that while Bob wrote seventeen books during his career there was no actual biography of Nevada's most acclaimed writer of the modern era.

"Why don't you write it?" he asked me over dinner one evening four years ago. "Why me?" I responded. "Because you knew Bob best and, if not you, then who?"

With that nudging I turned to the prime sources for any book about Bob, his wife of fifty-two years, Joyce, and their daughters, Monique, an attorney and novelist, and Kristin, a physician. They embraced the idea with enthusiasm and that led to many dedicated people with whom I have spent these four years researching, writing, editing and, finally, publishing.

I would like to acknowledge them as follows:

The Editorial Board of the Center for Basque Studies, affiliated with the University of Nevada, Reno (UNR) College of Liberal Arts, for deciding to publish this book. I credit the Center's founder, Professor Emeritus William A. Douglass, for seeing merit in the manuscript and writing a generous and insightful foreword. My thanks go to Professors Joseba Zulaika, Xabier Irujo, Zoe Bray, and Sandy Ott; managing editor Daniel Montero, editorial assistant Kimberly Daggett, and copyeditor Penelope W. Smith.

Thanks, too, for the support of the Center's Liberal Arts Deans Heather Hardy and Scott Casper.

UNR President Emeritus Joe Crowley, attorney/author Monique Laxalt, journalist Bruce Bledsoe, and author/journalist Alan Deutschman for giving invaluable counsel throughout the project. Special thanks go to Bruce for his challenging editing of the manuscript content.

The staff of the UNR Knowledge Center's Archives and Special Collections in my search though the 26.5 cubic feet of Bob's files and material kept in 33 boxes, Donnie Curtis, Jacque Sundstrand, Kim Roberts, Jessica Maddox, and Betty Glass. Thanks, too, for the support of Dean of Libraries Kathy Ray and development director Millie Mitchell.

Members of the Laxalt family, Bob and Joyce's son Bruce and his wife Pam, Bob's brothers Paul, John and Peter (Mickey), sisters Sue and Marie and Marie's son, Robert Bini, and nephew Paul.

Professional writing and editing colleagues Guy Rocha, Professor Emeritus Jim Hulse, Mike Sion, David Río, Sarah Pollock, Nick Cady, Barbara Land, Shawn Griffin, Caroline J. Hadley, Anthony Shafton, Jackson L. Benson, author of *The Ox-Bow Man*, Richard E. Osborne, author of *World War II in Colonial Africa*, Carmelo Urza, author of *Solitude* and Guy Farmer, author of *Gaming Regulation in Nevada: The First Sawyer Administration*.

The reader/referees selected by the University of Nevada Press who provided insightful critical examination of the manuscript.

Associates in politics Ed Allison, Greg Ferraro, Sig Rogich, Tom Loranger, and Jerry Dondero.

Lifelong friends of Bob, Bill Bliss, and Gene Empey, whose photograph graced the original publication of *Sweet Promised Land* in 1957.

Bob's students in literary journalism and magazine writing John Evan Frook, Verita Black Prothro, Chuck Alvey, John Metzker, and Shawn Griffin.

The Robert Laxalt Distinguished Writer Program Honorees William Albert Allard, Paige Williams, Alicia Parlette, Lou Cannon, Clay Jenkinson, James Houston, Isabel Wilkerson, Stephen Bloom, Rebecca Solnit, and Mark Kurlansky.

Reynolds School of Journalism Deans Al Stavitsky, Bill Winter, and Jerry Ceppos, administrators Barbara Trainor, Drew Johnson, Sally Etcheto and Derak Berreyesa, Professors Saundra Keyes, Howard Goldbaum, Jake Highton, David Ryfe, Donica Mensing, Larry

Dailey and his helicopter, Todd Felts, Rosemary McCarthy, Bonnie Scranton, Deidre Pike, Ben Holden, Eric Robinson, Caesar Andrews, Stewart Cheifet, Paul Mitchell and Bob Felten, and special projects editors Zanny Marsh and Melanie Peck and development director Kristin Burgarello.

Finally, as all authors note, and I cannot note it enough, my gratitude to my wife Janet who has endured my search for lost or rambling footnotes in the middle of sleepless nights and celebrated the struggle for the occasionally well-written sentence. There must be a special place in Heaven for the spouses of writers. I gratefully dedicate this book to Janet.

Preface

This is a story of a storyteller, Robert "Bob" Laxalt. This is not the definitive word that one day should be written by a literary historian or master biographer. Rather, this is a story simply about who Bob Laxalt was, his family values, his sense of place in the American West and internationally, and how he came to be a writer and an inspiration for other writers.

He was motivated by his father, Dominique, whom he admired as a heroic man of the great outdoors, particularly the mountains, and by his mother, Thérèse (Theresa), whom he worshiped as a kind and caring woman of fierce principle. Their Basque heritage became an important theme of his life. His writing about it was celebrated not only by the Basques but by immigrant families of varying origins and the general public.

I tell this story as one of the many writers Bob Laxalt influenced. But even more so, it is told by Laxalt himself through his thought processes and the experiences that took him to write seventeen acclaimed books, scores of nationally and internationally published magazine articles, and hundreds of daily newspaper and wire service stories. His own words, through careful attribution, frequently come to life in this story.

Laxalt, who died in 2001 at seventy-seven, left a legacy of evidence about the processes that created and drove his writing life. The UNR Archives and Special Collections at the University of Nevada Knowledge Center contain 26.5 cubic feet of Laxalt's papers spread through thirty-three rectangular boxes.

The papers cover a vast range of his complex and adventurous life, from his birth in the rugged sheep camp and ranch country of northern California to his growing-up years in Nevada's tiny capital, Carson City, to his distinction as one of the American West's finest writers. The collection is a treasury filled with his personal correspondence, early drafts and final manuscripts of his magazine journalism and literary books, his global travel adventures, and his home life contradictions from revered quietude to robust, competitive family camaraderie. I have focused on matters that shaped his life as a writer rather than pursuing a fuller saga of the entire Laxalt family's many diverse activities.

I have purposely included detailed examples from his early *Saturday Evening Post* and *National Geographic* stories to illustrate how he successfully ventured into major-league national publishing. Conversely, I have not used extraordinary detail in a chapter about an important trilogy on his family experiences because I drew from those books material that unfolds throughout the narrative and I did not want to burden the reader with repetition.

For me, going through the Laxalt papers was a journey into how much I knew—and how much I didn't know—about this friend of more than fifty years. Bob Laxalt's spirit came to life in the mesmerizing research.

This story is also told through the eyes of the people whose lives Laxalt touched, his family, his fellow writers and publishing colleagues, and the students who trusted him as counselor in the formative years of their own writing.

Finally, the story is a remembrance of Laxalt as a slyly good-humored and sometimes painfully sensitive companion through decades of writing, editing, teaching, and traveling—from sailing the windy waters of Lake Tahoe, to walking the hilly streets of San Francisco, to standing in awe and respect amid the towering peaks of the Sierra Nevada and the Pyrenees.

—Warren Lerude
Reynolds School of Journalism
University of Nevada, Reno
Reno, Nevada, May 2013

The Writer

Robert Laxalt stared at the blank piece of paper in the Royal typewriter. He wrote a sentence, pulled the paper from the Royal and read it carefully. With both hands, he crumpled the paper into a ball, and then he threw it into the wastebasket. The words weren't right. They weren't good enough.

He knew he could write. After all, his byline was well established in the intense United Press (UP) wire service newsroom in the old Gazette Building at 133 North Center Street a block away from the snow-fed Truckee River in downtown Reno, Nevada.

But could he write a book about his own father? And, ethically, should he write such a book even if he could? Their immigrant Basque family life was very personal. Would he invade his father's privacy? He just didn't know. He couldn't figure it out, the writing or the ethics.

Bob Laxalt had professionally covered his share of the news in the 1950s: A bloody, gangland-assassination attempt by close range shotgun in the silk-stocking neighborhood of wealthy Southwest Reno. The trauma of watching men die in the ghostly gray-green gas chamber of the ancient, foreboding Nevada State Prison beneath its dark stone gun towers in America's smallest capital, Carson City.

As a UP reporter, competitive with the rival Associated Press (AP), Laxalt's deadline journalistic prose had raced through Nevada newspaper and radio newsrooms and across the country and around the world at the teletype monotone clatter of sixty-six words a minute.

He loved writing even though the constant demands of daily journalism left him so exhausted he rarely could turn to more literary work. He was a perfectionist even when facing fierce news deadlines. Despite being pushed constantly for time against the racing clock, he carefully chose his words to properly write true and dramatic stories for his readers. He was caught up in the immediacy of the pressure-filled newsrooms of the competitive *Reno Evening Gazette* and morning *Nevada State Journal* staffs and the excited camaraderie of the cramped, windowless UP and AP bureaus with their desks overflowing in marked up newspaper pages, reference books strewn about amid story clips and photos from days, weeks, months, even years of news-gathering work.

As much as he loved writing stories, he was passionate about reading stories. As a child in Carson City, struck with a serious case of rheumatic fever that kept him bedridden for months, he turned to books that family and friends brought to him from the Nevada State Library. He wrote, many years later, in an essay entitled "The Library and I," about how he discovered the action worlds of such figures as Tarzan of the Apes.

"My memory fails me when I try to recall who first told me about the library and Tarzan. But once bitten, whole new worlds opened up for me."

The discovery of literature caused him to want to tell the deeper stories that lay beyond the fiercely paced minute-by-minute work of journalism.

One particular story wove its way through his reportorial and increasingly creative mind. It was the story of his own life as the son of Basque immigrants, that of his innkeeper mother Theresa and his sheepherder father Dominique. Dominique had talked many times, even yearned, to return to his roots in the Pyrenees mountains and grassy meadows of the Basque Country of France. The challenge was to write about the trip he had taken there with his father.

As a wire service writer whose stories reached beyond the local journalism of Reno and Carson City and Nevada's other towns and cities, he thought of storytelling in national and international terms.

But where to place such a story? As a journalist comfortable with news stories and magazine articles, he thought first about the *Saturday Evening Post*. He had broken into the magazine field with an earlier in piece in the *Post* about Nevada's legal gambling. But the consistent work of major magazines was dominated in New York City by established journalists and authors, novelists and biographers, poets, and essayists. They were the writers in and of the sophisticated metropolitan East, and even the historic literary South, but he was, despite his UP work, a journalist in the small town West.

Unsure, Laxalt turned to a *Post* editor with his thoughts about a magazine story, how poignant it could be seeing his father, this son of Europe, returning to the old country after years of sheepherding in the hills and peaks of the Sierra Nevada. It also could be a story of discovery about Laxalt himself as he learned more about who he really was, what truly mattered to him and why.

The editor questioned him. She probed his thinking. The story of Dominique could be a book, she told him. The story was bigger, fuller than a magazine piece could be. The story needed to be done at length in the emotional detail of the Basque immigrant's return to his homeland and the new understanding by the immigrant's son of their shared heritage.

But there was a problem. Laxalt had never written a book and he wasn't sure how to write one.

The year was 1954. Laxalt was thirty-one years old.

He had the material, a lifetime of it, from seeing his sheepherder father at work in the heavily forested, massive mountains that loomed above his boyhood home in Carson City.

He had closely watched, even studied with some awe, Dominique on foot and horseback, with his sheep dogs and, of course, with the sheep, around smoky campfires on hushed evenings beneath bright stars, on wind-whipped ridges in winter's driving rain and snow and summer's glaring sunshine.

Laxalt had seen his father, still lean and strong in his late sixties, take the long-planned and problematic trip to the land of his birth. The journey was problematic because Dominique really didn't want to make the trip he had so often talked about. He really wanted to remain at home in the new country he had adopted, America, where he had now lived for nearly half a century.

The journey was equally problematic because the son who would escort the father to his homeland had to figure out how get him to accept and wear a new suit. Dominique had only owned one suit in his life, the one he had been married in and then hung in a closet and never wore again in favor of the hardy blue denims and warm woolen shirts of the sheepherder.

The figuring was complicated. Laxalt knew that Dominique clearly remembered how it had taken him weeks, so many decades before, to travel by ship from France to New York and then many more days by train across the expanse of America to Nevada. Now, the son had to convince the father to take his first airplane rides from Reno to San Francisco and then to New York and on to France and finally, all in mere days, to the Basque Country to see his long-ago relatives.

Arriving there, and getting reacquainted with the lives of those who had remained behind when he had left as a teenager, the old sheepherder had made a discovery about his long cherished homeland. The sweet promised land of his many dreams was not, in fact, the Basque Country of his birth but, instead, was the America of his new life.

This was the book Laxalt could not decide how to write. He didn't know if it should be a novel or a memoir and he couldn't determine his own role in the storytelling. Should he be an interpreter of his father's emotions? Or should he be a first-person participant in the story? He thought it through and decided it was a true story, not fiction. He would have to write it as it happened.

He put another clean sheet of paper into the Royal typewriter there in the warm and comfortable knotty-pine basement room where he worked at an old rolltop desk in the family home on Cardinal Way in Southwest Reno. He wrote sentence after sentence and rejected them all. He continued to stare at the typewriter and more blank paper. He typed a few more words and examined them and filled the wastebasket near his desk with his lack of satisfaction. He wrote more words, carefully, again and again.

His wife Joyce, an experienced teacher of the complexities of both the English and French languages, was acutely sensitive as she watched him struggle with the words day after day. She knew he had to get them right and that they simply were not coming to him. He couldn't keep going unless he was satisfied. Frustrated, he tried one more time, wondering if he might continue to fail, hoping that he would not.

Then he wrote: "My father was a sheepherder, and his home was the hills."

That simple but eloquent prose unlocked the creative process and the book flowed.

Sentence after sentence.

> So it began when he was a boy in the misted Pyrenees of France, and so it was to be for most of his lifetime in the lonely Sierra of Nevada. And seeing him in a moment's pause on some high ridge, with the wind tearing at his wild thickness of iron-gray hair and flattening his clothes to his lean frame, you could understand why this was meant to be.

Paragraph after paragraph.

> My mother used to say a man like that should never get married, because he didn't go with a house. And in her own way, I think she was

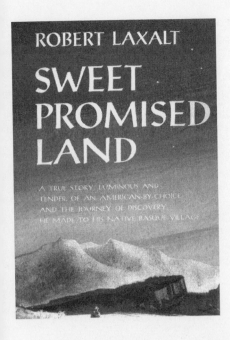

The original cover of Robert Laxalt's iconic *Sweet Promised Land*.

right, because I could remember thinking it and knowing it too when I saw him bent over a campfire at night, with the light playing against the deep bronze of his features and making dark hollows of his eyes, and with its own humor, etching more strongly a nose a little off kilter from where he'd been kicked in the face during his horse breaking days.

Harper and Row published *Sweet Promised Land* in the autumn of 1957. The book quickly became an international classic and a voice for many immigrants to America. Joyously, for the Basques both in America and in the provinces of France and Spain, *Sweet Promised Land* became a celebration of their roots, their spirit, and their lives.

A black-and-white photograph, taken by his University of Nevada journalistic colleague and friend Gene Empey, illustrated the back cover. Laxalt's dark eyes, known by family and friends to twinkle in moments of merriment, now stared seriously, almost studiously, away from the camera. His slightly aquiline nose appeared classically sculpted in angular half light and shadow beneath his high Basque forehead. His sleeves, rolled to the elbows above strong forearms, established an iconic literary demeanor and image that would be prominent in the writing years to come as he further developed the book's themes of family and immigration, rugged mountainous landscapes and fishing village seascapes, characteristic personalities, and mysterious intrigues.

Photo of Robert Laxalt for
the back of the original
publication of *Sweet
Promised Land*. Photo by
Gene Empey.

But the sudden acclaim with this first major book came as a surprise
to Laxalt. By his unassuming nature, he had no expectations of wide recognition, let alone global fame. He was naturally shy and modest about
the book's publication. He had hardly believed it when Harper and Row
offered him a contract based on the mere four chapters he had submitted.
But the laudatory reviews, nationally and internationally, came in quickly,
as they would for years to come.

William A. Douglass, a scholar of Basque culture and an author, wrote
in the forward for the 1986 republication by University of Nevada Press of
Sweet Promised Land:

> The book . . . represented a very personal statement of a son's love
> and respect for a father whom he scarcely knew prior to their shared
> journey. For Dominique had always been a distant figure, physically
> removed from the family circle for months at a time and aloofly patri-

archal in his Old World ways. The journey had provided father and son with the first real opportunity to share something together; the book had the potential of compromising this precious intimacy, or even of making it maudlin.

Guy Shipler Jr., a veteran writer from the sophisticated East with *Time Magazine* who had resettled in Carson City and come to understand the American West, analyzed *Sweet Promised Land* in a review in *The New York Times* on December 2, 1957.

> Robert Laxalt has written of his father and his world with a poetic beauty that helps define vividly both this little-known area of our nation's heritage and the earthy, hard-working quality common to many of our foreign born. As a first-generation American and trained journalist, Robert Laxalt has captured the quality and its relationship to the development of our country with such high literary merit that his book deserves universal regard as a classic of Americana.

In the London *Sunday Times*, J. W. Lambert wrote on February 23, 1958: "Mr. Laxalt has taken one of the great themes of humanity: exile and return, the divided heart, whose fading melodies sigh through the wilderness of history from Babylon on, I don't doubt, to the hundreds of thousands who, from choice or compulsion, are trying to make new lives for themselves all over the western world today."

David Río, author of *Robert Laxalt: The Voice of the Basques in American Literature*, published in 2007 by the Center for Basque Studies, had studied Laxalt's writing and saw the book as "an intimate story" showing "the affection and admiration he feels for his father" and a "biography of a Basque immigrant." Others thought the book, though nonfiction, read like a novel. Laxalt thought he couldn't write it as a novel because the poignancy of his father's actual return to the Basque Country would be missing in a fictional account.

Laxalt's impact on writing about the American West was described by another scholar and author, Ann Ronald, in the foreword of the fiftieth anniversary republication of the book by the University of Nevada Press:

> When Harper and Row first published *Sweet Promised Land*, formula fiction dominated readers' naive notions of Nevada and the Far West. Other western writers like Walter Van Tilburg Clark, A. B. Guthrie Jr. and Wallace Stegner, who also were finding eastern audiences and were gaining recognition for their accomplishments, often complained of

their treatment by critics. . . . When Robert Laxalt with *Sweet Promised Land* joined the ranks of his fellow emerging writers, he significantly helped stretch the boundaries of the western genre.

The *Los Angeles Times* picked up on the western theme in a review: "One of the most distinguished books of the year and one no Western reader should miss reading cover to cover."

But the appeal was not merely western. It was universal, as noted in a review in *The Miami Herald:*

> Laxalt speaks not only for Basques, but for the Italians and Yugoslavs, for the Swedes and the Irish, the Portuguese and the Greeks—all our second-generation citizens. Rarely have they had a more eloquent spokesman.

Others focused on Laxalt's skill as a story teller:

> "An example of the art of writing."—*The Washington Post.*

> "An American story in the best tradition."—*San Francisco Chronicle.*

> The book "has a depth and an emotional impact out of all proportion to its modest length."—*New York Herald Tribune.*

Years later, in 1984, Laxalt's literary voice, so internationally acclaimed in *Sweet Promised Land,* was put into a fuller perspective by Charles Kuralt, a noted CBS television commentator. Having read many of Laxalt's subsequent books, he told students at a journalism dinner at the University of Nevada's Reynolds School of Journalism: If you want to be a fine writer, do not emulate me on television, but go to the mountain. When you reach the top of the mountain, Robert Laxalt will be there for you.

Kuralt's endorsement would be echoed by many in years to come as Laxalt's career blossomed as both journalist and author.

The Birth, "No Name" Laxalt

Robert Laxalt's journey to acclaim began uniquely. His birth certificate was inscribed "No name" Laxalt because the physician had difficulty communicating with Laxalt's immigrant Basque mother who spoke little English. Dominique, who spoke English well, was in the hills, delayed by an early snowstorm, on the day of Bob's birth, September 24, 1923, in the small northeastern California town of Alturas a few miles from the western Nevada state line. When Dominique arrived and conferred with Theresa the "No name" Laxalt birth certificate was changed to Robert Peter Laxalt. He was their second son, following Paul who had been born a year earlier.

Robert, six months, brother Paul, 18 months, Alturas, California, 1923.

The years were hard for the couple. Their small family grew with the birth of daughter Suzanne in 1925 as they moved about from ranch to ranch. Theresa cooked three meals a day for thirty ranch hands and sheepherders and Dominique rode horseback and walked the rugged rain-pelted and blizzard-whipped ranges tending sheep. This was in stark contrast to their previous life operating Dominique's own prosperous cattle and sheep ranches in western Nevada. However, a dramatic economic downturn in agriculture, the precursor to the Great Depression, had forced him out of businesses and they had to become hired hands for others.

Dominique had come to America through Ellis Island in New York City in 1906 from his native village of Liginaga-Astüe (Laguinge-Restoue) in the French Basque Country at age nineteen. He immediately traveled west to Nevada where other Basques lived, including two of his six older brothers, Pierre and John Pierre. He joined them in their livestock work.

Dominique started out breaking horses and herding sheep for Matheu and John Jauregui in northwestern Nevada's Washoe County. In 1910, he joined his brothers as an entrepreneur in their own sheep business near Gardnerville. Together, they guided their 2,200 ewes from the grassy summer pastures in Lassen County in northeast California to the stubborn sagebrush of Nevada's winter range.

Eventually other partners joined with Dominique and expanded their holdings to twelve thousand ewes and six hundred cattle spread over thousands of acres of public and private land from the Nevada, California, and Oregon borders in the north, southward to the historic mining town of Bodie in the mountains of western California near Bishop and Tioga Pass leading to Yosemite.

They thrived from 1918 to 1920 but in 1921 a national livestock economic crash forced them to sell what they had in land, sheep, and cattle, at rock-bottom prices.

By the nasty cold winter of 1922 they were out of business, broke.

Thérèse had come to America in 1920 at age twenty-nine to assist her brother, a French soldier wounded by poisonous gas in World War I who was being treated in a San Francisco military hospital. She was born in the village of Baigorri (Saint-Etienne de Baigorry) in the province of Lower Navarre not far from the ancient city of Iruña-Pamplona in Navarre across the Spanish frontier that was made famous by Ernest Hemingway writing about the running of the bulls.

But she faced numerous problems because she was an illegitimate child. How this all came about was detailed years later when Laxalt researched his mother's background and wrote a biographical novel, *Child of the Holy Ghost*, telling how the young woman faced her fate with courage.

Her mother was a beautiful, dark-haired young woman named Jeanne Alpetche, who lived in the village of Baigorri in the low hills of the Pyrenees Mountains of France. She fell in love with an engineer visiting the Basque Country from his home in Paris. Unaware that he was married, they struck up a romance and she soon was pregnant, which was a disgrace in the Basque culture of her birth. The Basques would embrace an illegitimate child in a communal way while at the same time treating the child with disrespect as being shamefully second class. The father took the child to visit his own mother in their aristocratic home in Paris but the little girl's Basque grandparents retrieved her there and took her home to her mother in Baigorri.

Thérèse's mother eventually married a wealthy Basque man named Bassus who had left his village and gone to Bordeaux to make his fortune. He owned a small hotel, Amerika, where many Basques stayed as they made their way from their villages to emigrate to North and South America as sheepherders. From there, Jeanne and her husband moved to South America, leaving Thérèse to be raised by her grandmother and grandfather and an uncle, a brother of her mother. Her mother eventually had two more daughters and two sons whom Thérèse would come to know as her sisters Claire and Aurélie and her brothers Michel and Maurice.

One day a telegram arrived at Thérèse's grandparents' home saying her mother, whom she hardly knew, was moving back from South America and coming to visit. The excited grandmother helped Thérèse into her best little dress so she could greet her mother, a beautiful woman in grand clothes including a fine hat. Settling back into Bordeaux, Thérèse's mother took her to live in their new home, the Hotel Amerika, which her husband continued to own.

Thérèse learned of her illegitimacy when she attended her first communion and the church listed her birth as illegitimate. The awareness haunted her throughout her life and once she had become an American citizen she burned her French passport. She would never return to her natal country.

While living in Bordeaux, she remained close to her mother, who cared deeply for her. She ventured to Paris in her early twenties to attend the famed Cordon Bleu culinary school where she demonstrated a gift for fine cooking. But she returned to Bordeaux to be with her mother who was dying of consumption. She learned upon her mother's death that even though she as the eldest child would inherit the house they had owned in the Basque Country, an uncle had cheated her out of the property on the basis of her illegitimate birth. She returned to Bordeaux and never returned to the Basque Country.

She stayed there until traveling to America to help her brother, who she hoped was healing from his war wounds, and to take him home to France. She briefly found work as a cook, thanks to her Cordon Bleu training, in a well-to-do home in San Francisco. But Michel's health began to deteriorate and he eventually was moved to St. Mary's Hospital in Reno, where she then cared for him while working as a maid in a small Basque hotel.

It was in Reno where Thérèse met Dominique, who was a rare combination of Cadillac-driving boldness and charming shyness. As a successful livestock entrepreneur, owner of ten ranches, he stood out in the Basque hotel dining rooms from the other sheepherders. He pursued her and she fell in love with him. They were married on October 8, 1921 at Reno's St. Thomas Aquinas Cathedral and settled into what appeared to be a life of well-being as American immigrants.

Theresa—as she chose be called in the United States instead of the more traditional French spelling of Thérèse—wrote to her sisters telling them she was dropping any rights to inheritance, thus cutting all ties to the Basque Country. Then, suddenly, in the year of their marriage, Dominique and his partners went broke in the livestock crash, and Theresa found herself joining her new husband on a wandering journey through the Basque ranches in California.

By 1925, the little family of five—mother, father, three- and two-year-old sons, and one-year-old daughter—was living in a small shack in Bodie, California, which had been a mining community decades before but now was a dusty, windswept ghost town. Their makeshift home was a wooden shack with a dirt floor. And Theresa had had enough of the harsh life of mere survival in rugged mountains and far-flung cattle and sheep ranges. In 1926, after three years of working on the ranches, Dominique and Theresa decided to return to Carson City to raise their family near the western Nevada communities where he had originally emigrated twenty years earlier. Their two sons and one daughter would have to shift from Basque, their first language, to English for the educational years to come.

Robert, 7, Paul, 8, First Communion,
Carson City, circa 1930.

Theresa bought the French Hotel, a small Basque inn, on the main street of the little Nevada capital, with a population barely over a thousand, for a down payment of one hundred dollars and the family settled into the back rooms behind the kitchen, bar, and dining room. The hotel had been owned by another couple who had emigrated from the French Basque country, Bernard and Maryanne Supera. It was a boardinghouse affair that became a temporary home for Basque sheepherders when they came down from their lonely work in the hills and mountains of the Sierra. In the hotel, they found relaxing comradeship at hearty family-style lunches and dinners provided by Theresa, now seasoned as a ranch-hand cook. The sheepherders slept in small bedrooms on the second floor, sharing one bathroom.

Theresa's cooking drew a crowd of both locals and visitors to Carson City but it alone wasn't enough to keep her customers happy. Many wanted a drink of whiskey before dinner and red wine with the meal. So, against the laws of prohibition that banned alcohol throughout the country, Dominique became a bootlegger of sorts. The young Robert Laxalt accompanied his father under the cover of a dark night to fetch whiskey and wine made secretly by local area Italians. They drove north toward

Reno in Dominique's old Nash and turned off the highway at small road to make the exchange, money for alcohol. Bob watched as his father paid the whiskey and wine broker with cash.

While this was a great adventure for the boy, it also troubled him because other children called his family "bootleggers" and treated the Laxalts as though they were lower class. One young boy, the son of a clergyman, gave Laxalt a challenging look one day as if to say "How could you sell whiskey?" Laxalt was torn between loyalty to his parents and the shame and humiliation he felt they brought upon him in the schoolyard. Laxalt was further confused by the double standard of those of upper-class families who drank whiskey and wine with their meals at the hotel while seemingly disapproving of the alcohol-providing proprietors.

The French Hotel became a community gathering place in the center of Carson City across the main street from the Virginia & Truckee railroad depot just as small Basque hotels did in other little towns scattered across Nevada and the West. Among the clientele of railroad workers and state legislators from time to time was Nevada's nationally famed U.S. Senator, Pat McCarran.

"Senator McCarran was like a deity in our household," Laxalt's brother, Paul, recalled in a memoir. "The fact that he was a man of international renown and highly controversial in some circles was of no moment when compared to his real achievement: He was the champion of young Basque sheepherders immigrating to the U.S. At this time when his powerful voice was closing the door to many newcomers, he kept the 'Basque door' wide open."

Everyone in the family had chores in the hotel ranging from helping Theresa in the kitchen to cleaning up the dining room and bar to keeping the upstairs bedrooms properly made up. But Dominique soon grew restless with town life. He longed for the hills and mountains. He soon reentered the sheep business in the Sierra Nevada above Carson City, buying small herds at first and later expanding them with more ewes. He centered his camp two thousand feet above the eastern shore of Lake Tahoe at historic, snow-fed Marlette Lake, the source of water for Virginia City. The lake had been created with an earthen dam in 1876 to provide 6,600,000 gallons of water daily for the silver-mining boomtown.

Dominique's sheep fed amid the pines on the grassy meadows around the picturesque little lake from which water had raced in a thirty-two-mile network of flumes and pipelines, including four thousand feet of tunnel blasted through granite down to the Washoe Valley and then pressured up two thousand feet to Virginia City in an inverted syphon.

The family continued to grow as Theresa gave birth to son John in 1926, daughter Marie in 1928, and son Peter in 1931. They moved from the hotel in the early 1930s to a home at 402 Minnesota Street in a tree-lined, leafy green neighborhood close to school and church. Theresa paid three thousand dollars for the two-story, white-frame house with a large living room and dining room and two bedrooms. To increase the sleeping quarters, a screened porch was added in a makeshift dorm for Bob and his brothers.

Laxalt Family: John, Robert, mother Theresa, infant Peter (Micky), father Dominique, Marie, on lap, Paul, Suzanne, circa 1931.

This was in Carson City's historic district, west of the main street, with its two- and three-story Victorian homes handcrafted in decorative wood trim by designers and carpenters. Among the stately homes were two mansions: the governor's residence gleaming white with tall columns on either side of the double front doors; and, across the street, the stately home of the celebrated Bliss family whose wealth had come from the Tahoe logging industry that provided lumber for Virginia City's homes, businesses, and mines.

As a boy, Robert Laxalt loved to accompany his father into the hills but he especially loved his home. He and his brothers and sisters loved the safety and comfort of the neighborhood, so different from the sparse, rugged sheep camp, and Bob thought of the house as a haven—"When things had gone wrong during the day it was there I went to find refuge and solace."

He would walk through the gate and high hedges to the screen porch with its swing and oak chair to the glass panel front door, knowing he would find his mother, her graying hair tied in a bun, cheerfully at the stove in the kitchen.

Theresa's cooking aromas filled not only the kitchen but the entire house and beyond through open windows to the immediate neighborhood. Laxalt relished the warmth of the house with his mother cooking bread in the kitchen. Boyhood friends, scenting the fresh bread, couldn't resist their longing for it, and Theresa couldn't turn them away. She cheerfully fed the whole neighborhood.

She was old country by tradition, serving her family first at the rectangular table beneath the dining room's high ceiling, then eating her own meal alone. The four brothers and two sisters savored her French soups, lamb and pork chops, steaks and stews, and French fries.

In the absence of Dominique, who was away in the mountains for weeks at a time, the elder son Paul sat at the head of the table, a surrogate father to his siblings. They shared the news of the day, filling each other in on what was happening at school, in town life, and, for the boys, news of the sports they excelled at from fall football to winter basketball to spring baseball and track and the combat of boxing.

Occasionally, when Dominique would be at home, he would join them at the table, sometimes bringing along a young sheepherder just in from the Basque Country attired in his newly bought work clothing of blue jeans and woolen shirt. The sheepherders came from Theresa's Basque Country homeland province of Lower Navarre and she and Dominique spoke to them in the mysteriously rich, ancient Basque language. Bob and his brothers and sisters listened unknowingly to the words, for as children of proud-to-be immigrant Americans, their language, at the insistence of their parents, had to be English. In their parent's determination for assimilation, Bob and his siblings were denied development of the native Basque language Bob had first heard in the early itinerant ranch years of his infancy and that, with a certain degree of irony, is a fundamental part of Basque cultural identity, which would later form a cornerstone of fame as a writer.

Reading, Writing, and Exploring

As a young boy, Laxalt was stricken with a life-threatening case of rheumatic fever. He was confined to bed for months. This was one of many turning points that would occur in his life as he tried to balance resentment and anger over loss of restricted freedom with competitive overachievement in alternatives. He turned away from the hurt of hearing the joy of other children running, playing, and laughing beyond his closeted bedroom window by exploring the larger world through library books brought to him by family and friends. He couldn't read enough. The books came to life in his vivid imagination.

"I developed an insatiable appetite for all these treasures," he would one day write. The "treasures" included the jungles of Edgar Rice Burroughs's *Tarzan of the Apes,* the frozen tundra of Jack London's Yukon stories, and the collies of Albert Payson Terhune's *Sunnybrook Farm* as well as shelves of other adventure stories and action heroes.

Bob took the books to the sheep camps in the summertime when he worked with his father. He shocked the elderly, straight-laced, old-fashioned librarians who didn't like the books' smell of sagebrush when he returned them to the library. They insisted on airing them out before returning them to the bookshelves.

The library books developed his desire to write about such action heroes and awakened what he called the magic of words. He thought of the library as his second home during his 1930s boyhood, noting that libraries were scarce in Depression-era Nevada and that only the wealthy or die-hard book collectors had their own personal home libraries. But because Carson City was the capital of Nevada, the state library had a better collection of books than the small libraries of other communities, and he was grateful to be the beneficiary of the classics he found there. In elementary school, he was putting words to paper in *The Sixth Grade Chatter,* the student mimeographed newspaper of which he served as editor. The little

Robert, 6, during illness period,
sisters Marie, 1, Suzanne, 5,
Carson City, Nevada, circa 1929.

paper made a big prediction. It reported: "We believe that if Robert Laxalt, our editor in chief, continues his efforts as a writer, he will some day make a name for himself in the literary world."

Bob read a book a day, dropping one off at the library each morning on his way to school and picking up another on his way home after school. The books brought the sense of action and excitement that was denied him when he was restricted to his bedroom and, later, kept from being active in sports. Teachers, fearful of his heart condition, kept him on the bench during recess as others rousted about on the playing fields. He was humiliated when the teachers discussed his affliction with other students as they explained why he was restricted to the bench. He reacted with outbursts of frustrated anger when restrictions caused him to fail to meet his goals.

At the end of the eighth grade, Laxalt, once again, was so determined to overcome the pain and hurt of restrictions due to what was perceived to be his fragile health that he angrily declared he would go out for football in high school, as his brother Paul had done, and that no one could stop him. His mother was worried but when she saw his fierce determination she relented and allowed him to get active not only in football but all sports including the toughest of all, boxing.

New forces emerged in his high school years—romance and writing, with varying degrees of success. With his slicked back, jet-black hair and handsome chiseled facial features, all the girls liked him, so much so that his buddies called him Casanova. When they learned he was French Basque, they changed the tag to Frenchy, a nickname he would have all his life. His growing interest in writing attracted the interest of both a dubious girlfriend and a gifted teacher.

The teacher was Carson High School's Grace Bordewich who Laxalt frequently credited as an inspiration through her use of vocabulary and poetic prose. He dedicated his book *The Basque Hotel* to the gifted English teacher who taught at the high school from 1933 to 1965. She taught everything from Shakespeare to Greek mythology to the poetry of Emily Dickinson and inspired her students to use language well in their own writing.

Bordewich's class served as a turning point for Laxalt. She sent him to study hall for the first two sessions as punishment because he talked too much and sent notes to other students, disrupting her English class. When he finally got settled into the class, however, he heard a new and unique voice reciting poetry. Her reading expressed a pure love of language; she shared her own delight in the wondrous power of words to convey images. He had never realized that the English language could be so beautiful, that he could love each word.

Suddenly, he thought for the first time of a teacher being human. He saw her teaching as not coming from the tedium of grammar, but from poetry and short stories, what he sensed as the magic of writing. He saw her eyes brighten and her voice soften and thought a student would have to be dead not to be affected. He realized this teacher was giving him the love of language.

The teacher assigned the students to write a short story and gave them two weeks to do so. She said the story would be one half their final grade. The students moaned and Laxalt thought she was expecting them to write like Mark Twain or Bret Harte.

In the hallway after class his high school girlfriend asked him if he would write her story for her. She was afraid she would do a poor job and flunk the class. Laxalt told her he didn't know how to write his own story, let alone hers. But after she begged him, he agreed to try, making no promises.

Laxalt worked hard measuring every word, every sentence, on a story for her about a high school girl and her boyfriend holding hands at sunset. He gave it to her one day before the deadline and she quickly ran to class to turn it in, not bothering to thank him, not giving him the kiss he expected.

He was left with the realization that he had only one night to write his own story. He wrote a story about a detective and finished at midnight. The next day, the teacher praised Laxalt's story and read it aloud to the class. His girlfriend was waiting for him in the hall when class was over. He wrote years later in his memoir about her dramatic reaction: "'You creep!' she cried in a very audible voice. 'Do you know what she gave me for my short story? An F! I flunked the course, and it's your fault. You did it on purpose! Find yourself another girlfriend.'"

With that, Laxalt's teenage love life wilted and his love of words, first found in the Nevada State Library, blossomed.

Laxalt began to learn more about life as he and his brothers learned to thrive in the mountains with their father.

He was only eight when he got his first real feel for the grand scale of Nevada beyond his Carson City home. The experience was so powerful that it would stick with him and he would one day tell of it in a book about the state. The perspective came through a sweeping view from high in the mountains. His father had taken Bob and his brothers to the sheep camp where they amused themselves chasing lambs while Dominique tended to business with one of the sheepherders. The camp was simple and practical with its small canvas tent to shelter a herder through the long nights of cold wind and sometimes drenching rain. There was an open fire pit for warming coffee and cooking the staples of sheep camp meals: meat and potatoes.

When Dominique finished his conversation, in Basque, which his sons were now finding elusive, he motioned for them to follow him into the pine and fir forest that encircled the camp. "Come along. I want to show you something," he told them, shifting easily to English. They did so obediently for he, not they, was the master of this rugged terrain.

They walked briskly to keep up with their sure-footed father. They hiked with trepidation over the rocky ground and made their way upward through the pathless trees and thick willows. They eventually reached a small ridge where, suddenly, they saw the blue waters of Lake Tahoe spread vastly, two thousand feet below.

It was nearly the same scene Mark Twain first saw when working as a reporter in Virginia City in the summer of 1861. He called the lake "a noble sheet of water lifted six thousand three hundred feet above the level of the sea. And walled in by a rim of snow-clad mountain peaks that towered aloft three thousand feet higher still!"

Even as a young boy Laxalt had heard and read stories of how Sam Clemens took the pen name Mark Twain while working as a reporter and visiting his brother, Orion, the Nevada territorial secretary in Carson City before 1864 statehood.

Laxalt was in awe as he looked out over the twenty-two-mile-long, twelve-mile-wide 1,645-foot-deep lake that the famous author had described so eloquently—"As it lay there with the shadows of the mountains brilliantly photographed upon its still surface I thought it must surely be the fairest picture the whole earth affords."

Laxalt and his father and brothers carefully moved off the ridge, leaving the spectacular image behind but preserving it in his mind, and continued their trek toward a peak still higher in the boulder-strewn distance. They reached the peak at about ten thousand feet and searched for shelter amid the boulders and old trees that had been whipped by ferocious winter winds.

"Now boost yourself up and have a look," the father told the sons.

It was an awesome experience for Laxalt: "The wind tore at our hair and sucked the air out of our gasping mouths. Below us, the world dropped away dizzyingly. The forested slopes of the Sierra slanted down to a chain of valley floors, and we could see isolated ranch houses and cattle tiny as ants grazing in green pastures."

They stared down at Carson City with its capitol dome gleaming silver in the bright midday sun, tiny at such a distance but protected by the huge mountains to the west. From this perch on Snow Valley Peak near the 10,766 foot summit of Mount Rose, they could see Reno to the north. Its Truckee River appeared to the imaginative young writer-to-be as a vein of silver.

As they looked eastward they saw a series of desert mountain ranges running from north to south, colored by natural pastels of gray and soft reddish rose. The landscape went on forever with no trace of civilization, no houses, no towns, just mountains beyond mountains.

Dominique turned to his sons and said, "Well, that's your Nevada out there."

"'She's pretty big," Laxalt's older brother, Paul, said.

"She's big, all right," the father nodded. "And what you saw is only a little part of it."

Anything bigger was beyond the comprehension of the eight-year-old Robert Laxalt whose day of discovery would shape him for the rest of his life.

While Laxalt's love of words took him into the solitude of the Nevada State Library, his penchant for action heroes such as Tarzan brought out a personality far from that of a bookworm. All the Laxalt boys were active in sports of every season, including one of toughest, most competitive of all—boxing. And his competitors were the very scrappy fighters at the nearby Stewart Indian School.

"My real distinction in the fighting game was in being the only white guy on the Stewart Indian School boxing team," he wrote in an article in his typical self-deprecating humor. He saw the distinction as having peculiar shortcomings. The training sessions in the old gymnasium increasingly turned away from casual sparring into bloody brawls. He wondered if he'd get out alive. He began to look forward to the weekend fights as an escape from training sessions. He figured he had been hit in the head a thousand times in one year. He got punchy but noted "this was very good for my next career—writing. Because as everyone knows, all writers are nuts anyway."

The article was headlined "The Laxalts: Boxers In Spite Of Themselves."

He knew he and his brothers were destined to be boxers. The first book he remembered in their home was their very well read encyclopedia of the world's top prize fighters. World champion Jack Dempsey, who had boxed in Reno, got to know Laxalt's father and even tried talking him into becoming a prizefighter. The family spent a great amount of time at Steamboat Springs just south of Reno when Paolino Uzcudun, the "Basque Woodchopper," was training to fight the famed Max Baer. Laxalt revered the good sportsmanship of champion Joe Louis and saw the beer-drinking Tony Galento as just the opposite. On world championship fights nights, the whole family turned up the radio to follow the suspense blow by blow.

The boys thought of themselves as early professional prizefighters at ages five and ten years old, performing for their father's friends with the winner getting a quarter and the loser a dime. Big-time cash for the fledgling fighters but it didn't threaten their amateur status when it came time for boxing in Golden Gloves tournaments.

He described brother Paul as a scientific boxer with a really good left jab and said of himself: "I was mean enough but too nervous to be a good fighter. However if I were lucky enough to get hurt just short of being knocked out, I did all right, too. It is a huge risk, though, to leave yourself open for a Sunday punch that may or may not knock you out, and I don't recommend that strategy to anybody."

Laxalt described his brother John as tall, rangy, and fearless when throwing punches. He saw Peter, his youngest brother, who was nicknamed Mick, as the most clever boxer of all. But Laxalt noted Mick's career was stopped in its tracks by their mother when Laxalt himself came home with two black eyes and a broken nose.

In turn, Bob was described by his brother John as "a class act, kind of an old style boxer, not a fighter but a boxer." In one match, a Stewart fighter rabbit-punched Laxalt with a blow to the back of his neck below the skull so hard that John thought it severely inflicted him for the rest of his life. Laxalt took more punishment than he was aware of in fifteen to twenty amateur fights, John thought.

Just as Laxalt found heroes, such as Tarzan, in books, he came to worship those who stood out in his high school sports. Among them were a couple of Carson High School basketball standouts of Italian descent named Caesar and Geon who led their little school to an intense victory over the much larger and feared Reno High School. Laxalt watched from the sidelines as Caesar sank the winning basket which turned the tiny gym into bedlam as the hometown fans thronged over the court.

Robert, 16, junior at Carson High School, 1939.

"Hero worship was an integral part of my high school days." he wrote later. "Who could experience such a dramatic victory without becoming infected?" Of the sharp-shooting Caesar and his master dribbling brother, Geno, Laxalt observed: "I was one of their worshipers. The fact that they were Orphan Home kids did not demean them a bit."

He developed friendships with his boxing competitors from the Stewart Indian School who visited him at his Carson City home. His sister Marie greeted two of the Indian teenagers at the door as they asked if Laxalt were home. "Just a minute Mr. Cornbread," she said. "I'll get him." After they left, Laxalt chided his little sister: "His name is Buckwheat!" He was upset that she had offended them.

The growing up years in Carson City, both during their time living in the little French hotel on the main street and later in the fine home Theresa had bought on Minnesota Street, exposed Laxalt and his brothers and sisters to the racial and ethnic diversity of small town America that posed both threats to their security and self-esteem and pride in their family's self-reliance and hard-work ethic. An "American" classmate made fun of Laxalt's brother Paul's efforts at English, blended as they were with bits of Spanish, Basque, and Italian he'd picked up in the neighborhoods. That inspired the sheepherder's son who would go on to become governor of Nevada and represent the state as a United States senator to resort to a fist fight victory to win understanding and respect—in his first grade schoolyard.

The Laxalt sons and daughters did bond with other emigrant families such as the Superas who had sold the French Hotel to Theresa who became Godmother to her namesake, their daughter, Theresa though her name was spelled with an "a" as Theresa had taken to spelling her name in the United States rather the traditional French name Thérèse. The Laxalt and Supera families joined together in their small town summer picnics and attended church together. Paul Laxalt and Pete Supera were in the same high school class and developed the early social instincts that would eventually take them into politics, Paul as Nevada governor, Pete as justice of the peace in Carson City. Classmates John Supera and Robert Laxalt, Leon Supera and Suzanne Laxalt, Benny Supera and Marie Laxalt, and Theresa Supera and John Laxalt all became friends for life. The boys all played sports games through the seasons—touch football in the fall, softball and baseball in the spring and summer—in a big empty lot across the street from the Supera home at Curry and Washington streets.

Until 1937, school life was limited to a single building, three blocks from the Laxalt home, where students attended all twelve grades. In that year, however, a new high school was built that included a gymnasium seating five hundred fans for basketball and other sports the Laxalt brothers played competitively.

Bob Laxalt felt ethnic and cultural pressures from the more prominent Anglo-Saxon families, the main street merchants and state government employees who dressed not in the jeans and woolen shirts of his sheepherder father but in the more formal suits and business and commercial attire. And then there was the slight stigma of the one-time Laxalt home in the little hotel that had sold bootlegged liquor, ironic since all stations in life from cowboys and sheepherders to top politicians had enjoyed drinks before dinner and wine with Theresa's hearty meals.

"To have as neighbors immigrants who once ran a saloon did not sit well with the respectable occupants of the fine houses in our neighborhood. They never said so openly, but the pause in their hellos spelled out what they were thinking," he would write years later in his memoir.

Robert, 17, second from right, first row, Carson High School basketball team, 1940.

The Laxalt brothers and sisters' school work, aided by their excellent teachers and the constant discipline of their mother's watch, helped the family find acceptance with their more mainstream neighbors. All the Laxalt children earned places on the school honor roles which were published in the town's daily newspaper for all to see. And it didn't hurt when everyone in small town Carson City came to cheer as the Laxalts excelled in all the varsity sports.

To College, and to War

While Theresa insisted that her sons and daughters grow up as English-speaking Americans, as an immigrant she clung to old country ways, particularly in her deep Catholic faith she had learned as a child. As others of Anglo-Saxon background said "Amen" at the end of The Lord's Prayer there in the pews of St. Theresa's Catholic Church, Theresa could be heard softly saying "*Anise doit-il*" in French as native a language for her as the Basque of her birth. Laxalt and his brothers and sisters knew the discipline of daily Mass:

> It had to do with forty mornings of Lent, up when the sky was still dark and the snow was piled high on the ground, trudging a narrow path to the church, with her brood strung out behind her, little dark patches moving slowly through the white snow, huddled deep in their coats, shivering, and with eyes still stuck with sleep.

The devout Theresa insisted that Laxalt and his brothers serve as altar boys, a precursor of things to come when she would decide the proper course for their eventual college education. "We were subject to the authority of a succession of Irish priests with names like Murphy, Ryan and O'Grady," Laxalt thought. "There were so many that I began to believe all priests everywhere were born in Ireland and spoke with a brogue." They memorized the daily and Sunday morning Masses and Laxalt felt a mystical and peaceful aura amid the burning of incense and the pouring of wine for the priests as they spoke the foreign sound of Latin.

Theresa joined with the family priest in noting the exemplary altar boy service of Laxalt's brother Paul and decided that he should become a priest. None of the Laxalt children ever dared appealing to their father to overrule their mother's determined and, in his frequent absences, sole decision making. But Paul did just that, if timidly, when Dominique came home from the sheepherding hills and learned of the emerging plans for a seminary education and priesthood being visited upon his eldest son:

> "Pop," I said. "Mom and Monsignor want me to go to a school in California to become a priest. I know it would be an honor for the family, but I don't think I'm cut out to be a priest. Do I have to go?"
>
> "No you don't, Paul. It would be wrong for you, and the church, if you haven't been called. Don't worry about it. I'll talk to Momma."

On one rare occasion, Robert Laxalt spoke up to his mother in defense of his younger sister Marie who had drawn the disapproval of Catholic Church nuns over her picture appearing in the local newspaper. Marie had gotten her mother's permission to compete for Miss Nevada, she recalled years later. "The nuns came over to the house and were preaching about how young girls shouldn't go around parading their bodies in swimsuits. That is sinful. Robert was home at the time. He heard what they were saying. He came in and said he didn't agree with them and told them the body was beautiful. And then the nuns left. And Mom didn't speak to us for two months."

Theresa set aside her aspirations for a son becoming a priest but she kept a focused eye on what she considered an appropriate college education—the disciplined social and intellectual environment of the Jesuit priests at California's Santa Clara University. In September of 1940, Dominique drove Theresa and their four sons and two daughters in the family truck, some riding in the cab, some in the open back, from Carson City to the railroad station thirty miles away in Reno. Dominique remained behind as Theresa ushered the rest of the family aboard the Southern Pacific for their first ride on a train. They were wide-eyed as the scenic venture took them through sprawling forests and past the dramatic granite walls, giant boulders, and sheer cliffs of the Sierra Nevada to the spacious sweep of the Sacramento Valley on to the San Francisco Bay. Arriving at Santa Clara, near San Jose, she personally took the entire family to meet the president of the university so he could enroll Paul in the autumn semester. Bob thus got a first glimpse of the school he would enroll in one year later.

Santa Clara had five hundred students, all male, and Paul and Bob were to learn quickly that the Jesuits ran a tight ship with a multitude of confining rules, including curfews that limited their evening hours to the school's campus grounds. Rumors, they heard, had it that the Jesuits even had owned dogs in an earlier day to make sure the students didn't wander away to the nearby allure of tempting city life.

Bob found the studying routine to be disciplined. He and his first-year roommate Ray Callahan, who had come to Santa Clara from San Francisco, were in study hall lockdown in their dormitory room from 7:00 until 9:30 each evening under the strict Jesuit rules. At 9:30 p.m., they took a thirty-minute break to slip out of the dorm to a nearby café for a soft drink or a milkshake but they had to be back in their room by ten at which time the dorm doors were locked restricting them until morning. Bob had a heavy load of twenty-one units, which earned him the reputation of being an excellent, sharp student seriously tending to his books and his interest in literature. The weekends were more relaxed allowing time to explore nearby Stanford University and San Francisco.

As such, Paul and Bob found life at Santa Clara far different from what they had known in tiny Carson City. Students came from around the world to the small but heralded university. Classes ranged from politics to religion to history, philosophy, psychology, mathematics, and literature as well as military studies through the Reserve Officer Training Program (ROTC). The school's vigorous intramural program was loaded with all the seasonal sports the Laxalts had competed in back home in Carson City. The football team, headed by the celebrated Buck Shaw, was nationally known as the "Notre Dame of the West." The basketball team was nationally prominent, too, playing in New York's Madison Square Garden collegiate championship tournaments.

Paul noted: "For a youngster from Carson High where a 'crowd' at a football game would be fewer than a thousand fans, I was thrilled with my first visit to Kezar Stadium in San Francisco which was filled with 60,000 shouting fans."

Bob found himself in, among all the other classes, ROTC, which no one had taken seriously until, in Bob's freshman year, the shocking news swept the campus of the Japanese attack on Pearl Harbor on December 1, 1941. As America went to war, the Laxalts, like college students everywhere, continued momentarily with their classes as they began to make decisions about volunteering. The questions they pondered: where to serve—in the Army infantry or as pilots in its dramatic air corps, in the Navy with what seemed like the possibility of relative safety aboard ships at sea, in the challenge of the historically front lines fighting Marine Corps? Some tried to stay in school by joining the reserves which would delay the inevitable combat. But, unlike later generations when many young Americans tried desperately to avoid the draft by leaving the country or protesting in the streets against war, the Laxalt college generation by and large volunteered eagerly to fight for their country. By 1943, Paul was headed into the U.S. Army medical corps. He would eventually serve in combat in the Pacific, tending to his fellow soldiers in the bloody battle of Leyte in the Philippines. Also in 1943, Bob's roommate Ray Callahan's ROTC advanced class was called into the Army as a unit.

Bob would come to face a far different quandary: the lingering effect of his childhood bout with rheumatic fever. However, he knew nothing of this as he contemplated his future during the spring semester of 1942—a fairly calm period on the little Santa Clara campus following America's entry into both European and Pacific warfare. But he began to notice the absence of students he had come to know in his first year of college. They were gone from school life. They were off to war. For those who remained, there was a new energy on the ROTC drill field. Suddenly, cadets who had been lackadaisical in the military classes, many seeing them as an irrelevant waste of time, were responding to commands seriously, listening to orders as though they meant something, snapping to attention and saying "Yes, Sir!" One cadet approached a superior cadet officer, handed him a piece of paper and gave a proper military salute.

The commander barked: "Private Robert Laxalt! Fall out!" At first Laxalt didn't take the cadet commander seriously. He had never been given an order before in ROTC. And he suspected the commander probably had never given one since he repeated the order twice to get Laxalt's attention. Laxalt approached the commander but did not salute. Instead of saying "Yes, Sir!" Laxalt looked at the commander and said "Yeah?" The commander formally advised Private Laxalt that the proper response was "Yes, Sir!" Laxalt, suddenly sizing up the situation as serious, responded: "Yes, Sir!"

"I know this is going to hurt you but you are dismissed from the troop," the commander said with what Laxalt sized up as sarcasm. "You flunked the physical. You've got a heart murmur." Laxalt brushed it off as an unimportant token of his childhood rheumatic fever. He had a heart strong enough, he noted, to excel in varsity sports including the rigors of boxing. "It's enough to keep you out of the service," the commander said. It suddenly dawned on Laxalt, who had not taken the military classes seriously, that he might have to sit out the war involuntarily and not serve his country as Paul and millions of others would patriotically—and heroically—do.

Laxalt pondered the fate of returning to Carson City, a small town so relatively isolated that a trip to Reno was an event and the thought of going off to San Francisco almost a dramatic lifetime experience. Yet, he knew the war would change Nevada's little capital city. He knew that the young men who had proudly worn the blue and white colors of Carson City on their letter sweaters and jackets would be donning the brown, blue, and green uniforms of the United States Army, Navy, and Marine Corps.

Denied the opportunity to join them in the armed forces, he nonetheless stepped along with his friends as a sign of solidarity when they marched as a group down Carson City's main street to the Selective Service office. He was humiliated but it was the best he could do and he grew increasingly bitter about his rejection. He took it personally, deeply, that his country was rejecting his service because of the stigma of a heart murmur.

"That I was an athlete of varsity rank meant nothing. I was declared unfit, and the damage was done to my pride. The Selective Service System might as well have denounced me as subhuman." But, as he had done at earlier times in his life when his frustration turned to anger, he drew on positive energy and commitment and vowed to overcome the unfair stigma of a heart murmur that he knew didn't limit him in any way—physically, psychologically, or mentally. He was desperate to find a way to serve in the armed forces but he ran into rejection at every military recruiting office in the San Francisco Bay area. He kept notes that eventually he would use in writing a book about the personally devastating rejection.

Air Force, Marines, Navy, Army. The answer was always the same— physically unfit for military service. With each rejection, another door closed.

January, 1944, *San Francisco, California*
Sorry, young man. This war you sit out.

February, 1944, *San Francisco, California*
I appreciate how much you want to be a combat flier, but I can't pass you with a heart like that.

February, 1944, *San Francisco, California*
The Marines pride themselves on being tough. We've got our standards. They don't include accepting bum hearts.

February, 1944, *San Francisco, California*
Your heart muscle is strong. That's from sports. But you have a leaky valve in there somewhere. I just can't pass you.

Back in Carson City, he faced the agony of more rejection:

The taunts and contempt were, if anything, worse than formal rejection. There was no choice but to get out of town, out of Nevada.

March, 1944, *Carson City, Nevada*
Our son has to risk going to war while you stay home safe and sound. Something stinks here.

March, 1944, *Carson City, Nevada*
I didn't know they served 4F's in here. We'll do our drinking somewhere else.

March, 1944, *Carson City, Nevada*
Football star. Basketball star. Boxer. But not strong enough to go to war. Smells like draft-dodger to me.

Laxalt turned to Nevada's powerful United States senator, Patrick McCarran, who had often joined others at the long tables for Theresa's family style dinners at the little French Hotel in Carson City. Laxalt knew that the senator had great respect for the hard work and honesty of his father and mother and all the Basque immigrant families.

In a letter dated March, 1944, posted in Carson City and addressed to Senator McCarran in Washington, D.C., Laxalt explained how he tried again and again to enlist in every one of the armed services but had been rejected by all because of a heart murmur. Laxalt wrote:

> I am appealing to you to place me in the State Department in Washington, D.C. I would like to serve overseas, preferably in a dangerous post, so that I can feel I am helping my country in time of war.

The senator reacted positively. Laxalt was on his way quickly from Nevada's tiny capital to the nation's capital to join the millions of patriots awash globally in the work of war. He was designated a code officer to work with top secret communications in the United States Legation in the Belgian Congo. Leopoldville was infested with spies and intrigue, but the Allies had driven out the Germans ending the combat action in North Africa.

Laxalt was grateful to serve in the State Department assignment but he remained bitter about his country's rejection of him as unfit for combat duty. As his ship put to sea in the Atlantic and he watched the American shore slowly disappear on the horizon, he said of his homeland with frustration and anger:

> "Goddamn you. I hope I never see you again."

Spies and Death-Dealing Malaria

Laxalt was haunted by conflicting thoughts as he headed into harm's way. He was concerned about the threat of German submarines, called U-boats, prowling the seas on the very routes his ship was taking and, personally, he was worried about his uniform showing him to be different from his combat-bound shipmates.

He wore one of two new khaki uniforms issued to him at Camp Patrick Henry in Virginia just days before as he joined a long, single-file line of soldiers in steel helmets and full body packs to board the Liberty ship that would take them to Africa. But his uniform had no insignia and he had no rank—other than the secretive "code officer"—which could be met with scorn by a challenging shipmate.

He had learned during his indoctrination in Washington that German U-Boats haunted the Atlantic where Laxalt's ship would move with a hundred others in a convoy from the eastern seaboard to Casablanca in North Africa. In one month alone, thirty allied ships were sunk off West African coasts by six German U-Boats and an Italian submarine.

One incident became a well-known story aboard U.S. ships zigzagging their way through the deadly waters: A German submarine surfaced and confronted the American commercial ship *Robin Moor* in broad daylight. The U-boat captain ordered the American crew of thirty-eight and eight passengers to abandon the ship. They managed to get into four lifeboats from which they then watched the submarine sink their ship with torpedoes. The boats drifted for days before vessels came across them in the stormy seas and saved the survivors. In just one month, November of 1942, Germany's 196 submarines sank 117 allied ships. Hitler dispatched his U-boats from the North Atlantic to the Mediterranean and West African waters. Others prowled the coasts of the United States in search of troop ships and cargo vessels leaving or returning to American ports. By

February of 1943, the U-Boat fleet had risen to 212 which, by year-end, sank 597 ships.

Aboard ship, despite Bob's longed-for military uniform and wartime surroundings, his combat rejection kept him full of fury and he continued to feel deep humiliation as he found his way to a small compartment of six bunks. There he met his shipmates, all officers in uniforms bearing insignia and rank. His anger intensified as they questioned his noncombat assignment that, due to its secrecy, he could not explain. He couldn't even say that once they left the ship he would be assigned to the Belgian Congo.

Laxalt, lacking any real military training, made up his bunk loosely and was immediately questioned in a friendly way by an older officer with a Texas drawl: "Mac, in what man's army did you learn to make up a bunk?" Laxalt froze but the Texan eased his tension and cheerfully showed him how to stretch out the blankets to what Laxalt thought was taut as a sail in the wind. "Now, you pass muster," the friendly Texan said.

The cabin mates were surprised to learn Laxalt was from Nevada. None had been to Laxalt's home state nor had any of them ever known anyone from Nevada. But they had heard of it and immediately questioned him in easy banter about the state's legendary gambling casinos and brothels.

Suddenly, the mood changed when an arrogant officer with a Teutonic bearing and a cold voice stiffly questioned the rank-less Laxalt: "What's your outfit?"

"Lay off, Heinie," another barked in defense of what appeared to be an attack on Laxalt.

"What do you mean, 'lay off'?" Heinie rebuked. "It's the question all of you were asking."

"None," Laxalt said as he faced his challenger.

When he told them he was of Basque descent none knew what a Basque was, let alone a Basque from Nevada, which seemed strange enough by itself.

Heinie asserted that Laxalt was really a Jew who had gotten an easy war assignment, declaring: "Jews always come out on the easy end."

The dinner bell rang and all but Laxalt headed for the galley with Heinie saying: "Fucking New York Jew draft dodging 4F sonofabitch."

"Heinie! Shut your mouth," the senior Texan barked. "That's an order."

Alone in the cabin, Laxalt was so shaken his hands couldn't grasp a match to light a cigarette. Feeling deserted, he thought despairingly: *It's beginning all over again. I thought it would end when I left that damned country. But it's not going to.*

Laxalt gathered up his clothing and shaving gear and stuffed everything including his blanket into his duffel bag.

Heinie demanded, "What does that mean, 'None?'"

"Just what it's supposed to mean," Laxalt said. "I'm by myself."

"That doesn't make sense. What's your rank?" Heinie again demanded.

"I don't have a rank," Laxalt said. "I'm a casual officer."

"Well, what do you do?"

"I'm not supposed to say."

"What kind of bullshit is that?" Heinie threatened. "If you're in the Army, you got to have a rank and you got to have a reason for being here."

"I've got a reason," Laxalt started to say as he was cut off by the Texan, who came to his defense. Laxalt confirmed he was on a State Department mission but could give no more detail other than that he'd tried to get into the armed forces but was rejected for health reasons and then arranged through a U.S. senator for an overseas civilian assignment.

His cabin mates were astonished that Laxalt had voluntarily put himself in harm's way aboard a troop ship being hounded by German submarine torpedoes. With the exception of Heinie, who remained arrogant and hostile, the others wanted to know more about Laxalt. He would not stay in this cabin a minute longer. While the others joined in noisy camaraderie in the galley below, Laxalt took his belongings up to the main deck which was blacked out as the ship avoided the deadly German submarines. He climbed into one of the many life rafts rigged on the deck, covered himself with a piece of canvas and propped a life jacket into a makeshift pillow. Peering out of this nest, he tried to drift into sleep as he looked up at the stars. They were as clear in the dark night sky as those that twinkled above his father's sheep camp in the Sierra Nevada. He thought: *That part of America I will miss. That and my family, but nothing else.*

Laxalt thought he could avoid the arrogance of Heinie and the uneasiness of the cabin and its tightly crowded six bunks but he quickly learned he was involved with them whether he liked it or not. The others had noted his aquiline nose, flat to one side from having been broken in his young boxing days as well as scars near his eyes, another toll from his being pounded in the ring with the Stewart Indian School and Golden Gloves bouts. They had put two and two together and decided he was a fighter.

The Texan, being a senior officer, had approved a boxing match to ease tensions among the men and elected Laxalt to be the main attraction in a fight with a soldier named Batalucco who had been a Golden Gloves champion in Chicago.

Heinie was promoting the fight with hopes of seeing the tough Chicago boxer destroy Laxalt. Laxalt told the Texan he would fight. But that he wanted everyone to think he was way overmatched so Heinie and his friends would put up a lot of money betting that Batalucco would knock him out. Laxalt had no intention of allowing that to happen. He planned to win and force the Heinie to lose his bet and the considerable amount of money he had overconfidently and errantly waged.

Laxalt drew first blood with a left jab to the Chicago fighter's face and easily took the second and third rounds as Heinie grimaced with anger from ringside. As he went for the knockout in the fourth round the ship was rocked with an explosion that sent spectators and fighters running from the ring, chaotically fighting for the single ladder to escape to the higher decks of the shuddering ship.

Everyone shouted: "Torpedoes!" "Torpedoes!" Someone yelled: "We're going down!"

The MPs on the above open decks fired forty-five caliber pistols into the air to get the attention of the clamoring men and halt the panic. There were no torpedoes. The explosion came from an errant depth charge with a short fuse. The ship was not under torpedo attack. And the boxing match was over, without a finish, though Laxalt had won the respect of everyone other than the sullen Heine.

Laxalt's shuddered at his first sights, sounds, and smells of Africa . . . Casablanca's harbor a graveyard of sunken ships . . . a remaining Nazi sniper's bullet firing at a match, lit in the darkness, zinging off the ship's steel hull and someone yelling "No matches!" . . . a nightmarish scramble of poor Arabs in rags and turbans scrambling for coins in the streets and being beaten back into the alleys by Senegalese soldiers with long batons . . . a famed Dakar whorehouse in a white mansion with prostitutes from twelve countries strolling the gardens and working the upstairs rooms of exotic Arabic décor . . . taken on a tour by a merchant marine, visiting out of curiosity but not partaking . . . the green jungle set off from the blue Atlantic by the white sandy beaches . . .

As he and a companion flew from Dakar in French West Africa to Leopoldville in the Congo, the companion said: "I suppose you know what you're getting into . . ." Laxalt shrugged and shook his head in silence. "Malaria, dysentery, heat, humidity, jaundice, boils, blacks who will steal you blind, malaria, malaria, ad infinitum. In case they didn't tell you, you'll be straddling the equator."

Laxalt settled into the residences and offices of the American Consulate General attending the routine of cocktail parties that the many foreign legations, all located in the same traditional diplomatic neighborhood, put on to entertain each other socially. Being from small town America, he was dazzled when he found himself in the center of sophisticated formal manners, tuxedoes, white gowns, serious political conversations, flowing whiskey and vodka amid the endless background music of stringed instruments.

He quickly learned that all was not as friendly as it seemed because everyone at play in this international game was coyly trying to find out what everyone else knew. They then took the information, tidbit or major discovery, back to their respective consulates for code officers such as Laxalt to secretly transmit to their home countries. He had been trained in his brief time in Washington D.C. in confidential cryptography and was surprised to learn the American legation was using an old standard called Brown's Code Book which also was used by the other legations, those of enemies and allies alike.

Most of the conversation was mundane, much of the information being dispatched by ordinary code having already been published in the newspapers including old war news. But there was an exception when more vital information needed to be sent by confidential code including observations of the frequent visits by suspected German spies to the official Belgian offices. The tension grew when two men, a regular legation staffer and a visitor from Washington, D.C., called Laxalt into a confidential meeting in the vice consul's office.

They revealed they worked for the Office of Strategic Services, the OSS, which was the legendary secret intelligence unit of the U.S. government. Grim-faced, they told Laxalt their special confidential code officer was down with malaria and they wanted Laxalt to substitute for him by coding some highly secret material to dispatch to Washington.

"Bob, we have to be careful," the vice consul said. "This place is crawling with Nazi spies."

"You want me to handle your stuff?" Laxalt asked.

"Yep . . . until we can smuggle one of our own code men into the Congo operation," the OSS man from Washington said. Laxalt agreed but appeared uncertain and hesitant to ask what this was all about. Reading Laxalt's perplexed expression, the OSS man said: "Young man. For your own sake, it'd better that you don't know."

The OSS was created by President Roosevelt in 1942 to gather information and sabotage enemy military operations. With a staff of twelve thousand, it dispatched secret agents from its base in Washington to collect and study information in all U.S. theaters of war, many behind enemy lines. It countered enemy propaganda with disinformation activities and used sabotage and demolition to aid resistance and guerrilla operatives fighting allied enemies.

As Laxalt went to work coding the highly secret dispatches he noted information relating to mining that stood out to him because of his background in Nevada, which was widely known for its gold and silver mines. And he wondered about the word *Shinkolobwe*. He mentioned it as he was having a drink with the OSS man at a sidewalk cafe filled with Belgians. "Jesus Christ," the OSS man said. "Don't ever use that word in anyone's presence. Not ever!" He then revealed that the Shinkolobwe mine near the Congo's Elizabethville was the world's only mine producing uranium and that the Germans had been importing it for secret scientific research since before 1940. American scientists, who once thought the mineral to be worthless, had taken new interest in it and were now importing it, too. No one was saying why publicly. But there seemed to be a secretive race to get it.

Confidentially, scientist Albert Einstein had advised President Roosevelt in a letter dated August 2, 1939 that uranium could be used "in the immediate future" to build ". . . extremely powerful bombs of a new type." Einstein speculated: "A single bomb of this type, carried by boat and exploded in a port, might very well destroy the whole port together with some of the surrounding territory." Einstein told the president that "the most important source of uranium is Belgian Congo." By October, Roosevelt appointed a secret committee called the Manhattan Project to explore using militarizing uranium, which would open the Atomic Age.

The Shinkolobwe Mine was owned by Union Minière of Belgium, which produced the uranium and shipped it to its refinery near Brussels where it was stockpiled without much attention since it had no commercial use. Germany took Belgium in May of 1940 but did little with the uranium even though its scientists, who had been importing the mineral themselves to Germany, knew of its atomic potential. Hitler, preoccupied with the war, showed no personal interest in it. This resulted in Germany failing to develop the atomic power the Americans were exploring in the top-secret Manhattan Project that would create the atomic bombs used on Japan to end the Pacific war four years later.

The twenty-year-old Laxalt knew nothing of such worldly problems as he dispatched the top-secret coded messages, which he himself didn't fully understand, from Leopoldville to Washington. He was developing a significant new problem of his own.

There is no sense kidding myself. I have malaria, Laxalt thought. He had been warned of what the Americans and English called Annie—Anopheles, the deadly malarial mosquito that infested the Congo and that had infected the other confidential code officer.

"Holy Christ! You've got it," his Swahili errand boy said when he saw Laxalt shaking and sweating in the code room. Legation associates put Laxalt to bed and covered him with blankets. He was gripped by malaria's life-threatening fever, chills, thirst, and delirium. His skin turned as dry and brittle as parchment. He thought: *I could pinch the skin of my hands and it would crackle and tear like paper.* The attacks came, eased, and came viciously again and again for months as he rode through the terror of fever and debilitating pain. In his delirium, he had visions of blue Nevada sky and snowy mountains, even bleating sheep and barking sheepdogs. He thought: "My dreams began to show me where my heart belonged, and it was not in steaming Africa. Anger against my country was waning."

When the fever finally passed and his health returned to normal his thoughts about returning home to America intensified when he received a bundle of delayed mail from his war-divided family. The news was troubling and made him want to return home.

His father wrote from Carson City in October of 1944. Laxalt was heartened to learn that Dominique continued his way of life tending his sheep and protecting them from coyotes and mountain lions. "I don't worry about the coyotes because my two sheep dogs are big and good fighters. If the coyotes talk to each other, they know that Jumbo and Barbo will kill them pretty quick."

Paul wrote in November with news of having "a ringside seat for the biggest show on earth, the invasion of the Philippines. . . . If I get out okay, and there's no reason I shouldn't now, it will really be worth remembering." Laxalt longed for his family and was cheered by Paul's hopes for the bitter war's end within two years: "We'll be together again, and a wiser, happier group we'll be."

Laxalt was deeply concerned when he read a letter his mother had sent from Carson that same month: "We just received your letter about the malaria. I am so worried. What is happening to our family? Suzette is gone to the convent. In her order, the nuns are cloistered. It is like a daughter dying. . . . I pray every morning at Holy Mass that my sons will come home safe. I could not bear it I lose you two, too. . . ."

And he was inspired by a letter from Suzanne who told of her decision to become a nun. "My dear brother in Christ: I was so worried about my dear brothers that I almost made a pact with God. Unless He spared your lives and brought you home safe, I would not enter the order. Then I realized that I had committed a terrible sacrilege even thinking such a thing. My mind was made up in that instant. . . . Please understand me, and love me. I will love and pray for you both all the days of my life. Your sister in Christ."

Laxalt opened another letter sent from a friend in Battle Mountain, Nevada. In the envelope was a sprig of sagebrush. Its sweet pungent smell overwhelmed him. He knew it was time to go home:

> The word overseas has lost its glamour for me. Every letter from home was like a drawstring pulling me back to where I belonged—my country, right or wrong. I have learned a lot in this experience, but the experience is done and I am tired of it. This war has shattered our ordered family life, and all I want is to help put that order together again with my loved ones. The foolish things one does in an outrage!

Laxalt's deteriorating health resulted in his receiving orders for him to return to the United States in 1945 for debriefing in Washington about his Congo experiences. As he prepared for the voyage home, his health improved, and, once at sea, it continued to improve as he deeply breathed the fresh sea air during the long days and nights that his ship zigzagged its way across the Atlantic avoiding the deadly German submarines. As the ship entered the New York harbor, the Statue of Liberty stood out in the light fog. Laxalt didn't try to hold back his tears.

Coming Home

Laxalt found a phone booth near St. Patrick's Cathedral in midtown Manhattan and nervously but joyfully placed a call to his mother whom he had not been able to contact from Africa about his plans to come home. He located her in San Francisco.

With Paul, Bob, and John away in the war and Suzanne in a convent as a Roman Catholic nun, Theresa could not manage the French Hotel by herself. John, despite his youth, had helped by running important errands such as going to Reno to get the liquor for the bar and to the bakery for fresh bread. So she shut down the hotel and restaurant, turned the bar over to Dominique, closed the family home, and bundled up daughter Marie and son Mick for a Greyhound bus ride to San Francisco where she rented a furnished apartment. Dominique stayed at the Carson hotel.

Marie answered Laxalt's phone call in San Francisco and it took her by surprise. "This is Robert!" he exclaimed, shouting over the noisy din of the Manhattan street. "This is Robert!" "No it isn't," Marie responded. She told the caller her brother Robert was in Africa. "Goddamit, Marie, I'm coming home!" he shouted.

When Theresa got to the phone and heard his voice, she broke into tears, as did Laxalt, now only a continent's width away from his family. She told him to go home to Carson City and said that she, too, would return. Aware of his malaria, she immediately made plans to help nurse her son back to good health with love and her fine cooking. She gathered up their clothing for the bus ride back to Carson to reopen the house.

Laxalt took a train from New York to Washington, D.C. for a week of debriefing at the State Department, then took another train for the four-day journey to Nevada not knowing exactly who would be there to greet him. He had sent a telegram from Washington to Dominique but he had no way of knowing if his father would be in Carson City to get it or up in the hills with his sheep. In Reno, Laxalt boarded the Virginia and Truckee (V&T)

short line railroad for the thirty-mile ride to Carson City through the scenic pasture land of Washoe Valley at the base of towering Slide Mountain. How strikingly different from the jungles of Africa. How enriching to his soul, this deep feeling of being in his personal home country, the Sierra Nevada, once again.

"Are you Dominique Laxalt's son Robert?" a tall, lean cowboy asked as Laxalt stepped out of the V&T station in Carson. Laxalt looked at the cowboy with a sure sense of being back home in the West and said that, yes, he was Dominique's son. "Well he got word to me to pick you up and take you to the sheep camp. Get your bag. You can spend the night with me in my room. I'm a roomer at the Star Hotel. That's a little Basque Hotel down the street. You'll be on familiar ground, since you're a Basco, too."

The hotel was actually a rooming house owned and operated by the Supera family. Theresa Supera was happily surprised when she came home from high school to see Laxalt sitting on the porch relaxing. He told her, quietly, that he was glad to be home. He appeared to be thinner than she had remembered. The family had heard he suffered from a terrible disease in Africa but he did not talk about it, nor about his wartime experiences in the Congo, nor being at sea amid the threat of submarines. He just wanted to talk quietly about being home. She was relieved by Laxalt's gentle demeanor and thought to herself that, in this time of epic international violence, this close and warm friend of her family could never hurt anyone.

Laxalt felt comfortable in the familiar Basque family-style surroundings. He sipped a glass of red wine and ate the nourishing hearty Basque dinner of traditional salad, soup, stew, freshly made bread, crisp French fried potatoes, and hard jack cheese for dessert. He thought about his deep bitterness over his country's rejecting him from military service and the near-death brush with malaria and he welcomed his change of heart, happy to be home in Nevada and soon to be reunited with the family he cherished.

When Laxalt awoke, he welcomed the sound of the morning rain. As he and the cowboy drove from the city toward the high range country to meet his father, he savored the fresh sweet smell of the sagebrush bathed in the glowing raindrops. Suddenly, he saw his father's truck coming toward them. Laxalt yelled as Dominique passed them, then screeched to a stop. The cowboy turned around and the two trucks pulled up to each other.

Father and son, separated by time, distance and war, greeted each other with some puzzlement. Dominique knew his son was different, much thinner, exclaiming: "Oh, my God, what happened to you?"

Laxalt grasped his father's strong hand and said: "I'm all right now. I haven't had an attack of malaria since I left Africa." Laxalt reassured the ever-hardy sheepherder that he was well, having put on five pounds to compensate for the twenty-five pounds the malaria attacks had stripped from him. "The important thing is you're alive and home," the father said to the son. Laxalt thanked the cowboy and joined his father for the drive off the paved highway to the bumpy, rutted dirt road journey to the sheep camp.

The mountain air was refreshingly clear and clean, unlike the Congo's humidity he'd breathed with such dangerous difficulty. He studied the rugged landscape with deep appreciation and remembrance of his growing-up years in the Sierra Nevada high above Carson City to the east and the vast deep blue waters of Lake Tahoe spread before him to the west.

As he joined his father and his uncle Pete who was helping tend the sheep for dinner in the little canvas tent, he radiated with the cozy feeling of being home where he belonged. He remained in the sheep camp for several days awaiting his mother's return to Carson City from San Francisco and while he loved being there with his father he yearned to return to his boyhood home and the mother he had missed so much in his travels over the seas.

It was an emotional homecoming for all as the family began putting itself back together. Laxalt pondered the reunion with his mother, his younger siblings, Marie and Mick, and his thoughts embraced even more as he eventually noted in his memoir:

> My journey was over. The war was nearing its end, and the future seemed predictable. My brother Paul would be coming home his combat days behind him. My sister Suzanne, who had become a nun, was at least within telephone distance. The family home was filling with familiar voices and cooking scents. We were nearly a united family again.

Laxalt continued to have severe headaches in his bouts of recurring malaria. He tried to gain strength through diet and exercise, including helping Dominique in the rugged work of the sheep camp. He decided to resume his college education, not at the highly acclaimed, privately operated, Santa Clara University in California, but at his home state's public University of Nevada.

The pretty little campus had been the scene of Hollywood movies because it looked like a picturesque Ivy League school in the East with its autumn colored vines lacing red brick buildings and spacious, tree-lined quadrangle of grass. The university's quad was a replica of the University of Virginia's, which had been designed by Thomas Jefferson as an academic village with a large lawn surrounded by classroom buildings. A Nevada benefactor had sent an architect in 1906 to Charlottesville to study the Jefferson-designed quad.

The campus was perched on a slight hill a few blocks north of downtown Reno's gambling halls and saloons, banks and churches, and San Francisco–sized mansions overlooking the Truckee River. Nevada's only university had been founded sixty years earlier in the state's northeastern, sprawling cattle county of Elko and moved shortly after 280 miles to the west to Reno, which boasted itself as "The Biggest Little City in the World."

Laxalt's decision to attend the University of Nevada as an English major would profoundly alter his life, the cultures of Nevada and the West, as well as the world of European/American emigration literature.

Joyce Winifred Nielsen, a fourth-generation Nevadan of Northern European descent, was an actress in plays during each of her four years at Reno High School, an ardent reader of English literature, a special summer class student of French, and a writer of short stories and poetry by the time she graduated at sixteen and enrolled at the University of Nevada. She had been born to Grace and Henry Nielsen. Grace was a graduate of the University of Nevada who taught school in Reno and Henry worked in the Sparks hub center of the Southern Pacific Railroad. Joyce's maternal grandmother was Amy Heritage Parker, who had graduated from the university and became a roving rural teacher. These teachers traveled from one rural school district to another, living with ranch families. In one such ranch family's home, she met her husband to be, Harry Parker who later left ranching for the mining industry. Joyce's maternal great-grandmother was Sarah Baker Heritage whose husband George Heritage had fought in the Union Army during the Civil War, then struck out for the West and the logging business at Lake Tahoe. Joyce traced her family farther back—to Sarah Baker Heritage's own father who had galloped across the West as a Pony Express rider.

Joyce, despite her awareness of this family background of educated women and her own intellectual explorations, was shy by nature. She wore her blonde hair at shoulder length and was pretty with elfin eyes and a ready smile that she shared with her college chum girlfriends while being reserved when around the few boys on campus. (Many college-aged boys were away at war in 1945.) That fall, as the semester was beginning, she walked into Stewart Hall, a three-story Victorian architectural masterpiece of high ceilings, dark wooden stairways and curved banisters, and arched doorways, and ascended the stairs to her second floor French class. She was early and, while waiting for her classmates and professor to arrive, she looked beyond the curtains and sill of the tall window out at the gates that separated the campus from the little city.

She was transfixed at the sight she saw—an alarmingly handsome man with jet black hair, an angular face the likes of which she had never seen before on any man, and a stance of distinction. It was Robert Laxalt standing at a large bulletin board on the sidewalk leading from the campus gates to the quad. She could see he was reading notes posted on the board. His trench coat, collar turned up at the back of his neck, flowed from his shoulders to his boots, which were a style foreign to her and unlike the cowboy boots common in Nevada. A romantic, Joyce had heard of love at first sight and suddenly knew she was experiencing it. She watched him walk away from the board toward Stewart Hall and then lost sight of him.

As students entered the classroom, there he was, walking through the door. Bob took a seat directly behind Joyce and her friend Rose Meredith. She thought he didn't notice her, but, in fact, he had, because earlier at the nearby Wolf Den where students gathered for breakfast and lunch he had seen her sitting with her girlfriends. Now sitting behind her, he recalled having being smitten at first sight of her. Neither Laxalt, also shy by nature despite his aggressiveness in sports, nor Joyce spoke to each other. But she turned frequently, just enough to study his polished brown boots, which she later learned were African mosquito boots. Professor B. F. Chapelle greeted the students and acknowledged Laxalt by name as if he knew him. In fact, the professor recognized the Laxalt name as French Basque. Laxalt was the only male student and he was older than the girls in the class. Joyce thought he was strikingly mature, but she wondered about his strange name. She'd never heard of such a name, Laxalt. It seemed awkward as she quietly pronounced it to herself.

As the days turned into weeks, the professor encouraged the students to read aloud to each other from French literature. Laxalt had learned some

Robert and Joyce, students at
University of Nevada, Reno, circa
1945.

French from his mother singing French lullabies and his parents' conversations but the other students noted he didn't do well in past and future
tenses. "Present tense Laxalt" some joked. Joyce never said a word to Bob
even though she plotted with her girlfriends to ask him to go to her Delta
Delta Delta formal dance in November. As it turned out, he had something
in mind for her, too.

Finally, she got up the nerve to phone him at the Alpha Tau Omega
fraternity house where she had learned he was living. She dialed the number and asked the young man who answered the call if Robert Laxalt was
there. No, he was out. She left her home number with the fraternity brother
and asked him to have Laxalt phone her. Later that evening the one phone
in the Nielsen home, located in the living room, rang.

"This is Bob Laxalt. Is there someone there who needed to speak to
me?"

"Yes, this is Joyce Nielsen," she responded, embarrassed because she
had to talk to him in front of her whole family. It was made worse because

she had no privacy in suddenly asking him to go to her sorority dance. He accepted her invitation and then revealed he had planned to call her to invite her to his fraternity dance. She said she would be happy to accept and without much elaboration, due to her whole family listening to her end of the conversation, the two French classmates ended the phone call. And so they had spoken at last, after eight weeks of sitting next to each other, she in front, he behind, never uttering a word to each other though they obviously had kept a close eye on one another.

The dances were both on the same weekend, his at the Trinity Church community room on the southern bank of the Truckee River, hers at a hall on Sierra Street just north of the river. Both dances were formal, with orchestras, so Laxalt wore a tuxedo each night and dress shoes replacing the African boots he wore everywhere else. She wore formal dresses. The courtship was underway between the handsome, dark-haired, twenty-one-year-old son of Basque immigrants and the pretty sixteen-year-old blonde daughter of generations of Nevada university-educated women and business and professional men.

They began cordially talking to each other in class and occasionally cutting class to walk through the picturesque campus where, in an effort to demonstrate his skills, he taught her how to play mumblety-peg by holding a knife so it touched his head then flipping it through the air to have its blade stick in the ground. They held hands in the movies and met for dinner at the restaurants spread around downtown Reno including the Moulin Rouge, a tiny but sophisticated Sierra Street bistro, a block north of the river, that served fresh French bread and onion soup on tables with red-and-white checkered tablecloths and linen napkins. They visited Lake Tahoe for picnics and swimming and Joyce was shocked at the sight of his very white skin the first time she saw Bob in a swimsuit. They skated on the icy surface of Manzanita Lake next to the great brick library on the campus and at the frozen ponds of Idlewild Park adjacent to the Truckee at the west end of Riverside Drive. They gathered with friends to stay warm around bonfires on the shores of the ponds.

Bob missed class some days and Joyce learned he stayed in his fraternity house bedroom in the dark suffering from severe headaches from the recurring malaria. He didn't talk to her about the malaria but she learned from his fraternity brothers that he retreated in isolation to deal with the severe head-searing pain.

Many young men who had fought in the war were returning to college and, like Laxalt, found campus life quite different from their lives in war-torn Europe or the Pacific islands. Laxalt and long-time friend Pete Reading wanted to room together where they could also get their meals and that meant joining a fraternity. They browsed around the various fraternity houses and decided the food was best at the ATO house, which was located on a hill on University Terrace overlooking not only downtown Reno but three sororities including Joyce's Tri-Delta house.

The gap quickly became evident between what Laxalt saw as pink-cheeked freshmen students and the older veterans. They told stories about how a fraternity president welcomed new pledges, including a burly American survivor of German gunfire, with a vacuous lecture on various campus rules and penalties for violating the rules. When the burly pledge laughed at a rule that ordered pledges to walk around big quad rather than save time walking across the lawn, the fraternity president ordered up a paddle that Laxalt judged to be about as large as a tennis racket. Then the president ordered the combat-seasoned pledge to bend over and take ten swats on his "posterior." The pledge asked to examine the paddle. Taking it in hand, he broke it apart and returned the pieces to the president. That pretty much took care of hazing the veterans.

Bob studied literature but not journalism, figuring he could learn the latter by writing part-time during his school days for the local newspapers. He wrote sports for *Nevada State Journal* sports editor Ty Cobb, covering, among other topics, university basketball and his brother John, who had returned from the Navy to play for the team. Bob also began covering news of Carson City for the Reno newspapers and planned after graduation in 1947 to set up his own Capital News Service on a full-time basis to provide stories for the international UP wire service and California newspapers.

Joyce majored in theater and, as she had done in high school, acted in student plays each year at the university. She wrote a play about Judas betraying Jesus and it was produced on campus. Bob attended the play and watched her act in other plays as well, and she, in turn, went to the university boxing matches to watch Bob fight. She hated the fights even though the crowd loved the sport and cheered, "Frenchy!" "Frenchy!" as Bob entered the ring in his long red robe. She couldn't stand seeing others hitting the man she loved. She would not go to the fights alone. She always had her sister accompany her.

Robert boxing
at University of
Nevada, Reno,
circa 1946.

With the exception of the torturous malaria headaches that attacked Bob and the prize fights that Joyce hated, their first semester together was blissful at the little university. They joined their classmates, settling into the peacefulness of post–World War II America, and continued their courtship through their college years. She could not anticipate anything but their happiness together. There were no signs of the turmoil to come.

Marriage and the Writing Life

Joyce Nielsen had never seen anger in the Robert Laxalt she fell instantly in love with when she was sixteen and he had just turned twenty-one. She knew he was tormented by the horrendous malaria-driven headaches and she knew he relished boxing even though she thought it to be a dangerous and cruel sport. She knew Bob not as a combatant but as a gentle, soft-spoken, sometimes slyly humorous, intellectually inspired English-literature student with an aptitude for writing journalistically

So Joyce was not prepared for what she saw on a mild spring evening in 1947 after three-and-a-half years of courtship when Bob, by now her steady boyfriend, came to her home on Mary Street in Southwest Reno to take her out to dinner. As they left the house to walk to his car, Joyce's mother, Grace, called out, "Oh, Bob, come back in here. You know, have you set a wedding date?" Joyce was shocked at her mother's blatant question. She had never mentioned anything to her mother about getting married.

Bob didn't respond. He just stared at Grace Nielsen. Then he asked Joyce to get into the car. He started the engine, looked straight ahead and pulled the car away from the curb. He drove in silence. It seemed forever to Joyce, who could tell something was seriously wrong. This was a very different Bob Laxalt. She knew him to be a sensitive person who could be hurt by what he perceived as a slight or an insult and that he could retreat into quietude. But she'd never seen what she saw now as an extreme icy silence. He finally spoke out in anger. "You tell your mother that what I do is my business," he said furiously. Then he drove the car back to her house, opened the door, and let her out. She walked into the house and to her bedroom and went to bed, shaken.

Bob graduated from the University of Nevada that spring and did not speak to Joyce again that summer nor in the fall when she returned to the campus for her final year of school. Having graduated, he was not around campus but one day she did see his car nearby. She placed a rose on the window but did not leave a note. She did not phone him, nor did he phone her. Then in November, five months after the angry evening, her phone rang at the university office where she had a part-time job. It was Bob. He asked Joyce if she would like a ride home. She said yes. Neither mentioned the flower she had placed on the window.

They began dating again. Their life together returned to the literary, theatrical, and recreational adventures they had enjoyed before. He gave her a ring during dinner at the little bistro, Moulin Rouge. They planned a wedding at St. Thomas Aquinas Cathedral in Reno for May 29, 1949, the Memorial Day weekend. Part of the planning didn't sit well with Joyce or her family who were Episcopalian Protestants. Bob's mother, Theresa, was what Joyce thought of as a radical devotee to the Catholic Church with pictures of Jesus Christ on every wall in the house. Theresa insisted that Joyce not only study Catholicism but also convert to the Church of Rome, which she begrudgingly did.

Robert and Joyce's wedding at Saint Thomas Aquinas Cathedral in Reno, 1949 following his college graduation in 1947.

Joyce was about to join the large Laxalt family and its even larger extended family of Basque immigrants and offspring. They all gathered at St. Thomas for the formal wedding ceremony at two o'clock in the afternoon, Bob in a dark suit, Joyce in a flowing gown she had purchased in San Francisco. The reception followed at the nearby 20th Century Club. Bob, never one to like big crowds, preferring a quiet, more private life, suggested they duck out of the reception early and go home to the apartment they rented at 244 Hill Street a couple blocks away from the downtown courthouse where Bob had spent time during his college years as a part-time reporter gathering the news. On their two-week honeymoon, they drove through the Pacific Northwest to British Columbia.

Joyce returned to finish college with a teaching credential and went to work at B.D. Billinghurst Junior High School in a leafy green neighborhood on Plumas Street in Southwest Reno whose rebellious students kidded her about being too young to teach teenagers. She was twenty-one. After a year at the junior high, she moved to McKinley Park Elementary School where she felt more at home with the younger pupils.

Bob thought about someday writing the kind of literature he'd been reading from childhood through college but his days were consumed now as a full-time reporter doing stories for the Capital News Service he had created in Carson City in the spring of 1947 to serve the UP and Reno and California newspapers.

A brief story appeared in the *Nevada State Journal* headlined:

Laxalt to Open News Gathering Agency in Carson

Items appearing in the Nevada State Journal and bearing the credit initials, CNS, are disseminated by the Capital News Service, which will begin full-scale operations in Carson City on Monday.

The news agency is being founded by Robert P. Laxalt, well known Carson City resident, who has been one of the Journal's Carson City correspondents for many months.

CNS is offering daily and weekly coverage of events in the state capital to a number of Nevada newspapers and radio stations.

Mr. Laxalt was graduated last week from the University of Nevada.

CNS stories written by Robert Laxalt began regularly popping into print and would continue to do so from 1947 into 1949 when he joined the UP as a staff correspondent.

Human Skeleton Found in Carson

Carson City (CNS). A human skeleton was unearthed here today by a city grader during development work on the capital city's Sierra Heights project. Lester Smith, Ormsby county sheriff, will begin an investigation immediately. Current conjectures as to the age of the bones date it as a fatality of old Indian and white settler skirmishes in the Carson City area . . .

Miller of White Pine to Continue Fight for War Bonus, He Announces

Carson City. Branding the current session of the Nevada legislature as "the most apathetic in the United States of America," E. R. ("Boots") Miller, assemblyman from White Pine County, stated today he would fight to the last ditch for passage of his proposed veterans' bonus bill . . .

Carson Residents Facing another .22 Rifle Scourge

Carson City (CNS). The capital city's .22 caliber rifle scourge, dormant for several weeks after the confiscation by authorities of firearms belonging to potential young Jesse James, flared anew here recently.

Carson's citizenry pulled their heads a bit closer to their shoulders today when reports were publicized to the effect that people were getting their tires punctured and their hats blown off by erstwhile young marksmen . . .

Big Gold Nugget Causes Commotion in Carson Office

Carson City (CNS). A quartz lump of exceedingly high gold content, displayed this week in the office of John Koontz, secretary of state, caused quite a commotion.

The nugget was shown simultaneously with the filing of incorporation articles for the new El Dorado Syndicate by R. M. Sanderson, widely known Nevada mining operator.

When questioned by a nearby reporter as to whether the nugget came from the new El Dorado mine in Goldfield, Sanderson refused to say a word, but snatched the Nugget and his papers from the filing desk and scurried out of the capitol building . . .

Laxalt's Capital News Service coverage ranged from deadline pressure breaking police news of crime and tragedies to the financial and political complexities of government as well as nondeadline feature stories, mostly about people and human character or lack of it, to sports including boxing which he championed.

A *Nevada State Journal* Sports Editor's Note introduced Laxalt to the readers: "Robert Laxalt, the author of this article, speaks with authority when he writes on collegiate boxing. He is a veteran of the University of Nevada rings and one year recently was voted the 'Best U. of N. boxer.'"

The story was headlined:

Nevada Athlete Proposes Boxing as School Sport

The analytical story opened dramatically:

By Robert Laxalt, Capital News Service
Carson City, Nevada. From days of old when gladiators bound their hands with metal strips and went forth to pound each others' faces into bleeding pulp, the manly art of boxing has often been proclaimed as the nearest throwback to barbarism that any age could offer.

Even today, with boxing civilized to a high degree by the intensive effort of generations of athletic authorities, fighters are gazed at askance by a good share of the public.

Laxalt goes on to acknowledge the dangers of professional prizefighting for those without championship ability as a potential "wobbly stroll down rum-dum alley." But he raises the argument that through strictly enforced rules, controlled collegiate boxing is safer in minor injuries than football, wrestling, soccer, water polo, baseball, basketball, "and get this, even track."

And when it came to serious injuries such as fractures, stitched cuts, concussions, torn or pulled ligaments, analyst Laxalt wrote: "Boxing ranked below football, wrestling, soccer, basketball, track, and remained on an even keel with baseball."

Laxalt vouched for controlled boxing as a good sport for Nevada's high schools to develop physical fitness, agility, quick thinking, self-confidence, courage, skill, and *"above all sportsmanship."* What's more, Laxalt, the advocate, argued *"Financially, the advantages are nothing but good,"* citing strong fan-paying customers turning out at popular matches and bringing in much needed funds for all high school sports.

The twenty-four-year-old Laxalt was comfortable when writing about people, an instinct he hoped would serve him well as he aspired in years to come toward major magazine writing and authorship of fiction and non-fiction books.

Report on Orphans Home
By Robert Laxalt, Capital News Service
Carson City. Best tribute that can be paid to the Nevada Orphans Home here in the capital city is that in every sense of the word, it is just that—a home.

Any resemblance to an institution ends at the white gateway to the 16-acre tract of hayfields, milking barns, and gray stone buildings. Inside is a large turbulent family of homeless and orphaned youngsters.

A child need not be a complete or even part orphan to be cared for at the state orphanage. Many children have been plucked from the pits of poverty and sent here for a clean, happy, and healthy rearing in Nevada's salubrious western mountain climate. Youngsters from families in desperate plights have time and again been turned aside from what may well have been a miserable existence and instead have grown into substantial citizens . . .

Home youngsters have established some of the highest scholastic ratings ever earned in Carson City. In the field of athletics, however, the healthy life, the wholesome food, and the regular hours kept by the home kids have really paid off. It is hard to remember when home athletes have not starred on Carson City aggregations . . .

Laxalt added a light touch when writing about whimsical topics.

Capitol Is Described as "Glorified Outhouse"
By Robert Laxalt
Carson City (CNS)—Nevada's capitol corridors ran rampant with varied comments here today when the people who make their livelihood beneath the dome read that the building had been described as a "glorified outhouse."

The decidedly derogatory description, appearing in this week's *Life* magazine, was uttered by one John G. Nichols of Chicago.

The youthful Nichols recently completed a tour of the nation's capitols and compiled a complete album of photographs showing him standing on his head before each building.

Laxalt could not reach Governor Vail Pittman, who was out of town, for comment but the intrepid investigative reporter did quote a number of other state officials by name who issued light-hearted rejoinders to the *Life* magazine writer as well as one anonymous state worker who opined:

"That's a devil of a thing to say about our capitol—even if it is true."

The young reporter started developing a style of his own when writing a feature called:

Spirit of the West

By Robert Laxalt

In the days when Nevada was a wide expanse of frontier plains, over which bands of Indians roamed at will, the early settlers carved out of the wilderness a civilization founded on the principles of fortitude and human kindness.

Out of the mountains to the east came a never-ending train of covered wagons bearing families in search of "a place to settle down." The arrival of a family to one of these frontier outposts was a signal for all the men of the community to drop whatever they were doing and help the new "neighbor" build his home.

The West grew up and things like this were forgotten, but every once in a long while a dead harkening back to the old frontier days showed that the spirit was not dead.

Floyd Wishart and his family came to New Empire a few months ago. The little community, situated a mile or so east of Carson City, looked good to them and they decided to "settle down."

Laxalt wrote about Wishart going to work for the Sierra Pacific Power Co., earning money for materials to build a home while living in a tent on the property. Eventually, working late each night, the man built a small three-room house and the family moved in and all was well. Then, without warning, when the family was away from home, the house burned down and everything they owned was lost.

Laxalt continued:

Things looked black for Floyd Wishart as he moved his homeless family into an abandoned box car. He forgot one thing, however.

He was a "neighbor."

That word meant a lot in this lonely little community of Empire.

In three short days, the residents of New Empire, headed by Pete Pistisa, had collected more than $350 in cash, plus numerous contributions of food and clothing for the destitute family.

From nearby Carson City, gifts of building materials poured in a steady stream to the Pistisa home.

At nine o'clock today, the men of New Empire will begin work on a new and larger home for the Wisharts. With luck and hard work, the house will be ready within a week.

The young reporter, seasoning himself as a writer, was learning what good writers know: save something rewarding for the reader at the end of the story. Laxalt pondered, then finished the piece:

And just to make sure the new stove doesn't try any disastrous antics, the Carson City Sheet Metal Works has donated a patent flue!

Laxalt's reporting and writing for his Capital News Service clients earned him increasing respect from the pros in the busy UP bureau in the Gazette Building next to City Hall on Center Street in downtown Reno. When UP offered him a regular staff writer job, he jumped at it. His own little news service had provided stories on a piecemeal basis for UP in Reno and a handful of Nevada and California newspapers. But reporting and writing officially as a staffer for UP meant his stories would be dispatched across the country and around the world and put him into the legendary "deadline every minute" wire-service competition with the Associated Press (AP), UP's arch rival. Though still working in Carson City and Reno, this meant "By Robert Laxalt, United Press Staff Correspondent" was a move of his byline to the big leagues of national and international journalism.

Laxalt used the new opportunity to explain Nevada to the outside world. A 1950 broadcast carried a note for radio stations to use to explain the story their listeners are about to hear:

Station (——) presents the last of a series of United Press Radio stories about western prosperity. The preceding stories have shown that there is prosperity in the West . . . this last one provides the final proof. The story today is about the western state of Nevada, prepared by Robert Laxalt of the Reno bureau of United Press Radio.

Laxalt wrote the prose in the pronunciation-style of combining numbers with spelled-out figures and the separation of phrases by three dots or two dashes for easy conversational reading over the air by broadcasters:

Leading economists who regard the gambling barometer in Nevada as a true indication of the state's economic health say they are more than ever convinced that the state is on sound footing. And there's proof from other sources, too.

The economic status of Nevada is backed up by these facts. Gambling proceeds are running high . . . they hit a record in 1949 . . . industrial expansion is booming in Southern Nevada . . . oil fever is sweeping the state . . . and mining is showing a steady recovery.

Moreover, the population of Nevada is more than 50-thousand over the 1940 census of 110-thousand . . . and employment is reaching new records in all sections of the state.

Laxalt went on to describe in detail the economic strengths in industry, construction, mining, oil, and gambling with the flair for words he was developing as a professional writer:

In the wide expanses of desert in Eastern Nevada, oil fever has been mounting steadily for the past two years—first with the advent of Continental Oil Company and then with the sudden influx of more than a dozen similar firms. At present, some 16-hundred oil leases issued to these firms cover one-million-220-thousand acres of hitherto worthless land.

Laxalt loaded the story with more facts and figures:

Retail sales in 1948 and 1949 ranged in the neighborhood of 200-million-dollars yearly—last year an estimated 860-million-dollars passed over Nevada's gambling tables to establish an all-time betting record. The figure is almost double that of 1945—considered a good year, incidentally—in which 441-million dollars was wagered. In 1949, gambling operators in Nevada grossed approximately 43-million-dollars, two per cent of which went to the state in taxes.

And Laxalt saved something of a twist for the listener to punctuate the close of the radio story:

But here's a conservative note to end the story of prosperity in Nevada. The economists know that the boom can't last forever. They feel that there'll be a tapering off generally in the state this year . . . followed by a leveling off at a good point of economic health.

In a May 31, 1950 story published on the front page of the *Nevada State Journal* and dispatched on UP wires to newspapers across the nation and around the world, Laxalt harked to the spirit the West that would lead him eventually to authorship of seventeen books and publication of hundreds of other authors through his creation of the University of Nevada Press.

> *V. & T. Making Final Run of Its Career: Chapter in Passing of Old West Is Closing*
>
> By Robert Laxalt. United Press Staff Correspondent
>
> Another chapter in the passing history of the Old West will be closed today when the Virginia and Truckee Railway makes its last run.
>
> The 81-year-old shortline, whose story is the story of Virginia City, will be laid to rest this afternoon—the loser in a hopeless battle with the modern age, its highways, its faster modes of transportation.
>
> As in the days of its birth, the Virginia and Truckee's yellow wooden coaches will be filled with passengers for its last trip; but the ride will not be a joyous one. For one and all, the "last ride" on the V and T carries the sadness of farewell.

The now-veteran newsman and journalistic writer moved into a literary narrative that drew a sentimental picture through prose and let the reader feel a part of the western saga.

> As the railway's last locomotive tugs its way laboriously up the grade from Carson City to Lakeview Hill and across Washoe Valley, farmers in their fields will stop their work to watch the train go by. For as long as many of them can remember, the piping blast of the V and T's whistle has marked the start of the day, and its return in the late afternoon across the shadow of the looming Sierra has been the signal that the day's work is done.

Laxalt added descriptive color and the kind of storytelling detail about people that he was developing as a journalist and would eventually master in his books and teach in his writing classes:

> Noticeable in the faded plush seat of the coaches are the old timers.
>
> A few of them can remember how the ox-teams labored to pull the first shining locomotive up the precipitous Geiger Grade to Virginia City for that first welcome; they can remember the V and T's first trip in that year of 1869 amid the tumult of cheers from Virginia City's teeming thousands in the lusty heyday of the Comstock Lode; they can remember the proud days of the railroad's glory when it carried the rich gold and silver ore—"the wealth that built San Francisco"; they can remember President U.S. Grant's gasp of admiration at the gaudy yellow coaches, the plush-lined seats, and the shining new track.

Laxalt continued the writer's style of taking the reader, through the personal experience of others, deeply into the story:

> And they can remember the time when the V and T began to die, when Virginia City's thousands had vanished, when its mines lay abandoned, when voices sounded hollow in the once-roaring saloons. And, finally, they can remember the death blow—when the track to Virginia City was abandoned, when the railway fought for survival, selling off its locomotives and coaches to movie studios, to world fairs, to museums.

Laxalt's detailed reporting and descriptive prose established the story for the minds of national and global newspaper readers who had been to, or knew about, Virginia City in its glory days. But he brought the story to a close as local news in the romantic and idealistic style that he would develop in years to come as an author.

> And today, as they climb down from the little shortline for the last time, they will have the memory that ends the chapter—"the last ride on the V and T."

The spirits of the Old West and the "New West" weren't all that much different when it came to UP reporter Laxalt training his eye on dramatic detail for breaking news. He captured the color in a July 5, 1950 story datelined Lovelock, a small ranching and farming town ninety-five miles northeast of Reno.

> *Bartender and Miner Engage in Shotgun, Cutting Scrape at Nevada Club in Lovelock*
>
> Fireworks in the form of flying beer bottles and a shotgun blast erupted in the Nevada Club here at 2 a.m. today, resulting in the serious injury of two men and the superficial wounding of two other persons.
>
> Injured in the affray were:
>
> Pete Fontana, 65, owner of the Nevada Club, who reportedly was struck on the head with a beer bottle . . .
>
> Edward A. Lynch, 29, employee of a tungsten mine north of Lovelock, who was struck in the back of his right leg by a shotgun blast fired by Fontana . . .
>
> W. L. Harper, about 30, fellow worker and companion of Lynch, who was struck in the lower part of the back by stray shot from the load which hit Lynch . . .
>
> An unidentified Southern Pacific worker who was hit in the ankle by a stray shot as he walked out of the Nevada Club . . .

Laxalt reported the sheriff giving eyewitness accounts about the fracas starting over Lynch being accused of stealing drinks from other patrons in the crowded barroom, bartender/owner Fontana ordering Lynch to leave the premises, Lynch responding "by sailing beer bottles through the air" and crashing one bottle over Fontana's head.

> Despite his wounds, Fontana went behind the bar and grabbed a shotgun, which he fired at Lynch . . .

Laxalt chronicled other stories of the New West, circa 1950s, this one in Reno:

Stage Is Set for Showdown on Prostitution in Nevada

Mae Cunninham's house of prostitution in Reno was put out of business last spring without due process of law and without sufficient cause, Emerson Wilson, attorney, told the supreme court yesterday in a brief filed in Carson City.

Filing of the brief set the stage for an important final showdown on the question of legalized prostitution in Nevada . . . because if the high court upholds the action of the Washoe County Commissioners, steps will be taken to abolish all the existing houses of prostitution now operating in other Nevada counties.

The legal prostitution question wrangled its way through Nevada for decades, eventually resulting in county discretion with a ban in high-population Las Vegas's Clark County and Reno's Washoe County and brothels operating legally in rural counties including Storey, where the internationally celebrated Mustang Ranch was an inexpensive taxi ride from nearby Reno.

Laxalt wrote about human drama locally and nationally, some of it bizarre, the kind of wire-service story that telegraph editors across the country and around the world loved to feature with big newspaper headlines.

Chicago Socialite Nearing End of Wait for Husband She Had Sent to Jail

CARSON CITY, Nev., October 6 (UP)—A wealthy Chicago socialite hoped that she was nearing the end of her wait for the man she sent to jail because he married her while he had another wife.

The socialite, dark-haired Mrs. Frances Taft Pollack, began her wait for the man she loves in December, 1947.

At that time, 40-year-old William Witkowski entered the Nevada State Prison to serve a one to five year sentence for bigamy.

The day he entered prison, Mrs. Pollack, who is the mother of two children, announced she was sorry she had been responsible for putting Witkowski behind the grey stone walls. She said she planned to wait until he was released and then re-marry him . . .

Laxalt, in these days of journalistic development, learned as an emerging writer how to approach a human interest story to capture the reader's imagination in-depth.

Four Convicted Murderers Present Striking Contrast

By Robert Laxalt

Four condemned men are spending their last days in death row at the Nevada State Prison.

Number one on the execution list is 19-year-old David Blackwell, sullen, dark-haired killer of two Reno police officers. Number two is Owen Bunter, 33-year-old former policeman convicted of murdering his ex-wife. Laszlo Varga, a blonde Hungarian refugee convicted of the brutal rape-slaying of a minister's wife, occupies cell number three. In cell number four, a 44-year-old San Francisco bartender, Eugene Gambetta, awaits execution for the murder of his former wife.

Young Blackwell, however, shows the same bitterness towards death that he has shown towards life. A psychological puzzle because of his twisted career of crime that evolved from a normal, religious home-life, he spends most of the time staring moodily into space.

Varga is a surprising contrast to his unflattering pictures. Short, pink-cheeked, and blue-eyed, he actually looks more like a schoolboy than a condemned killer. Varga spends most of his time writing letters to relatives and friends in his native Hungary, and Warden Richard Sheehy reports that he has not once displayed any of the violent outbursts that characterized his trial and early imprisonment.

Laxalt took the reader through the detail and mood of death row. He used little of the attribution most journalists provide the reader to illustrate credibility and accuracy. Rather, Laxalt wrote authoritatively from his own in-person, on-site research in the style of most magazine and book writers.

Death row itself is completely isolated from the prison proper by a succession of long corridors and steel doors fitted with special locks. Guards are sealed into the death block with the condemned prisoners. Since the door to the block itself is locked from the inside, the guard can only be released by relief guards coming for an eight-hour shift.

Each half hour the death row guard signals that everything is all right by pressing a buzzer that rings in the prison arsenal.

Once a week, with three armed guards on hand, the prisoners are let out one at a time to clean up in the death block's shower. They are allowed to have a weekly visitor from a minister of their own choosing.

On the last night, they are granted a last request, almost invariably some special meal they would like. At this time, they are allowed to send a last telegram to their families or friends.

Then, on the morning of their execution, they are awakened shortly before dawn and taken down the last mile to the end of the road—the lethal gas chamber.

Laxalt developed a sense of expertise in what he covered. He remembered the earlier story about the Hungarian refugee Laszo Varga on death row whom the warden described as showing no signs of violence as the tale turns dramatically.

Wounded Prison Guard Tells Full Details of Death Row Battle with Condemned Man Seeking to Kill Him with Butcher Knife

By Robert Laxalt. United Press Staff Correspondent

From his bed in an Carson City hospital, prison guard Jack Parker yesterday described the knife attack of Laszo Varga, 19-year-old Hungarian refugee under sentence of death at the state prison.

By nightfall yesterday, Parker—a former Carson City chief of police—was able to receive visitors. He suffered five deep knife wounds, a broken nose and minor abrasions from Varga's attack.

Varga, meanwhile, is recovering from a torn shoulder and swollen nose and eyes as the result of a direct hit from a gas gun.

Laxalt reported that the condemned prisoners had just completed their noon meal and were lining up in the kitchen area to return to their cells when Varga attacked.

"The first thing I knew, he had kicked me in the face, knocking me against the door. He reached into his pants pocket and pulled out a long butcher knife, curved into a skinning knife and sharp as a razor.

"Death row guards are not armed so there was nothing I could do but try to get away. He aimed for my stomach, and I pulled up my arms to block it. The blade laid the side of my hand open."

Laxalt told the story with the unfolding suspense he would eventually use as an author and in a style he would counsel writing students to use, such as short sentences and active verbs when writing about violence.

"The wound sort of paralyzed my right arm and I turned my back and ran into the guard's corridor. I knew he was going to kill me. He ran right after me, stabbing me once in the back and again in the right arm.

"I ran for the little table in the guards' room and put it between us. He picked up an armchair and threw it across the table. It hit me in the left shoulder and almost knocked me down . . . when he couldn't reach me, he kept swiping for my throat across the table. Finally he ducked underneath it and stabbed me in the back again."

Laxalt knew that great writers such as Hemingway, Steinbeck, and Crane had learned their early craft by covering dramatic action as newspaper reporters. He put that dramatic detailed suspense into his own coverage:

"When he straightened up, I kicked him with everything I had in them groin. He doubled up and went back. When he started to come forward again I thought I was a goner. I was losing blood fast and things were beginning to black out."

Laxalt then broke away from the dramatic first-person quotes and in his own person narrative reported that as other guards arrived at the bloody scene, Vargas ran to his cell where, back against the wall, knife in hand, he yelled at them:

"Come in, you ____. I dare you."

Laxalt wrote: "A shot from the tear gas gun tore open his shoulder and knocked him to the floor."

The veteran reporter was finding the factual news more and more violent, a long way from the literature, fiction and nonfiction he had read as a boy and aspired to write during his college studies.

From News to Magazines

Ernest Hemingway broke into writing covering routine news as a reporter for the *Kansas City Star,* but, later, as an author, he found more dramatic reality when he wrote about "death in the afternoon" in the bull rings of Spain. It was a way of observing not only the killing of the bulls but also what Hemingway saw as the bravery of the killers, the matadors. He described the matador's "courage" as "grace under pressure."

Laxalt didn't see death on Hemingway's terms but Laxalt was writing about the death of human beings, not bulls or the rare death of a matador. Laxalt commented, many years later:

> Watching an execution isn't like watching an accident. It is much more protracted. Something very deliberate and calculated.

Laxalt covered his first execution at the Nevada State Prison on April 22, 1949. It was published in newspapers around the world. The *Nevada State Journal* headlined it on the front page when it went to press nineteen hours later, about midnight.

> *Blackwell Smiles as He Is Executed: 19-year-old Youth Spends Last Hours with Bible and Ministers*
> By Robert Laxalt. United Press Staff Correspondent
> David Blackwell, teen-aged killer of two Reno policemen, died with a smile on his face at dawn yesterday.
>
> The 19-year-old former high school youth from Tacoma, Wash., was strapped into the execution chair in the gas chamber at the Nevada State Prison at 5:14 a.m.
>
> At 5:17 a.m., the lethal hydrocyanic fumes were released and five seconds later he was unconscious.
>
> Breathing stopped at 5:22 a.m. and at 5:26, nine minutes after the cyanide tablets tumbled into the vat of sulphuric acid beneath the chair, Blackwell was pronounced dead.

The breaking hard news out of the way in four terse paragraphs, Laxalt turned to the human interest detail he knew readers wanted to know.

> Blackwell had a final visit with his parents and brother yesterday after-noon. He was calm and outwardly cheerful during the farewell scene, and when one minister said goodbye, Blackwell answered "it's not goodbye—it's so long."
>
> Blackwell's final request, ironically enough, was for a "great big chocolate milkshake."
>
> Blackwell consumed not one but three such milkshakes furnished by Warden Richard Sheehy. He had a chicken dinner.
>
> He passed the long hours of the night reading a Bible and talking with Rev. George and Rev. Dewese of Faith Temple Church in Tacoma . . .
>
> At 3 o'clock, little more than two hours before his execution, Black-well and Rev. George had knelt beside the youth's bunk to pray. When Blackwell arose, he was crying.

Laxalt continued with the detail he gathered after the execution from those inside the death row cell where reporters were not allowed. The UP was competing with the rival AP and reporters from major newspapers who had come to Carson City to cover the execution. Laxalt's storytelling instincts drove him into the detail that would make his story stand out amid such competition.

> When the guards arrived thirty minutes later, Blackwell faced them smilingly. There was no need to help him along the 200 yards down the long prison corridors and across the outdoor yard. He led the way himself.
>
> When he first entered the execution chamber, he insisted upon shak-ing hands with Warden Sheehy and the guards. His last words were, "I'll be seeing you."

Laxalt was twenty-six years old when he witnessed his first execution. He covered several more but with little appetite for what was required as part of the job of a UP reporter. He finally reached his limit. He told an interviewer: "They messed one up and I went back and pulled my hitch. I told 'em that was it, to get somebody else. They could have their job before I'd go back. . . . It just took too long to die."

Growing restless about covering such news, Laxalt moved toward book authorship and planned to turn several feature stories he had written into a book to be called *The Violent Land—Tales the Old Timers Tell about Nevada.* At night, after dinner, Laxalt went back to work, not at the UP bureau but in the living room of the Hill Street apartment near the courthouse that he and Joyce rented when they were married. He wrote on the Royal type-writer his mother had given him in high school at a walnut-colored desk Joyce's mother had given her. In addition to magazine pieces and short stories, he continued the nocturnal writing when they moved with their six-month-old baby, Bruce, in 1951 to a small house at 620 Cardinal Way in Southwest Reno. He wrote at the living room desk into the night long after Joyce went to bed and didn't disturb her sleep when he finally joined her. When she awoke in the morning, she wasn't sure when he had come to bed.

Life was full with movies and get-togethers with family members and friends from college and dinners at the small French restaurant, Moulin Rouge, on Sierra Street where he had proposed to Joyce. On weekends, they drove to Carson City to visit his mother, who in her highly devout fashion routinely quizzed her adult children about the priest's message from the pulpit. To be ready for her questions, since they had not gone to mass, Laxalt asked Joyce to reach into the car's glove box and retrieve a booklet that had the sermon topic for the day.

They also drove to Lake Tahoe for snow-capped winter beauty and summer's warm sandy beaches. But during the week, Laxalt wrote news all day and magazine features much of the night. He also began writing short stories as he increasingly thought about developing a career in writing fiction. Joyce grew increasingly concerned that he was overworking.

Laxalt brought his day-time work home with him mentally and talked continuously about details, a common trait among journalists but not nec-essarily all writers, particularly authors. Many authors keep their writing projects to themselves, not wanting to lose their unfolding creativity in casual conversation. Joyce, creative and industrious in her own right as a veteran of high school and college plays and, in fact, a college playwright, seldom got a word in and listened mostly in silence. "He never gave me a chance to talk. I couldn't stand it," she jokingly but honestly told me when I was working on this book many years later. Laxalt had the public persona of a quietly thoughtful, almost shy, person. But at home after a long day of UP reporting and writing, and before taking up a long night of more literary-style writing, he unburdened himself of the day's details, many of them minor. Joyce, having many other things on her mind, felt somewhat neglected and turned from time to time to having an extra brandy and water cocktail, sometimes three, before dinner. Laxalt usually had one cocktail.

Daily journalism itself, however, kept Laxalt intrigued—and busy—with stories that continued to break in Reno, which, because of its infamy as a gambling and divorce town, made it a hot dateline for national and international news. Such was the case on November 18, 1949 with the attempted assassination of Lincoln Fitzgerald, owner of the Nevada Club. Several stories, some by Laxalt, others by local newspaper reporters in Reno, still others by metro reporters from big city papers, pieced together the news. The *Reno Evening Gazette* reported in bold headlines:

Wounded Gambler Faces Fight for Life

The newspaper reported Fitzgerald was blasted by unknown assailants using a sawed-off shotgun at close range in the driveway of his Southwest Reno home that left him severely injured and hospitalized for months. The stories tied the then-legal Nevada gambler in with earlier alleged illegal gambling in Michigan; the speculation was that he had been gunned down by Detroit mobsters.

The shooting made headlines across the country as Laxalt's factual UP dispatches were merged into the sensational reports of the major newspapers. The news had been splashed across front pages just two years earlier about the gangland shooting of Bugsy Siegel, the one-time mobster who put Las Vegas on the map by building the Flamingo Hotel. That, the Fitzgerald shooting, and another at Lake Tahoe, caused the Kefauver senatorial hearings to explore Nevada mob activity.

Fitzgerald eventually recovered and went on to live in seclusion in a specially protected upstairs apartment in the Nevada Club. He subsequently built a high rise hotel in downtown Reno, expanded his gaming operations to Lake Tahoe, and, with his wife, contributed major donations to the University of Nevada. Upon his death in 1981 at eighty-eight, Fitzgerald was hailed by Laxalt's brother Paul, then a U.S. senator from Nevada and former governor, as "one of Nevada's 20th Century pioneers."

But for Laxalt, now a veteran reporter whose byline was traveling at the top of news stories being dispatched across the country and around the world. The Fitzgerald story was the stuff drama of life and death.

The dramatic news kept breaking. On March 4, 1952, the *Nevada State Journal* headlined twin stories on the front page, the lead story by Laxalt's colleague, Robert Bennyhoff, and a colorful sidebar by Laxalt. Laxalt's wrote the color story, which he did in the feature style that filled in background to accompany the hard news of breaking stories.

Redfield Has Bitter Taste of Notoriety

By Robert Laxalt. United Press Staff Correspondent

The private life of La Vere Redfield is a thing of the past.

And Redfield—target of a brazen $2,500,000 burglary—is a bitter man because of it. The reason: he prized his anonymity more than money.

Before the sensational burglary flared into the world's headlines, Redfield was perhaps the least-known multi-millionaire in the United States. With his usual attire of run-down shoes, plaid shirt and worn denims, he had enjoyed complete freedom of movement.

For years he had wandered through the hills and ranches of western Nevada, leaning idly against corral posts, talking to cowhands, or stopping for occasional meals in the remote camp of a sheepherder. To all of them, he was known only as "Redfield—lives somewhere around Reno."

But today, all that has changed.

Now, his name is on everybody's lips. Everyone knows he's a multi-millionaire. And, like it or not, Redfield knows it will make a permanent difference in his status. For the first time, he will be treated with deference by his cowboy and ranch hand acquaintances

Laxalt drew a picture for the reader with the detail good writers use to place the story in easily understood, everyday terms.

For the first time, his name will have special significance in the corner grocery stores where he personally shopped with his own market basket, and in the gambling halls, where only a few knew he had very much money.

Laxalt quoted Redfield directly and took the reader to the scene.

"When the burglary happened, I had a premonition of what was to come, and it scared me," he said.

This was the reason newsmen and police first found him sitting on a rock in a field near his home. He asked everybody then not to say very much about the burglary.

But that was impossible. And today, Redfield has accepted that fact. But in his contrastingly mild yet determined manner, he is trying to salvage something of his privacy.

The reporters and photographers who daily mob the home are permitted to enter the kitchen only. They have a "gentleman's agreement" that they will leave all cameras outside, that no pictures will be taken of Redfield or his wife.

Laxalt rewarded the reader with final paragraphs that joined the reader directly to protagonist Redfield through dramatic quotes.

"This thing was so cruel," he said. "Not in the fact of the money, but in what it's doing to my life. When you've got money, your right of privacy and anonymity is a tough, tough one."

"Now it will be almost impossible."

The investigation led to the arrest by the FBI in Flagstaff, Arizona, 13 days after the February 29, 1952 leap year burglary of a blue-eyed, French Canadian songwriter named Marie D'Arc Machaud on a charge of interstate transportation of stolen property. A frequent guest at the Redfield home, she was carrying $50,000 in cash, securities that included 179,721 1/2 shares in 57 corporations and 28 pieces of jewelry. She was identified as the ringleader or "finger woman" of an odd group of "bunglers" that included:

A casino bouncer and ex pugilist;

A casino janitor;

A guest ranch caretaker;

An ex-convict;

Two house-to-house soap salesmen.

The woman had been a dinner guest in the Redfield home so often, the AP reported, that Redfield, was "shocked and greatly upset" when he learned of her arrest. "Why, I trusted her implicitly."

In fact, the so-called finger lady accompanied Redfield and his wife, Nell, to downtown Reno on the day of the burglary supposedly as a friend while actually working as a lookout to make sure the Redfields were safely away from the thieves, who were busy at their stone mansion on Mt. Rose Street in Southwest Reno.

Eventually, it turned out that the burglars made off with a haul of $1.5 million, not $2.5 million. In a June trial in U.S. District Court in Carson City, Michaud was convicted of the federal crime of transporting $147,000 in cash, jewels, and securities across state lines and sentenced to five years in prison. Wearing a tight black dress and red scarf, she was taken away in shackles. Others in the gang received a variety of sentences when convicted of various crimes in the caper.

Laxalt had broken into longer form magazine writing with several articles in *The American Weekly*—some factual journalistic reporting, some in an emerging effort at largely fictional Western lore. So he pitched the true story of Redfield as a follow up human-interest feature for the magazine. He wrote to Charles Robbins, the story editor of *The American Weekly* with offices at 65 Vesey Street in New York City, addressing the editor informally as "Charley." He enclosed the copy he had written for a feature story that would concentrate as a profile of the eccentric Redfield and explained how he got the story by earning the trust of the millionaire.

> He did me a terrific favor and slipped me into the house after FBI agents had left. The result—I got a terrific philosophy drawing the difference between a man and a millionaire. I certainly hope you like it.
>
> I laid off the crime angle as much as possible, since the newspapers will be hanging their stories on that peg for a long time to come. This one stands despite any developments in the criminal case.

The magazine, known for publishing melodramatic content, ran the feature story with a dramatic drawing of a man wearing a cowboy hat, a wrinkled shirt, and old jeans rolled up at the cuffs sitting in a field with his black dog where police had found him. The drawing illustrated two uniformed policemen interviewing the character depicted as Redfield. The headline:

Down to His Last Million

Laxalt's style as a beginning suspense writer emerged in the lead of his story. It read like fiction but in this case it was as factual as his UP news stories had been.

> For years the forbidding house on the hill had been a source of curiosity to most residents of Reno.
>
> Its high towers, its shadowed grounds, its barrier of high walls were in sharp contrast to the white frame houses surrounding it.
>
> People called it the "house on the hill" and wondered idly why its occupants were never about.

Laxalt, the student of literature and the craft of writing, knew how to paint a picture with words that required the reader to see more.

Occasionally a man in blue denims and shapeless hat could be seen with his dog, a Kerry Blue terrier, wandering around the grounds. He was assumed to be the gardener.

Then, on February 29, 1952—the extra day of the leap year—burglars brazenly entered the house in broad daylight and hauled off a safe containing a staggering amount of currency, jewelry and negotiable securities.

Laxalt introduced the reader to Redfield with suspense, the kind of approach that requires the reader to continue whether it be in a news story, a feature story, a magazine article, or an epic book.

What manner of man was this who kept millions hidden in a bedroom closet, who left his house untenanted and his money unguarded, who could honestly say that he would rather lose $3,000,000 anytime than lose his dog? . . . La Vere Redfield is a slight man who looks 20 years younger than his 55 years. He is mild mannered and extremely soft spoken.

After chronicling details of the burglary and the colorful band of thieves and how Redfield's choice of insulation made him vulnerable to such a spectacular crime and public notoriety, Laxalt delivered a crafted conclusion to satisfy the reader, a virtual reward for sticking with the story to the end.

Today, Redfield still believes he can salvage something of his past life. He has accepted the fact that publicity of the robbery and his habits is inevitable. All he desires now is that people understand him as a man— not a millionaire.

Laxalt had a string of feature stories published in *The American Weekly* from 1949 to 1952. One story ran in December of 1951 along with photographs of slot machine and roulette players and headlined "Nevada's undercover gambling spies." A sub-headline reported "Dumb blonde, naive college boy, carefree cowboy, all suckers at the gaming table, very often are shrewd tax agents on the trail of crooked operators." The story was accompanied by a prominently placed editor's note that explained: "Robert Laxalt, University of Nevada graduate, has spent more than four years in intensive research of Nevada history and is the author of 100 features dealing with the state. His 'Violent Land,' a collection of early Nevada stories, will be published next spring."

The American Weekly was a Hearst Sunday newspaper supplement that claimed a circulation of 50 million readers. It was started in 1896 and continued until 1966. It "was sort of the *Parade Magazine* of its day, it was also the precursor of the *National Enquirer* and could have given the *Police Gazette* a run for its money," wrote Jim Vadeboncoeur, Jr., a bookseller and publisher who researched the magazine's exquisitely drawn illustrations. "It was filled with scantily clad showgirls and tales of murder and suspense."

Laxalt didn't write about scantily clad showgirls but he did research and write about historical adventures for *The American Weekly* and his stories were full of suspense. Later, he would include some of the stories in a history of Nevada.

Most of Laxalt's after-hours feature writing for *The American Weekly* contrasted sharply from his day-time UP fact-filled journalism as he moved toward the challenges of fiction by blending facts with folklore and his own imagination. The shift toward fiction came when Laxalt moved way from contemporary events such as the Redfield and gaming spy stories and toward historical sketches based on facts but emboldened by his own imagination.

One story, published in June 1952, was headlined "Riddle of the Golden Ledge" and included a sub-headline that asked "Was It only a Dying Convict's Dream . . . Or Was It One of the Richest Treasures a Prospector Ever Stumbled Upon?" The story was accompanied by a drawing of an old prospector and a caption reporting "The miner in the lead, they dragged the burros down hill—only to discover that the car had vanished." The magazine was known to carry sensational stories that stretched the truth but this story by Laxalt was topped off by an Editor's Note that reported:

> This is a true story. Though the warden recently died, the guard is now a respected Nevada businessman and the miner is a public official. We feel that nothing useful would be accomplished by printing their real identities. Therefore, all names here are fictitious.

The story with the byline "By Robert Laxalt" told of a dying prisoner giving a guard who had been kind to him a map leading to a ledge of gold he had found in the Feather River country of northern California's Mother Lode, which had started off the Gold Rush of 1849. With suspense at every turn, Laxalt wove a story of the guard enlisting the help of the warden to find the gold, the prisoner miraculously recovering and leading the prison officials to the mountains and then escaping in the warden's car, with none finding the gold. Embarrassed, the warden hushed up the story but it eventually leaked out and became part of Nevada's exaggerated folklore.

Another was titled:

The Challenge of El Dorado Johnny—He Said He Was Happy to Take the Chance When He Deliberately Became the Notorious Killer's Rival for the Company of the Beautiful Singer

By Robert Laxalt

When Eldorado Johnny came to Virginia City in 1866, there were only three reasons to suspect that he might be a killer—four if you counted both the guns that were strapped low on his hips. The other two clues were his quiet, unobtrusive demeanor and the white softness of his face and hands.

The community remembered only too well another soft, white-faced youth, Billy the Kid, and so when Johnny walked into the Brass Rail saloon and up to the crowded bar, the other customers rapidly made room for him.

He drank slowly, glancing neither to the right or left, but when the gray lilt of a tune rose above the hum of voices in the rear of the room, he turned slightly and watched the singer over his shoulder.

She was worth watching, a slim, dark-eyed girl with shadows in her cheeks and in her rippling black hair a rose that matched the carmine of her lips.

Laxalt then reported with lingering suspense that her name was Julia Niles, she was a regular entertainer and she was the girlfriend of a man by the name of Farmer Peel who was no farmer but, as Laxalt reported, "the symbol of sudden deaths in the saloons and gambling halls of three states." Laxalt then reported how El Dorado Johnny showed his affection toward the singer and, in so doing, deliberately provoked Farmer Peel's anger into a gunfight by declaring to all he'd be waiting for Farmer Peel outside Pat Lynch's saloon at four o'clock.

Faced off at twenty feet outside the saloon, Farmer Peel declared:

"You better draw, stranger!"

Johnny reached awkwardly for his guns. Neither had left his holster when the first shot struck him in the shoulder, spinning his slight figure completely around. The second hit his heart.

The seemingly deserted street was filled in a minute's time.

"It beats all how slow he was," someone remarked wonderingly. "He never had a chance."

Laxalt then reported El Dorado Johnny really wasn't much of a gunman at all and had told Pinkie, a barber who had cleaned him up with a nice shave just before the shooting, that he'd never shot anyone in his life and just wore his guns as a disguise to keep people from bothering him. Then Laxalt wrapped up the tale with a classic ending for the reader.

"But why did he get all prettied up like he was going to a party?" Pat Lynch asked.

"On account of his girl," Pinkie explained. "He said he wanted to be remembered as looking nice when he was in his coffin."

Well, as noted historian Sam P. Davis wrote in *The History of Nevada*, there really were a Farmer Peel and an El Dorado Johnny and there really was a Pat Lynch's Saloon but the gunfight wasn't over the affections of a singer named Julia Niles who, if she existed, was nowhere to be seen. Rather, in Davis's telling, it is a rather banal killing. As for the community shying away from El Dorado Johnny in 1866 for fear he might be another Billy the Kid who Laxalt had arriving in Virginia City earlier, William H. Bonney aka Billy the Kid was seven years old and living with his mother in New York City, where he had been born, in 1859.

Laxalt was having fun with imaginative storytelling based on facts. He was beginning to spread his wings from the rigid accuracy of journalism to what many consider a better way of getting at the truth through the flights of fiction. Many writers of Western lore in the 1950s were blending fact and exaggerations including Lucius Beebe and Charles Clegg, publishers of the famed Comstock Lode newspaper *The Territorial Enterprise*.

Nevada advertising man Tom Wilson did just the opposite when he rounded up a batch of historical tales that seemed like folklore but had them meticulously researched for factual accuracy in a book called *Nevada: The First Hundred Years* that was produced as a state centennial promotion for the vintage gambling casino Harolds Club. Veteran writers know that most stories start with some kind of fact but in the repeated retelling can take on a life of their own if the facts start to wander. The old saw is that "the facts never stand in the way of a good story."

Laxalt was a stickler for factual accuracy in his UP journalism. But literary writing with its license for imagination in fiction was increasingly on his mind even though he was tentative about his talent. He was about to take a serious step toward answering his own questions about himself.

A New Way of Life

At night, away from the news, Laxalt turned his creativity toward short story writing. He was inspired by the extensive reading of his childhood as well as his devotion to literature in college. Short stories allowed his imagination to escape the pressure and factual boundaries of daily journalism. The journalism was a benefit, however, because it exposed him to what he called "a treasure trove of experiences: gambling clubs and dealers, politicians, prisons, murderers, and . . . lethal gas executions" that would serve him well as he turned to literary writing.

One short story, "The Snake Pen," would eventually become the seed of a novel about a man who charmed rattlesnakes in front of a horrified crowd. Laxalt sent the fictional short story off to *Esquire* with high hopes he could develop more contacts in the New York City magazine world. He received a rejection note and he was disappointed. But he saw the comments offered by the highly respected editor, Frederic Birmingham, as constructive criticism given to him personally with compassion and honesty.

"I am afraid," the editor wrote to Laxalt, "that you have repeated yourself in moiling about in topics which tend to be effective as literary tour de force, but almost impossible to think of in a commercial sense . . . THE SNAKE PEN is a damn good story . . . but my candid opinion is that you must turn your talents to more digestible backgrounds if you would succeed financially in your writing."

Laxalt turned out more than twenty-five short stories in his late twenties. He set the stories in the American West; it was a setting that he knew personally from his boyhood, as well as from his extensive reading of many types of Westerns. They ranged from the serious fiction of James Fenimore Cooper and Owen Wister's *The Virginian* to the so-called dime Westerns with identical plots that he saw as escape and enjoyable reading.

Laxalt experimented with short stories to determine what kind of writer he really wanted to become, turning out both serious and humorous pieces ranging from "Old Button" about an old buckaroo to "Sixty Miles Is a Long Trip" about two whiskey-drinking Indians beating and stabbing a white man to death during a long pickup truck ride from the ruins of the Army's frontier Fort Churchill in Western Nevada to the bright lights of Reno and a jail cell. Both of these stories would be published forty-five years later by The University of Nevada Press in *Robert Laxalt's A Lean Year and Other Stories.*

To augment what he described as the modest salaries of his work as a reporter and that of Joyce as a schoolteacher, he wrote dozens of news stories as the Nevada stringer (freelance correspondent) for the *Wall Street Journal,* a novella entitled "Rimrock," and the whimsical sketches that blended historical fact and fiction for the Hearst Sunday newspaper supplement *The American Weekly.* He also wrote a series of columns for the *Nevada State Journal* called *Tales the Old Timers Tell about Nevada,* which he was pulling together to be his first book *The Violent Land.*

The Violent Land eventually would be published in 1953 by Nevada Publishing Company with typography and lithography by Silver State Press in Reno and illustrated by Richard Allen. It ran sixty-eight softbound pages with twelve stories including: "The Cursed Mine," "The Lieutenant's Uncertainty," "The Gentleman Leaves Town," and "The Horse Traders." One, entitled "Mercy and The Soldier," hooked the reader with a dramatic first paragraph:

> The private's face was rigid and expressionless, but there were deep flushes of red about his eyes. Before him raged the hulking figure of Sergeant Anson Kelly.

That enticed the reader to move on to the second paragraph.

> "You're soft, Newton," the sergeant cried in his low, bull voice. "You're as soft inside as a woman. But I'm going to take it out of you. I'm going to take it out of you if it's the last thing I do."

Laxalt devoted the next seven pages to the private deserting, the sergeant and two troopers searching for him, the sergeant falling from his horse while separated from the other troopers, the private killing the injured sergeant with a crack shot and the troopers coming along from behind to find the sergeant dead and the private gone. Laxalt's prose was that of the journalist turned author, short sentences, active verbs, dramatic detail, high human foible interest and punchy ending.

"Well, he got what he wanted," one trooper said. "Even if things were twisted a little."

"What do you mean?" the other trooper asked.

"He made that boy hard inside. But still, I never figured he would get hard enough to kill a hurt man."

"Bitter, maybe. But not hard."

"If that boy was hard," the trooper said, "he would've let the sergeant lay here in pain until he froze to death."

Then, for good measure, Laxalt had the first trooper climb down off his horse, pull out his knife, and scalp the dead sergeant. And then, the punch ending:

"What the devil was that for?" the other asked. "We got to take him back, you know."

"I know," the first trooper said. "But we can't have that boy taking the blame for something the Indians did. That might make him hard."

Laxalt would write on the title page of the book in pen and ink:

—*for my Joyce*—
—everything I ever do will be for you.
Bob

Laxalt thrived on using his own experiences growing up in a livestock family in Nevada as he experimented with all kinds of writing—serious stories, humorous, satirical, fantastic, and, as he noted, years later, "even western cowboy" including his witnessing "the coming of poets and artists and Old West types to Virginia City."

The year 1950 proved to be fateful when he met one of those celebrated artists who had come to Virginia City and moved into one of the town's famed old mansions, the Chollar House.

Laxalt knew about Walter Van Tilburg Clark, who had gained fame for his realistic western novel *The Ox-Bow Incident*, but he had never met him. Despite having broken into national magazines and covered more than his share of major breaking news stories Laxalt had been hesitant about making a cold call to such an important writer without some kind of third-party formal introduction.

"If I had the good manners enough to read Walter Van Tilburg Clark's novel *The Ox-Bow Incident* first, I would never have made the telephone call," Laxalt wrote forty years later in a foreword for the University of

Nevada Press republication of Clark's famed novel, *The City of Trembling Leaves*. "I would have been, I guess the word is—awed. But all I knew then was that he was an established writer and I was just a beginning writer. I was looking for someone to provide me with the key to the magic kingdom I knew nothing about."

So Laxalt made the phone call and introduced himself by saying he had written a short story and that he was hoping Clark would look at it. Clark responded in a low, resonant, somewhat intimidating and authoritative voice. There was a moment of hesitation. Then, after the pause, the writer invited Laxalt and his wife Joyce to come up to Virginia City from Reno and visit with him and his wife Barbara.

Clark had been born in East Orland, Maine, but he was raised in Reno where his father had served as president of the University of Nevada. By age forty-one, when he met Laxalt in 1950, Clark had become Nevada's most distinguished writer since Mark Twain had told tall tales as a reporter for Virginia City's *Territorial Enterprise* in the early 1860s. The meeting would be a fateful turning point for Laxalt, then twenty-seven, and, by extension, legions of readers and writers whom he would eventually inspire. And it would prove to be historically significant for Clark himself in years to come.

Clark's first novel, *The Ox-Bow Incident*, was published in 1940 and earned him instant national acclaim. It was about a posse turned lynch mob killing three innocent travelers falsely presumed to be rustlers. Clark examined the flaws of Western law and order. The novel won praise as the first modern Western. Sixty years later, Jackson J. Benson, in his biography of Clark, *The Ox-Bow Man*, described it as going beyond the traditional romanticism of the Old West and as being firmly in the realistic tradition.

Clark's literary fame widened after director William Wellman based a 1943 film on the novel starring Henry Fonda and including other prominent actors such as Anthony Quinn, Dana Andrews, and Harry Morgan. The Twentieth Century Fox film was nominated for Best Picture in 1943 but was beaten out by *Casablanca* starring Humphrey Bogart and Ingrid Bergman.

As Laxalt knew, Clark's renown had spread even more with the publication of *The City of Trembling Leaves* to critical acclaim in 1945. The novel drew attention to Reno, the small but nationally known "Biggest Little City in the World," where Clark grew up, attended grade school, high school, and the University of Nevada. In that year, 1950, Clark had just published

The Watchful Gods and Other Stories, short stories he had written earlier in the 1940s.

But it was the author's third novel, *The Track of the Cat*, published in 1949, that prompted Laxalt to make the phone call from his home in Reno to Clark in Virginia City. Laxalt had read a *Nevada State Journal* story, headlined "Walter Clark Does It Again," about the new novel and thought the accompanying photograph of Clark "did not look too forbidding" despite his chiseled high cheekbones and piercing blue eyes.

After all, Laxalt assured himself, he faced a whole line of potentially intimidating characters in his UP reporting, characters whose voices ranged from "politicians' oratory to the dead tones of Mafia executioners."

Six decades later, reviewers continued to marvel at how *The Track of the Cat* captured the drama by describing the isolated, self-loathing, tormented ranch family in the Sierra Nevada and its cattle being menaced by a large black-hued mountain lion that eventually killed one of two brothers searching for it in a blizzard while the rest of the family destroyed itself through alcoholic and religious hatred. Amazon.com user "Michael Barb" commented in a July 2000 review of the Western Literature Series paperback re-publication: "Often melodramatic, this tale of a classically dysfunctional family of ranchers living in the Sierra Nevada is most notable for one extended tour-de-force sequence: Clark's detailed, snowflake by snowflake description of a man's disorientation and eventual descent into madness as he tries to find his way out of a mountain blizzard. This harrowing section of the book may be justification enough for reading *The Track of the Cat*."

Clark hit Hollywood pay dirt again when the director of *The Ox-Bow Incident*, William A. Wellman, cast Robert Mitchum and Tab Hunter in starring roles and John Wayne served as co-producer of the film adaption of *The Track of the Cat*.

Bob and Joyce Laxalt drove through a light storm of "dancing snowflakes" from Reno up the narrow, two lane, steep, and winding Geiger Grade highway. When they rounded the final bend they saw the full panorama of the "Queen of the Comstock Lode" with its boot hill cemetery on the immediate left and, in the distance, its centerpiece St. Mary's of the Mountains Catholic Church steeple.

As he approached the town, Laxalt was stunned at his lack of knowledge about its place in the nation's history. Its rich silver mines had played an important part in the Union victory in the Civil War and its newspaper, *The Territorial Enterprise*, had launched the literary career of a reporter named Sam Clemens who took the pen name Mark Twain. Laxalt wondered how he could have been so ignorant of Virginia City having grown up a mere twenty miles away in Carson City when, as he recalled his troop ship World War II days, his shipmates knew all about the great silver ore strike and its impact on the nation.

They approached the frayed old nineteenth-century mansion, the Chollar House, and knocked on the door, hearing the knocker's impact echo from within the walls. Clark opened the door, his startling blue eyes boring directly into Laxalt's. The journalist immediately sized up the author, thinking there "was a magnetism about the man that flowed like a physical force."

Clark invited them into the house and guided them to the kitchen where they met his wife Barbara who, Laxalt noted, was the opposite of the tall, muscular Clark "small-boned but wiry, with a birdlike face framed by graying hair . . . a New England face for sure" with warmth and compassion in her eyes.

The four sipped cocktails and Barbara Clark put the Laxalts at ease by talking about horses and growing up in America's northeastern countryside. The women remained in the kitchen as Clark led Laxalt up a creaking stairway to small room "with plenty of cobwebs." Clark sat at the one piece of furniture in the room, his writing desk, and motioned Laxalt to sit in one of two old chairs that appeared to be on their last legs.

At the desk, under a dusty dormer window, the wintry light filtered over the distinct features of Clark's face. Laxalt handed Clark a manila envelope containing the short story he wanted the author to read. Clark quickly scanned the first page. "Well, we'll talk about it when I've had a chance to read it," Clark said as he shifted to questioning Laxalt about how much actual writing he had done. After Laxalt said he had written several short stories and popular magazine pieces, Clark asked him what kind of writing he hoped to pursue. Laxalt found it to be a difficult question to answer. After a pause, he said he thought perhaps he might write about sheepherders and cowboys and life on the range.

Clark then shifted from writing to reading with the expression that *serious* reading was the fountainhead for *serious* writing. He asked Laxalt what he kind of books he read and Laxalt responded that he read *Beowulf,* Shakespeare, and British and American poetry taught by his Carson City high school teacher Grace Bordewich as well as some philosophy during his Santa Clara University days with Jesuit professors. He noted he read *War and Peace* during his University of Nevada English major days but mentioned that his "literary education" ended when his favorite professor,

Paul Harwood, left the university. As the conversation dwindled and they walked back downstairs, it dawned on Laxalt that Clark was separating Laxalt's literary wheat from Laxalt's literary chaff.

The Laxalts and the Clarks left the old mansion and walked through the light snow to Walter and Barbara's favorite saloon, the Sazerac. The saloons on C Street served as social gathering halls for Virginia City's eclectic population that ranged from serious intellectuals such as Clark to professional and amateur historians smitten with the romance and danger of the Comstock mining days to gamblers, seasoned drinkers. There were also a smattering of curious tourists, they proliferated during high season summer months and virtually disappeared on such snowy winter days.

They ordered drinks and as they visited at the bar, Clark laid out a piece of paper and began making notes. "I think these books will help you in your writing," he said as he handed the list to Laxalt.

Joseph Conrad
Heart of Darkness,
The Nigger of the Narcissus

D. H. Lawrence
Sons and Lovers
The first *Lady Chatterley*

Stephen Crane
The Red Badge of Courage

W. H. Hudson
The Purple Land
Green Mansions

Knut Hamsun
Hunger
Growth of the Soil

Turgenev
Fathers and Sons

Dostoevsky
Crime and Punishment

Faulkner
The Sound and the Fury
As I Lay Dying

Rolvaag

Giants in the Earth

Graham Greene
The Heart of the Matter

Richard Hughes
High Wind in Jamaica

Willa Cather
Death Comes for the Archbishop

Laxalt examined the list, folded the piece of paper neatly and placed it in his shirt pocket. He would keep it handy for rest of his life and he would be inspired by it to create his own list of *serious* reading for development of *serious* writing that he would, in turn, share with students and fellow writers for decades to come.

Laxalt's list:

Jack London
Call of the Wild

John Steinbeck
The Red Pony
Of Mice and Men
The Grapes of Wrath
East of Eden

Hugo's *The Hunchback of Notre Dame*

Dostoevski's [sic] *Crime and Punishment*

Chekhov's *Cherry Orchard*

Turgenev's *Fathers and Sons*

Tolstoy's *War and Peace*

Jules Vern's *20,000 Leagues under the Sea*

Bram Stoker's *Dracula*

Flaubert's *Madame Bovary*

Mary Shelley's *Frankenstein* about which Laxalt commented, "That's a real sleeper. It's a little bitty book. She was the wife of Percy Bysshe Shelley and she wrote this little masterpiece, from which all the Frankenstein things have come."

James Thurber's *The Thurber Carnival*

Mark Twain's *Tom Sawyer* and *Huck Finn*

Cervantes' *Don Quixote*

Laxalt added to the list other books with his own comments:

One of my beloveds is Thornton Wilder's *Bridge of San Luis Rey.*

One that's chilling is Joseph Conrad's *Hearts of Darkness.*

Theodore Dreiser's *An American Tragedy* is ponderous but worth something.

One that's delightful is Fielding's *Tom Jones.*

F. Scott Fitzgerald's *The Great Gatsby*

Hugo's *Les Miserables*

And then one I always go back to, Erich Maria Remarque's *All Quiet on the Western Front.*

And then one just to keep you awake at night, Kafka's *Metamorphosis.*

And George Orwell, of course, and *Animal Farm.*

Thomas Wolfe's *You Can't Go Home Again*

Pasternak's *Dr. Zhivago*

Hemingway's *Old Man and the Sea, Men without Women, For Whom the Bell Tolls*

And Lewis Carroll's *Alice in Wonderland,* which curiously I did not read until I was out of college because we were from an immigrant household and that wasn't standard.

Laxalt made a note: "I could give you a hundred more."

Clark's warm collegiality on that snowy Virginia City day in sharing his thoughts and list of books, and thus inspiring Laxalt into new directions of thinking about reading and writing, was a significant turning point in the life of the now-veteran reporter who yearned to become a writer of literature. Though grateful, Laxalt was cautious in not wanting to label himself as a writing protégé of Clark and, in fact, proceeded to develop a concise writing style through his journalistic approach more in the line of other journalists such as Hemingway who had matriculated to book authorship.

Laxalt continued writing short stories at night at home to develop his craftsmanship. He pursued UP journalism to make a living for his and Joyce's family, which expanded with the birth of a son, Bruce, in 1951. And he continued to break into the New York magazine world.

Laxalt's serious magazine journalism hit the big time when the *Saturday Evening Post* published his story on gambling September 20, 1952 under the title:

What Has Wide-Open Gambling Done to Nevada?

The sub-headline provided part of the answer and introduced Laxalt's text:

> *Twenty-one years ago Nevada legalized gambling—and started a boom that hasn't stopped. The state has gained millions of dollars and tourists—and quite a few despicable criminals. Here is the case history of Nevada's unique experiment.*
>
> By Robert Laxalt
>
> In the year 1931, an Eastern newspaper editor said: "If you can't do it at home, go to Nevada." The reason for the quip was that Nevada had just shocked the moral boot tops off the nation by legalizing gambling. The action was not born of madness. There was an argument for it. But in the furor of outraged criticism that followed, that timid voice of argument was hopelessly lost. It was only when the verbal smoke had finally cleared that the question arose, "How did this thing come to be?"

Laxalt put his newspaper and particularly tight-writing wire service training into play with a series of short, punchy sentences. He declared his own suppositions and facts without bogging down in an attribution of experts. He knew the pure style of the magazine writer who is supposed to know what he is writing about from his own research and knowledge rather than simply quoting others. Laxalt offered his own voice on the subject with dramatic use of composite quotes representing not one speaker but the attitude of many—in Laxalt's view:

> The answer did not lie in an economic maze, but simply in the fact that Nevada liked to pride herself on liberal tolerance. "Have done with hypocrisy" her lawmakers stated. "Get gambling out of the back rooms and into the daylight."
>
> Which is exactly what happened. The green-felted tables crept into the neighborhood bars and lounges. Slot machines made a brassy appearance in grocery stores. And casinos suddenly flared into being with dazzling displays of roulette wheels, craps and 21 tables.

Laxalt made his own voice authoritatively clear to the reader:

> It is hardly likely that the crusading liberals of the Nevada of 1931 were clairvoyant. They could not have foreseen the repercussions of their action—repercussions that were to sound the biggest boom the state had known since the mining heyday of the Comstock Lode. . . . Now, twenty-one years later, gambling has again shifted to the limelight. Crime-investigation committees, so-called syndicate gangsterism

and bookies are all common fare in the language of today. And, again Nevada has come under the sharp scrutiny of a nationwide society of crime watchers. It rests in an uncertain vacuum. Twenty-one years of legalized gambling. What has it accomplished for Nevada? Has it been a success or failure?

Laxalt answered his own questions by explaining legal gambling was an economic success for the state. He proved his point by citing figures. Within twenty years, millions of tourists flocked to the once barren state that claimed a population of less than one person for each of its 110,000 square miles. In 1951, Laxalt wrote, 3 million tourists came through Reno and stayed an average three days apiece, spending over $32 million, while another 2.5 million stayed an average of four days in Las Vegas and spent $43 million.

Laxalt explained how gambling casino taxes were a bonanza for building the state's infrastructure, thus keeping other taxes low which attracted wealthy new residents and new businesses. He was candid about mob elements arriving in the state, mostly in Las Vegas, where Benjamin (Bugsy) Siegel got The Strip going with construction of his $1 million Flamingo Hotel Casino. He cited the Tahoe shooting of Harry Sherwood, a partner in gambling boats, by one Louis Strauss who Laxalt identified as the "notorious 'Russian Louie' of Eastern Racket Fame."

(Laxalt could write with authority drawing on his early experiences as a reporter including when he actually encountered Strauss, reputedly a member of the mob's Murder, Inc., in the Carson City jail where he was held following the shooting. Laxalt described the gangster in his earlier reports as having "a long face and dead eyes" but "affable" and quite willing to tell the reporter he liked the nickname "Russian Louie" and, what's more, he was related to Charlie Fischetti who "had taken over the action in Chicago when Al Capone was sent to Alcatraz." Strauss claimed self-defense and the charge was dropped when a battery of witnesses said they never saw the shooting even though they were in the room where it took place.)

In this *Saturday Evening Post* piece, Laxalt went into detail about the state's early problems with weak gambling control that allowed questionable people with criminal backgrounds to get casino licenses. He then answered his own questions about gambling's impact:

> Though legalized gambling has been somewhat a moral failure, it has spelled economic prosperity for Nevada. But economic success or

moral failure, Nevada has paid the inevitable price for her experiment—hopeless entanglement with gambling and all its embellishments. The state cannot discard the industry. Such a move would mean economic ruin. . . . If Nevada can clean her house hold and keep it clean, then the future is fairly certain. If not, economic disaster both for the state and her gambling experiment may be very near.

Tough new state government gaming control would emerge in the late fifties and develop in sixties and seventies with major American hotel corporations building and operating extravagantly expensive casinos. Laxalt's brother Paul, as governor, welcomed Howard Hughes to the state and Hughes bought and cleaned up several of the hotels that had been infiltrated by the mob. As for the morality issue, legal gaming spread across the nation in the late eighties and nineties and Native American Indian casinos flourished throughout the country. Suddenly, if one could play legal slot machines in Cedar Rapids, Iowa, then Reno and Las Vegas began to lose their once highly noted "Sin City" reputations.

The success of the *Post* story was a significant move for Laxalt toward more distinguished national journalism. But he suddenly faced a major career decision when the UP asked him to move from the Reno bureau to the larger journalism worlds of its Los Angeles or Mexico City bureaus. It was routine for the wire service to move correspondents to new posts after five years and Laxalt's five years in the Reno bureau were up. But, having been born in California and raised in Nevada, he knew through his unique Basque upbringing that he was meant to be in the mountain West not in the big cities of metropolitan America or Mexico.

So he made a decision that would alter his career and his family's life and, ultimately, the futures of hundreds of writers and millions of readers. He resigned from the UP and found himself jobless while needing to support a wife and an infant son and a mortgage on their small house on Cardinal Way in Southwest Reno.

A Move toward Destiny

Robert Laxalt set out quickly to find a new job in local journalism. He had the credentials of five years' journeyman work as a reporter in the high-speed world of the wire services, as a stringer for *The Wall Street Journal*, and as an in-depth writer for national magazines. "I had just about covered the waterfront—politics, the legislature, murders and executions, and the workings of state government. To my surprise and anger," he would recall later, "none of these accomplishments seemed to matter. The only thing that counted was that there were no openings anywhere. All the news media—newspapers or radio or the new public relations field—were staffed up. I found out what it was to pound the streets looking for a job, and for the first time, I felt panic." Then he heard that the University of Nevada, from which he had graduated five years earlier, was planning to create a news service and publications office.

Laxalt decided to seek the university position. It would be a shift, in effect, from his seasoned work in hard news and investigative and in-depth reporting where his allegiance was to his readers—the mission of the independent-minded journalist—to the world of public relations. In such a new world, the mission still would be to seek the truth as a writer but in a way that put the university in a good light. He knew he would not compromise his storytelling integrity. He also knew that a major national controversy was brewing on the Reno campus with many conflicting points of view being exercised in a fight over professors' academic freedom and the board of regents' call for greater administrative control. He would join neither side in his coverage but be impartial in his writing.

The job would have to be approved by the board which would take some time. In the meantime, the Laxalts were involved in a family plot involving how to get Dominique Laxalt to return to the Basque Country for a visit. Dominique's two brothers had come to America and died after years in the sheep business but he still had four sisters living in their homeland.

Laxalt Family: From left, top row, Marie, Dominique, Theresa, Suzanne; bottom row, Peter (Micky), Paul, John, Robert, circa 1950.

Dominique had long talked about returning to the Basque Country to visit his sisters whom he had not seen since had he immigrated to America forty-seven years earlier, but nothing ever came of all the talk. But a new development occurred when the Laxalts received a letter postmarked in the Basque Country and addressed to Dominique. He had heard that one of Dominique's sisters had had a stroke and he suspected the letter would contain news of her condition. So Bob, Joyce, and their infant son Bruce set out in their car to find Dominique's constantly moving sheep camp and bring him the letter along with an apple pie and recently published newspapers and magazines. They spotted his tent across a mountain meadow, parked the car on the side of the road and walked toward the camp. Dominique saw them approaching and waved a welcoming greeting.

After dinner of lamb chops, potatoes, red wine from a goatskin pouch, and sourdough bread that Dominique sliced with the large knife he always carried, as they finished up with the bread and cheese and coffee, Dominique opened the letter. Without facial expression, he began to read, then stopped and said: "She's better. They don't know how long she's going to last, but she's better."

"Can she talk?" Laxalt asked his father.

"She's in a good mind and they say she can still bring the words out good. But they don't hardly think she'll walk any more." Then Dominique added: "It's a shame."

"Was she pretty?" Joyce asked.

"Yes, she's pretty, and the liveliest thing. But I guess she must be old by now."

Then, touching his own gray hair, he said: "I can't bring myself to think her hair is like this, but I guess it must be."

Dominique reminisced about his sister meeting him in Bordeaux when he came down from the high Pyrenees so long ago, buying him a new hat and taking his beret as a keepsake to remember him in times to come, then helping him board a train for Paris to continue his trip across the Atlantic to New York and eventually to the mountain West.

"Pop," Laxalt said, "Why don't you think about going back for a visit?"

"They want me to. They wrote it again this time. She wants to see me awful bad."

Laxalt reasoned with his father suggesting that since he had sold his own sheep earlier and now simply hired on with others for the love of being in the mountains—and not being in town—he no longer was required to work, and, what's more, the fact was that if ever he was to make the trip he should do it while his health remained good. He began to quibble about how long a trip it would be. That was met by Joyce pointing out how actually short a trip it would be. She reasoned that he could fly out of San Francisco on a Friday, arrive in Paris on a Saturday and be home with his sisters for dinner on Sunday.

Dominique then quibbled about the complexities of getting a passport, a medical checkup including potential shots, and a new suit which he was steadfast in declaring he did not need since he still had the suit he had worn thirty-two years earlier at his wedding. It was virtually still brand new, hanging at home in a closet. What's more, he pointed out, he didn't have a suitcase. As Bob and Joyce wore the old sheepherder down with their positive rejoinders to his flow of negative speculations, Dominique, forever a boxing fan, perked up and said:

"Well, you know, I had a notion. If I was to leave in September, I could see the Marciano-LaStarza fight in New York on the way. They're going to fight in the Polo Grounds, you know."

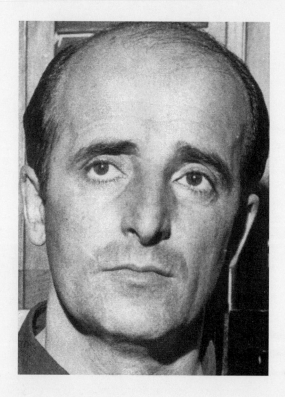

Robert shortly before taking his father to the Basque country, circa 1953.

Laxalt thought for a moment that this would end as had all the other talk through the years, as a fading dismissal of the idea of actually making the trip. And noting how Dominique fit so naturally into the mountain setting that had become his true home, the son could understand how the father felt. Then, suddenly, a new twist of fate occurred when Dominique raised the goatskin pouch and squeezed a stream of red wine toward his mouth. He just as quickly lowered the wine pouch, coughed and said: "I can't swallow so good." He pointed to his neck and explained how, though at sixty-six generally fit from his rugged life in the mountains, he thought he had suffered a slight stroke. He had fallen when gathering wood for his fire pit at the sheep camp and was unconscious for several hours before awakening and crawling to his bedroll. By the next day, he was able to move about with the sheep but he began to ponder whether he had become "an old man." This twist of fate suddenly added something entirely new to the years of talk about the return to the Basque Country by Dominique—a sense of urgency.

The Laxalt family was spread around the country by 1953 both geographically and vocationally.

Paul Laxalt, the eldest at thirty-one, had married Jackie Ross in the fall of 1946 after returning from the war where he served as a combat medic in the Philippines and, following Denver University law school, had joined her father John R. (Jack) Ross in his Carson City law firm in 1949. He was now district attorney for Ormsby County, the first step that would take him on to Nevada's governorship and eventually to the United States Senate where he distinguished himself as a good listener and became the fabled "First Friend" in Congress to President Ronald Reagan whom he helped elect to the White House.

Suzanne Laxalt, twenty-eight, had taken her vows as Sister Mary Robert and served as a Holy Family Order nun in Modesto before moving on to other California convents.

John Laxalt, twenty-seven, served as a U. S. Capitol elevator operator in Washington, D.C. under the patronage of Senator Patrick McCarran, the powerful Nevada Democrat, and was working in the senator's office staff while attending Georgetown Law School.

Marie Laxalt, twenty-five, had married Louis Bini, a San Jose engineer, and, pregnant with first child, had retired as an elementary school teacher to raise their family.

Peter (Mick) Laxalt, twenty-two, had graduated a year ahead of his class at Santa Clara University and served in the army at Camp Roberts, California before winning a scholarship to Catholic University in Washington, D.C.

So the face-to-face discussions in Carson City to persuade Dominique to take the trip fell to his wife Theresa, then sixty-two, and sons Paul, a gainfully employed attorney, and Bob, a momentarily unemployed journalist who had free time on his hands. It was quickly decided that if the trip were to actually happen, Dominique would not be able to successfully negotiate the complex travel through Reno and San Francisco and Paris airports or the overland travel to the high Pyrenees village of his birth Liginaga-Astue (Laguinge-Restoue) near Atharratze (Tardets) in the northern Basque province of Zuberoa (Soule). What's more, Theresa feared that if he made it back to the Basque Country he might never return to America. "Listen to me," she told her sons, "you don't know these Basques like I do. Once he is there where he began, he will forget he ever lived in this country!" It was decided that Bob Laxalt, a seasoned reporter who had handled the many complexities of journalism and public affairs, should accompany his father on the trip, not only to get him there safely but to make sure he returned home to Carson City.

But first they had to persuade him to finally do what he had so long talked about. Paul Laxalt's skills as an attorney would come quickly into play. He opened the dialogue by asking Dominique about the letter from the Basque Country, then shifted to the potential trip.

Paul: "Robert was saying you were thinking of a trip back there."

Dominique: "Well, they said she wanted to see me pretty bad."

Paul: "But now wouldn't be a very good time to go, would it? The sheep will be heading back into the hills soon, and you'll have to go with them, won't you?"

Dominique: "Oh, I don't hardly have to go back to the hills. I was talking to the foreman, and he said they was going to bunch the ewes and I could get off for a while if I wanted to."

It now being late summer time, they chatted about what time of year would be best for such a visit. Paul set the trap, suggesting springtime, almost a year away, anticipating that Dominique would disagree. He did: "No, no. It happens to rain too much in the spring back there and the roads and trails are muddy. The autumn is always the prettiest time."

Paul: "Well, why don't you go back then, Pop?"

Dominique: "I been thinking about it all right."

Paul: "Do you want to go back?"

Dominique: "You know I had a notion to go back for a long time."

Paul: "Maybe you'd better wait until next year. Maybe next year would be better for you."

Dominique: "No, no. Now would be the best time."

Paul: "Well, that's what we thought, Pop. And since you were so busy. We went ahead and made the arrangements. . . . You have a reservation on the plane for September."

Dominique quickly made a deft move to undo the plan and reverse the conversation by pointing out how he really did need to be with the sheep come fall.

Dominique, shifting: "Maybe next year . . ."

Paul countered: "But, Pop, the reservations have been made."

The deed was done. Dominique would return to the Basque Country of his birth.

After a quick flight from Reno to San Francisco, Dominique and Bob boarded a TWA airliner that headed east and quickly took them right back over Lake Tahoe and the Sierra wilderness where the sheepherder had spent so many solitary years. He looked out the window and recognized the rugged landscape.

"I know that peak," he pointed out for himself as well as for his son. "I made my camp in that funny hollow one night. There's a pretty little spring of water in it, you know."

"Well, we're over Nevada," the son said.

As they flew high above Colorado's Rocky Mountains, Dominique reminisced about taking the long train ride westward from New York through these same mountains now sprawled below. Laxalt, always the reporter, listened and took notes as he contemplated eventually writing a magazine article about the trip.

In New York, they were joined by Laxalt's brother John who broke away from his Washington, D.C. law school studies to come to the city, escort them to dinner and see the Marciano-LaStarza fight at the Polo Grounds.

The brief stay in New York was captured in Laxalt's notes as he chronicled how Dominique had to be culled from the decades old, out-of-style, wedding day suit he had brought along and, instead, put on the handsome new suit the family had cajoled him into buying in Reno especially for the trip. They did so by having a hotel valet come to the room and take the aged suit away for dry cleaning, explaining to Dominique he surely would want to save that suit for the trip to look nicely fresh on his arrival and when greeting of his sisters in the Basque Country. Meantime, the new suit looked just fine as they went to dinner.

Laxalt noted one particularly interesting moment at dinner when the waiter attempted to clear the empty salad plates to make way for the fresh entrée plates. Dominique held his hands firmly to the salad plate and refused to allow the waiter to take it. The perplexed waiter retreated from the table.

"Pop," said John, "Why don't you give him your plate?"

"It's clean enough," Dominique replied.

"I don't understand what you mean," said John.

"They shouldn't waste a plate. This one's fine," Dominique said.

John then explained to his father that he was about to get the waiter in trouble by not letting him do his job in gathering up the used plate.

John: "They're supposed to put a new plate on for each course. . . . If the waiter doesn't do it and one of the manager sees him, he gets fired on the spot."

Dominique: "I never heard of such a thing."

John: "It's true. That waiter's probably worried plenty by now."

Dominique: "Well, hell. Tell him to take it then."

As the waiter moved to retrieve the plate from Dominique's now loosened grip, Dominique looked at him and said: "I'm sorry, poor fellow. I didn't know you was that close to losing your job."

After dinner, they went to the Polo Grounds and watched Rocky Marcianno, heavyweight champion of the world, who was undefeated in forty-five fights, defend his title with an eleventh round TKO over challenger Roland LaStarza before the largest attendance, 44,652, at a professional fight in 1953. It was the thrill of a lifetime for prize fight enthusiast Dominique and his sons who had grown up with their own boxing gloves. The celebrated fight had receipts of $435,820 and was the first televised nationwide—to forty-three theaters in thirty-four cities.

The next day, John boarded a train for Washington and Bob and Dominique headed for the international air terminal for the flight to Paris. In Paris, as they checked into a small hotel, arranged by Air France since their flight from Paris to Bordeaux was not scheduled until the next day, the front desk clerk said to Dominique, "Eskualduna?"

Stunned, Dominique replied, "Bai. Eskualduna naiz."

The clerk explained that he was Basque and recognized Dominique's unique facial features, high forehead and cheekbones, piercing eyes as characteristic of his fellow countryman. The clerk said much had changed in the old country as many French Basques had left the Pyrenees and Bay of Biscay seashore villages to find opportunity in the large cities of Bordeaux and Paris. What's more, he told Dominique the small villages, including where his sisters lived, now had electricity and paved streets. Later, as he and his son strolled the Champs-Elysées, Dominique was flooded with youthful memories of horses and buggies as he watched shiny new cars drive by, and he noted the modern apparel in store windows, just like in America, far different from the long dresses he had seen women wear when he was last in Paris on his way to the New World.

The cultural differences between Dominique and Theresa throughout their long married life became apparent quickly in Bordeaux when he met her sisters Claire and Aurelie and Claire's husband Maurice. These were the more refined Basques from the gentle lower countryside of the Pyrenees and they had been raised in the sophistication of the city. As such, they were brought up to be cautious of the *zhibero* or "wild" Basque boys from the rugged mountains which, of course, Dominique represented even though he had met and married their sister in America. They seemed however to readily accept Laxalt since he was of their own blood through his mother Theresa.

The caution gave way during dinner of oysters and steak and fine wine served with silverware and crystal when the conversation slipped from the formal French language into their native Basque which Dominique spoke warmly.

"Dominique," said Maurice, "you don't talk too much like a *zhibero*. You talk almost like us, like a *manesha*."

"Well," Dominique replied, "that could mean only one thing. Since I got married, I've been doing most of the listening."

Maurice laughed and the sisters smiled as the conversation settled into detail about Theresa's life in America, the cheerful times of children being born and growing up and the solemnity of their brother's death in the Reno hospital where he had been treated for his World War I gas poisoning. They learned that Dominique and Theresa lost everything that he had built up in the livestock business when the prices crashed in the calamity of 1921, the very year they were married. And they were surprised to hear that she had accompanied him to the scattered ranches when he found work as a herder and she, a Cordon Bleu–trained chef, took up the dawn to dusk labors as a camp cook preparing breakfast, lunch, and dinner for herders and cowboys. Laxalt noted how intensely they listened as Dominique told stories of their survival and Theresa's courage in providing for and protecting their six children including marching them through early morning darkness over snowy sidewalks to Lenten Mass at Carson City's little Catholic church.

In the fading dusk of the next evening, Maurice drove the car slowly into the village of Atharratze and Dominique saw, for the first time in forty-seven years, the slate roofs of the houses and spires of the church in the town square where he had played handball as a boy. The cobblestone streets were quiet but Dominique could hear the river's waters rushing through the village from the high Pyrenees beyond.

Dominique identified the house of his sister Marie-Jeanne as the car pulled up. He walked up the path to the darkened door which, when suddenly opened, revealed the glowing brightness of the warmth inside. Someone exclaimed, "He has arrived!" His sisters, laughing and crying, greeted him with hugs, and he tried to get his arms around them all at once. The village came alive as other doors opened, neighbors streamed into the street, children shouted and danced about to the joyous calls, "Happiness to you all! May you always be together!"

Laxalt contemplated his father's triumph. He had come home from his faraway life in America and was being celebrated for what the family saw as the major success of a native son in the New World. Laxalt watched as the celebration grew in jubilation and realized that the warmth of humanity playing out in front of him was his own shared heritage.

The sisters fussed over Dominique as they gathered around the dinner table:

"How well he looks! How finely he carries himself!" And he objected: "You're going to spoil me. Sit down and have your dinner. You've gone to too much work already, fixing all of this. You shouldn't have done it."

Marie-Jeanne: "It is little enough. How humble this must seem to you after the richness of America."

Dominique: "You're talking to one whose tablecloth has been a piece of canvas on the ground."

They talked into the night about how his sister Marianne was recuperating following her stroke which kept her at home this evening in the nearby village of Montori (Montory), how proud of him their mother and father would have been, and how appreciative they were when they received money from him that helped them in their old age. They reminisced about their joys of their childhood, the festivals and music and food, and sports contests.

Laxalt noted how Dominique and his sisters shifted to talk of death, their mother's, their father's, their two brothers in America who had never returned as Dominique had now done, and they talked about how, despite him being their brother, they hardly knew him after so many years apart. And then with the urging of the upbeat Maurice's toast they poured more wine and broke into native *zhibero* songs that Maurice acknowledged with the surprised grin of the lower land, nonmountain Basque who he was. Soon the nephews from nearby homes joined in the merriment.

Dominique went to the home of his ill sister Marianne where Laxalt noted they held hands like sweethearts and looked so much alike they could have been twins. Marianne took a moment to look closely at Laxalt, then turned to Dominique and said: "America must be good. He holds his head high." Then she turned to Robert and said: "I cannot yet believe it. How many times have I prayed to Him for this one blessing before I died, to see my Dominique and one of his children from America."

After more days visiting with relatives and recalling his youth, including going to the original family house where he had been a child to see his long ago bedroom, and sharing the stories of becoming a livestock man in the rugged mountains and deserts of the American West, stories his Basque countrymen found enthralling, Dominique turned to his son with a look of discovery on his face.

He suddenly spoke of Nevada's admission to statehood day coming up October 31 and its traditional parade of high school and university marching bands, homemade historical and civic floats, and politicians riding in convertibles. He said he'd heard there would be more horses than ever this year. Laxalt noted he'd heard there would be more Indians in the parade, too.

And Laxalt knew it was time for the old sheepherder to leave the Basque Country of his family and birth and return to Carson City and the Sierra Nevada of his new family and permanent world.

As they flew over the Atlantic and farther across the wide spaces of America, Laxalt thought about what homage the trip had been not only for the father but also for the son who had come to learn so much about who he was and where his family roots had forever been. As he thought personally and poignantly about this discovery, his professional journalist mind pondered whether there was a magazine story in it.

Home to Nevada

On Bob's return home to pursue the new job as director of news and publications, he found the once serene Reno campus full of turmoil.

At the center of the fight stood the university's combative president, Minard W. Stout. Hailed as a pragmatic Midwesterner, Stout had been hired by the board of regents to bring order to a group of faculty who were seen as disruptive because of their views on shared governance with the administration. This brought the small university in Reno into the larger national context of Red Scare McCarthyism sweeping the nation. Senator Joseph McCarthy, a Republican from Wisconsin, created the furor in national headlines exploiting fear over the spread of Communism. Campuses were seen by crusading politicians as potential Communist hotbeds where liberal faculty could mislead students.

Stout was recruited by long-time regents' chairman Silas Ross, a staunch conservative and funeral home operator, whose attitude about faculty was that they should "stick to their classes" and leave governance of the university to the administration. "I guess you're all wondering what kind of S.O.B. I am," Stout said to the faculty when he first addressed the professors in September of 1952 about the same time Laxalt was planning to leave the UP and look for a job at the university. Many of the professors had come to Nevada's small campus from larger, prestigious universities where there were traditions of shared faculty/administration governance and academic freedom was well established. These professors were teaching many mature veterans who had returned home from combat in World War II to earn their college education through the G.I. Bill. In such a serious environment, Stout, in partnership with the overseeing regents, created a national scandal that Laxalt, as the eventual public information officer, would have to deal with one way or another.

In his inaugural visit with the faculty, Stout declared he "assumed that all faculty members felt that a president had to be some kind of overbear-

ing character to get to be president . . . While that might be true," he told
the professors, he would try to be clear and understood in his presidency.
And he added: "To be a president, you might have to be rough at times."
Years later, Stout would confirm he had been hired by the regents to "clean
things up."

Stout, educated and oriented by Midwestern values, found in Reno
a gambling casino town that billed itself "The Biggest Little City in the
World." It boasted twenty-four-hour bars, had legal brothels in a nearby
county only a half hour or so from the city, and traded in highly publicized
celebrity divorces. To be sure, Reno had more than its share of churches
within blocks of the university, but its "sin city" side was known to shock
conservative people from elsewhere.

Stout had served as an educational laboratory director at the University
of Minnesota where he trained teachers. He held degrees from Midwestern
colleges, a B.A. in economics from Northern Iowa, an M.A. in political science, and a Ph.D. in administration from Iowa. He had also taught classes
and served as principal of an Iowa high school and he had trained teachers
at another laboratory at the University of Iowa. His World War II military
management style was from top to down, commander to subordinates. He
referred to a Plato dictum in explaining managerial attitude: "Some have
the power to command; and these (God) has made of gold; others of silver,
to be auxiliaries; others again, who are to be husbandmen and craftsmen,
he has made of brass and iron."

Author J. Dee Kille would sum up the Stout conflict in her book *Academic Freedom Imperiled: The McCarthy Era at the University of Nevada*:

> He apparently did not recognize that there was a significant difference
> in administering in the highly structured public school milieu and the
> more self-governing atmosphere of higher education. Paralleling that
> outlook was a lack of commitment to what local physician and UN sup-
> porter Fred Anderson called the "Academic Holy Trinity" of "tenure,
> academic freedom and research, and faculty participation in university
> decisions and governance."

Though he had reservations about Stout and the controversy, Laxalt
was considered a shoo-in for the new position—and indeed he did get it.
He was however, somewhat reluctant to give up his writing life, as he
wrote to his agent on January 15, 1954: "Anyway, I'm taking an
unromantic post at the University of Nevada here, as director of their
campus publications, news, and radio programs. So it's back to burning
the midnight oil."

Different stories emerged about his appointment and the role that Stout played. Alice Terry, secretary to the president and the board of regents, was quoted: "He was really the only one considered. When he learned that we were going to start a news service, he was so anxious for the job he really applied before the university started searching. He was so interested, and had ideas, that Dr. Stout, with very little consideration, recommended him to the board of regents.... It was rather logical, his being a university graduate and a Nevada person, for him to have the job. Obviously, he was talented. I remember one of the girls in our office, shortly after he took his office, remarked that even his interoffice memos were good reading."

Laxalt remembered his hiring differently.

> The new president of the university, Minard Stout, was locked into a death struggle with his faculty over the firing of three professors who had challenged his policy of "professional educators." In my interview, I made the mistake of saying that I wanted no involvement in the controversy. That was enough for the president to turn me down for the news service job. I had gotten to know some members of the board of regents of the university well, and I went to them to appeal my case. By some miracle, they chose to side with me and I won the job. My position in the academic freedom controversy was not mentioned, and I was not about to bring it up.

Whether Stout turned down Laxalt or, in fact, hired him, or whether Laxalt went around the president to the regents to get hired, was unclear but Laxalt said he took to the job quickly and that "the regents and the new president were pleased" with his work.

Laxalt covered the university much like a reporter at a newspaper covered his or her "beat" at the courthouse, city hall, police station, or legislature. He dug up news that told the story of what happened on the campus of interest to the public and supplied the public relations–oriented news to the media. He responded to queries from the media about life on the campus.

And while he didn't take sides personally in the dispute, even though he leaned naturally toward academic freedom, his professional neutrality was a responsible position for a campus information officer who had to work with the news media covering the raging controversy that continued dramatically in the years beyond 1954 when he joined the university staff.

The controversy heightened when Stout used a small committee of hand-picked professors, without consulting the entire faculty for a broader view, to get regents' approval to lower admissions standards for high school graduates. Before the regents had given approval, when faculty were still discussing the options, Dr. Frank Richardson, chairman of the biology department and president of the Nevada Chapter of the American Association of University Professors, distributed to various colleges on campus a nationally published report called "Aimlessness in Education." The report criticized policies of some teachers' colleges and university education departments and cited the need to develop higher academic standards. Stout called Richardson to his office and criticized him for distributing the report. He chastised Richardson as being unworthy of being a department head, for attempting to be a critic of higher education, and suggested the professor would have to make a decision about remaining on the faculty.

Word of Stout's reprimand spread immediately through the faculty, and when Stout subsequently tried to limit faculty involvement in general university matter, tensions rose. Added to that was a revelation by Stout that he knew of a small group of professors who opposed his policies and were trying to damage the university before the legislature. What's more, Stout told the faculty the administration was gathering detailed information about the dissidents to "deal with the situation."

The news media, from Reno, Elko, and Las Vegas daily newspapers to rural county weeklies, began to cover the breaking story when the legislature formed a committee to examine the Reno campus dispute. The newspapers had great clout with legislators who sought editors' editorial page endorsements at election time and the coverage created more statewide interest. The campus was subjected to the constant clamor by reporters for news of the controversy that widened as students including the reporters and editors at University of Nevada weekly *Sagebrush* joined the fray with their own news stories, opinion columns, and editorials.

Stout and the regents were emboldened when the legislature dismissed the issue of the small group of dissident professors as a campus personnel problem with the inference the administration could handle it. This resulted in Stout sending letters of dismissal to Richardson and four others. The letters claimed that a "small, dissatisfied minority group" was spreading false information and alarming the legislature as well as the general citizenry. Richardson and the others asked Stout for detail about the claims but he declined to provide it after getting advice from the attorney general. The others' dismissals eventually were dropped but Richardson remained the firing target for Stout which caused professors from across the country to rise to his defense.

The campus became not only the center of statewide news but it also drew focus as the site of a national education scandal attracting the attention of media from San Francisco to New York. According to former *Nevada State Journal* reporter, long-time university professor, and author of several Nevada history books James W. Hulse, the regents held a three-day "half judicial, half-theatrical" hearing to take testimony in an attempt to prove Richardson was a troublemaker.

"No event in the history of the university had so polarized the academic community," Hulse wrote in his book *The University of Nevada: A Centennial History*. Following testimony for and against Richardson, the board voted unanimously to fire the biology professor for being insubordinate and uncooperative and because his conduct had not been "in accord with the welfare of the University of Nevada." At the same time, the regents showed support for Stout with a formal recognition of his presidency at the spring commencement ceremony.

Laxalt saw the controversy boil into nationally inflammatory news when Walter Van Tilburg Clark, the writer he so deeply admired, resigned his professorship in the English Department in a letter condemning the regents for condoning and perpetuating Stout's "autocratic administration." Clark, whose father had served as a highly regarded president of the university, said he could not remain in the "manageable mediocrity" that Stout had created. Another eruption followed with the resignation of nationally acclaimed faculty member Thomas Little who cited Stout's "chain of command" and declared: "The bald fact remains that we do not have freedom of speech and that many of us have been punished for attempting to exercise it."

Richardson's attorneys appealed his dismissal to the Nevada Supreme Court which held in 1954 that Stout had not proved that the professor was insubordinate or uncooperative enough to be fired and that some of Stout's charges were nothing more than trivial. The court said the administration could not fire a faculty member without sufficient cause simply because he took a position on university policy. The court ordered Richardson reinstated with compensation for salary lost during the controversy. Richardson returned to teaching but eventually grew tired of the poisoned academic atmosphere on the Reno campus and continued his career at the University of Washington.

Following the Richardson case, which journalist/historian Hulse called "a humiliating defeat for Stout and the regents," the campus atmosphere continued to erupt with new controversies involving the legislature, the faculty, and the students that would require Laxalt's deft hand as a public information officer. One involved a complex land trade by the university that left Stout and the regents squirming in embarrassed defeat at the hands of the governor. Another broke out when more professors turned in resignations including sociology professor Dr. Allvar Jacobson who decried during the 1955 legislature what he called the "inhuman and capricious" treatment of faculty by Stout. More controversial focus came through a major, twenty-five thousand dollar legislative-financed, investigation by out-of-state educators into how the Reno campus was administered by Stout.

The American Association of University Professors joined the inquiring chorus with its own investigation that resulted in the AAUP censuring Stout and the regents for their administrative practices.

By 1956, with Laxalt's information office fielding calls from an increasingly aggressive press covering the controversial Reno campus, the students added their voices. They voted with their feet by marching in protest to the president's house near the iconic Morrill Hall on the picturesque quad and then downtown to string up, hang, and burn Stout in effigy from the world famous Reno Arch. The *Reno Evening Gazette* headlined "Two Hour Demonstration Staged by U.N Students" and the *Nevada State Journal* blazed away with "U of N Students Stage Riot Here." Joining Stout dangling in effigy were the likenesses of two deans. The students shouted, "Down with Stout" and carried banners protesting that the president was treating the Reno campus like a high school.

Seven students were detained and subsequently dismissed from the university. But in still another embarrassing setback for Stout, his administration reversed the dismissal when legal authorities pointed out no hearings had been held for the protesting students and no proof was shown of any wrongdoing. The *Sagebrush* declared that a dangerous precedent was set by denying the students due process of law.

In the flurry of the increasing discontent, two important reports would be crucial in what would happen next. One would be produced by Laxalt's office in support of Stout's administration. The four-page report, "Highlights of Progress," cited achievements at the university under Stout's leadership including the founding of two major colleges, Education and Business Administration. The report also noted achievements in the graduate school and School of Nursing as well as increases in student enrollment and faculty pay.

The effort by Stout to bolster public support for his administration was met by more powerful criticism in a report by the out-of state educators appointed by the legislature to investigate the Reno campus controversies. Dr. Dean McHenry, a UCLA political science professor, headed up the team of seven educators, which found that while Stout did, in fact, have notable achievements, most of the claims of his high-handed policies were valid and confirmed in the committee's investigation. Importantly, the McHenry report encouraged the legislature to increase the Board of Regents from five members to nine. Silas Ross, the powerful chairman and Stout supporter, upset by all the turmoil, decided to retire and the newly elected and diversified board decided the problems could not be overcome with Stout in the presidency and fired him.

In the meantime, the situation was wearing on Robert Laxalt. An April 1, 1957 to his agent shows the toll that the controversy was taking on him:

> Otherwise, things are in a vacuum state. I'm still not certain whether I'll be leaving the university this summer. Things have come to a climax there, with the legislature overwhelmingly passing a bill designed to fire the president. However, he can't seem to take the hint, so he's going to fight it. I guess blood will be awful deep before it's over. And by then, my nerves will be so shot I'll be swinging from the chandeliers.

The mood of the campus changed when the regents turned to the faculty for insight about a successor to Stout in 1958. Dr. Charles Armstrong, president of Pacific University in Oregon, a student of the classics who had been educated at Harvard and had taught in the diversified academic landscapes of the Pacific Northwest, Florida, and New England, was selected to be the healer of the fatigued Reno campus.

Armstrong's appointment was good news for Laxalt who had traded the journalistic intensity of his twenty-four-hour, seven-day UP wire service work for the even greater and troubling intensity he faced as a publicist on the once peaceful little Reno campus. Laxalt, himself a student of classic books from childhood through his own college years, was delighted to learn that Armstrong not only referred to the classics in his speeches but also was predisposed toward creation of a university press on the Reno campus to publish the work of local, regional, and national authors.

The regents provided wide freedom for Armstrong to pull the campus community together with a new sense of teamwork. Unlike Stout who had first addressed the faculty with his infamous "s.o.b." remark, Armstrong opened his dialogue with reason and clearly reached out to the faculty and students by saying that he wanted to create "an atmosphere in which all members of the university community, students, faculty, and administration, may work toward our common goals in mutual confidence and respect."

In his first five months on the job, Armstrong joined with the faculty in creating a new plan for campus governance to replace Stout's hated chain of command military style. The new university code provided for a faculty council to advise the president and regents on educational policy and specified that most of the council's members be elected from academic colleges and professional units.

Laxalt found the new mood on campus more relaxing and he was happy to have settled into a job that would allow him to pay the mortgage and provide for his growing family that now included daughter Monique, born in 1953, and Kristin in 1956. It was during the academic anguish of the Stout years, however, before the warmly welcomed Armstrong arrival, that campus information officer Laxalt had covered university news during the day while turning to personal writing in the evenings, including a story that would shape his life forever and give voice to immigrants the world over.

Sweet Promised Land

As a veteran reporter, Laxalt knew there was a story in his father's homage to his family roots in the Basque Country but he didn't know what kind of story it might be. Laxalt looked over the tablets full of notes he had taken during his travels with Dominique. But he wasn't sure what he should do with the notes. Before the trip, he had thought that perhaps the story might be best for a magazine, so he wrote to Peggy Dowst Redmond at the *Saturday Evening Post* with whom he had had contact when the magazine published his story on Nevada gambling. He had shared with her the plans for the trip. She was immediately interested, but she advised him to think in terms of a book. The *Post* editor then put Laxalt in touch with New York agent Naomi Burton of Curtis Brown, Ltd., who was similarly intrigued by the book and pitched it to New York publishers. Laxalt received fairly positive responses from Doubleday, Simon & Schuster, and, especially, Elizabeth Lawrence at Harper's, who wrote:

> If he could use the experience and revelations of this trip as springboard for the larger story of his father in America—he might have something unique and delightful. It would, however, take doing. And a lot would depend on his father's reactions to the trip.

However, none of the publishers were willing to take on an untested book author with a proposed manuscript about a trip that had not yet happened! Laxalt's reponse to this letter from Naomi Burton is a quite remarkable document in its own right and from it one sees, while the actual voice of the book may have eluded him, that the stories he would share were firmly entrenched in his mind:

> Interspersed with the trip chapters would be the scenes of coming and living: for example, one would be his meeting and friendship with another Basque youth on shipboard, a youth both rebellious and tortured. It was not until they were nearing America that this youth finally

confided in my father that he was a priest, running away from the bonds of old-world religion.

Again, for example, there is the time of money in the United States. . . . The bankers, in their bowled hats and stiff collars and striped suits, came out to the sheep camps in their ponderously metallic Cadillacs, sat down on battered old pack bags and ate out of a blackened dutch over, and pretended to like it all. . . .

For a while, it was funny—if you can imagine rough sheep and cattle men in striped suits and Cadillacs and owning a dozen ranches. But then, it wasn't very funny. One year, the prices dropped 80 percent, and nearly everyone was crippled. My father held on, for one more year, and then came the winter in which more than half his remaining sheep were frozen to death where they stood, in the desert. I don't think I will ever forget his grimness when he told me of whipping himself to walk through all that frozen silence of sheep, so that he would never forget and be a sheepman again. But he was.

And then there is a little bit of tragedy in the fact that after a lifetime of sheep, not one of his four sons wanted the sheepman's life. I was the closest to it, and I knew it well, but I wavered and went this way. A little while later, my father sold his sheep. He never mentioned once that he wanted us to be sheepmen, and never mentioned afterwards what he felt about it.

Miss Lawrence mentioned something about my father's reactions to the trip. I don't think she has to worry. He is sharp of mind, and though he doesn't know what it means, I don't think I've ever seen more of an identification with life in many other people. My earliest memories are those of—in a way I can't fully explain—of his being part of the mountains. Even to this day, it's a jarring experience to see him in a closed room.

The agent encouraged his writing. Upon his return, Laxalt sized up the possibilities. He knew he had a good protagonist in Dominique whom he thought of as a gentle man who could be sturdy and tough because he had survived in the American West of his era. Laxalt thought one element would be Dominique's emotional goodbyes to fellow sheepherders since he would be first among them to return to their homeland. He had extraordinary amounts of background material on his father's life and experiences in the early West. In fact, he thought he had way too much background including all those notes. Another element would be the emotional reunion in the high mountains of the Basque Country with Dominique's aged sisters and their families who saw him in legendary terms. And, finally, there was the storytelling about America that goes with all immigrants who return to their homeland.

Laxalt wrestled with his own role. "Should I be a participant or an observer and interpreter?" he asked himself. He confided later that he really did not know which way to go. He had once been advised to write a long epic novel but he was never able to pull it off. Something never worked when he tried to write a novel. Then, pondering the story of Dominique, he hit on a new notion about his failed attempts at writing a novel:

> What was missing was the poignancy of my father's return to his native land. That, and the discovery I made against my will, finally, that this wasn't a work of fiction. It was actuality. It was non-fiction. It really happened. It wasn't invented.

Still, he couldn't figure out how to write the proposed book. Again and again, he put a piece of paper in the typewriter. Again and again, he tossed the wrong words he had written into the waste basket. Then, in a last almost unconscious effort with little thought, he typed, in the lowercase habit of wire service reporters, "my father was a sheepherder, and his home was the hills."

Laxalt looked at the sentence for an eternity of five minutes and then realized he had unlocked the creative process. He said to himself: "That's it. You've got a book. And I did. It started from there. The story felt itself along word by word, line by line, paragraph by paragraph, chapter by chapter. There was no outline. To lock the flow of the story into a framework would have been a disaster. The story found itself." As for all those notes he had made? He never used one of them. He simply began writing the story directly out of his heart with the enormous help of a brain he had seasoned in the storytelling suspense of journalism.

Laxalt put the first four chapters in the mail and sent them to the Curtis Brown agent who passed them along to Elizabeth Lawrence at Harper's who quickly offered him a contract even though they were concerned about how he would handle the actual moment of Dominique's homecoming with his sisters as well as how the book would end. Laxalt continued to write and later noted that the editors' concerns were relieved when he sent in a chapter about the homecoming.

> He was the adventurer who had braved the unknown land across the sea and found his fortune. He was the rebel who had broken the bonds of their own longings and fought the battle and come home victorious

He was the youth who had gone out into the world in beggar's garb and come back in shining armor. This was the moment of fulfillment. This was the moment of reward he could never have known in America.

As Laxalt continued to write more questions arose. How should the story end? And where? Lewis Carroll had written in *Alice's Adventures in Wonderland* about the reading of a letter: "Begin at the beginning . . . and go on till you come to the end: then stop" which many writers translated humorously about the quandary of writing—"Begin at the beginning and end at the end." Laxalt had struggled to find the beginning and he had found it. But was there a natural place for an ending? He thought the story should end with Dominique returning to America thus completing the circle of the trip. But he discovered that the natural ending was there in the Basque Country where the old sheepherder came to realize he had become an American. The startling moment came as father and son completed dinner and were descending a trail from Dominique's sister's house. Someone called out, "Come back! Come back!"

Laxalt wrote it as it happened:

> I looked at my father, but he did not seem even to have heard. His face was white and grim and violently disturbed, and he was breathing in quick gasps. I reached out and touched him on the arm and said uncertainly, "They want us to come back."
>
> Without turning, he shook his head and cried shakenly, "I can't go back. It ain't my country anymore. I've lived too much in America ever to go back." And then, angrily, "Don't you know that?"

Laxalt thought about the America Dominique had come to know as his new country, the mountains and the deserts, the sage and pine, the sheep and their tinkling bells, the sheepherder and his dog.

> Then I saw the cragged face that that land had filled with hope and torn with pain, had changed from young to old, and in the end had claimed. And then I did know it. We walked in silence down the wooded trail, and in a little while the voices died away.

Laxalt had found the ending. He turned to Clark's reference to a ballad in *The City of Trembling Leaves* for a serious—and biblically inspired—title:

> Oh, this is the land that old Moses shall see,
> Oh, this is the land of the vine and the tree,

Oh, this is the land for My children and Me,
The sweet promised land of Nevada

The title would take on a more personal meaning for readers of *Sweet Promised Land* who associated it with Dominique's discovery that his new land of Nevada had replaced his old world in the Basque Country.

Harper & Brothers published *Sweet Promised Land* in 1957, four years after his trip to the Basque Country with his father, to instant acclaim not only in the august *New York Times' Book Review* but in other celebrated newspapers and magazines around the world. Laxalt had not won the Nobel Prize, nor even the Pulitzer for which he would eventually be entered. But seven years after he had summoned the courage to show Walter Van Tilburg Clark a short story, three years after he left the UP to dwell in a strife-torn university campus as a publicist, he found he had become what he always wanted to be, an author of a serious book.

Sweet Promised Land became a selection of the National Book Society of England and an alternate with the Literary Guild in the United States and would be translated into German and French. William A. Douglass, a Basque culture scholar and author, cited other distinguished authors' praise in a foreword in the 1986 republication of the book by the University of Nevada Press:

William Saroyan said in a letter to publisher Harper & Row "*Sweet Promised Land* really delighted and moved me—the anger (rage) of the old man at the cougar (mountain lion) is magnificent, unforgettable , profoundly meaningful—about the relationship between righteousness and risk." Douglass cited western writer Tom Lea's testimonial: "The power of *Sweet Promised* Land has stayed with me. I have reread it more than once. I have been an advocate, admirer and frequent mentioner of that book's qualities since its publication."

Douglass called the book "an American original and a harbinger of things to come" with Laxalt rising as the "literary spokesman" of Basque Americans who had by and large kept to themselves in the lonely reaches of the sheep camps or in their mingling in the little Basque hotels and in the family privacy of their homes. "Robert Laxalt's simple eloquence in narrating it captured the imagination of the wider public," Douglass wrote. "In a sense, for Basque Americans the book's success legitimized their own ethnic sentiments—even to themselves. Laxalt received poignant letters from Basques throughout the American West thanking him for reinforcing their pride in their heritage."

Laxalt Family at first Basque Festival at John Ascuaga's Nugget in Sparks, from left, Robert, Kristin, Bruce, Monique, Joyce, 1960.

Two years after it was published, the book was a catalyst to the creation of a national Basque Festival in Reno's neighboring city of Sparks. Laxalt helped organize the event that drew thousands of Basques and their family friends as well as people of many ethnic backgrounds who suddenly found, to their enthusiastic liking, the hearty cuisine of the little Basque hotel kitchens. The festival inspired more such gatherings in Nevada and eventually around the West as Basques and friends of Basques celebrated their culture by dancing the traditional native jota and rooting for Basque strong men who, as they had done in the old country, lifted competitive weights and raced against each other in spirited wood-chopping contests that occasionally saw blood spurt from axe-stricken feet.

Basques celebrated with *bota* bags squeezed at arms-length sending thin streams of red wine accurately from hands to open mouths. Tables of traditional Basque food were set with chorizo sausages, lamb chops and stew, French fried potatoes and bread, green salads with fresh vegetables, bowls of homemade soup, and the unique Picon Punch cocktail. The Picon is a staple drink in the Basque restaurants of the American West. It is usually mixed in a bell shaped Irish coffee–type glass full of tiny ice cubes with a very slight splash of grenadine, an equal amount of soda and an original French aperitif called Amer Picon, or an adapted American version, Torani Amer, over which is floated a touch of brandy and into which is dropped a thin slice of lemon rind. The taste is bittersweet but eventually gets acquired repeat Basque cuisine aficionados.

Sweet Promised Land also inspired the creation of a Basque Studies Program in 1967 at the Desert Research Institute. The Basque Studies Program was incorporated into the University of Nevada in 1972. The program grew to become the Center for Basque Studies and became the most important center of such culture outside of the Basque Country itself. "This book was fundamental in starting the program because in a way it distorted the wider public's understanding of Basque Americans," said Douglass, who had become its director. "I mean that it exaggerated their importance. . . . You would have thought there were at least 30,000 Basques in Nevada, which, of course, there never were."

The book stirred pride in Nevadans who, Douglass pointed out, saw their state portrayed in the national media for its legal gambling, legal (in some but not all counties) prostitution, and divorces which welcomed a steady stream of people from out of state for the relatively quick "Renovations" as columnist Walter Winchell called the unhitching of marriage under liberal Silver State laws. As Douglass wrote:

> *Sweet Promised Land* provided a welcome relief from the imagery of easy money and a sleazy lifestyle. It was a simple morality play set amid the soaring mountain ranges and searing deserts far removed from the gambling glitter. For Nevadans, *Sweet Promised Land* became *their* book. It was an antidote for lurid depictions of the state, and one could read it for personal assurance and then send it to friends and relatives out of state as a way of saying "I do not live in Sodom and Gomorrah."

It also caught the attention of Hollywood's Columbia Pictures, Warner Brothers, CBS, MGM, Universal, and even Playboy expressed interest through Los Angeles literary agents or production company associates. Betsy Cramer of Playboy Productions wrote to Laxalt: "It is not very often that I am moved to want to write a fan letter. But then again it is not very often that a story is published that is as lovely, evocative and moving as SWEET PROMISED LAND. As an acquisitions editor by profession and a closet writer by desire I have always felt that the quality of a story can only be judged by its ability to move and touch. Thank you for reaffirming my belief that there are writers who can still do that." She went on to report that she had always wanted to develop and/or write a story for a movie dealing with the Basque people.

Included in the Hollywood correspondence was word from agent Marjel De Lauer about Peter McCrea, son of western movie star Joel McCrea, taking an option on *Sweet Promised Land* and possibly renewing it several times for about $22,500. There were various discussions as to who would play Dominique and the possibilities included the senior McCrea or Anthony Quinn. Over time, Joyce Laxalt, a playwright and actress in college, turned to writing copy for a screenplay. But, in the end, as happens to many if not most plans for book/movie deals, no film was developed.

The enormous success of the book set the scene for what was to become one of Laxalt's most permanent literary achievements, the founding of the University of Nevada Press. Laxalt could explore the establishment of a university press because of the new mood of academic freedom created on the campus after the classical scholar Armstrong replaced intimidatingly controversial Stout as president.

As Laxalt set about the complex planning for the press, consulting with colleagues, writers, and officials at other universities with successful presses, another idea was nagging at him. He had begun writing another book. And he knew he couldn't stop, that he had to continue to write. He also knew he needed time and space away from the pressures of the job he had taken six years earlier. The job had intertwined him with the stress of the Stout administration dark years and the new hope of the Armstrong enlightenment.

So, in 1960 in the midst of his planning for the press, having not yet attained tenure at the university, Bob, along with Joyce, took some of their savings and financed his own sabbatical leave to the French Basque Country with hopes of finding inspiration for writing but, in reality, only a vague notion of what future awaited them. Because of the uncertainty, they decided, as Bob put it in his memoir, "to take America with us." He watched in astonishment as Joyce packed thirteen suitcases and two trunks with clothes for the entire family over four seasons including party dresses with matching hats for what he described as "the gay Parisian life she anticipated." They bundled up their children, Bruce, nine, Monique, six, and Kristin, four, and flew to New York where they boarded the SS *Rotterham* for the voyage to Le Havre.

The Writing Life

After several days crossing the Atlantic, Bob and Joyce Laxalt arrived at Le Havre where their wide-eyed young children were suddenly enveloped in the sound of rapid-fire French on the docks. They retrieved the thirteen suitcases and two trunks from the hold of the SS *Rotterdam* and squeezed themselves and the luggage into a "pint-sized" taxi for the drive through the port city's busy streets to the countryside and the journey inland to Paris. The French taxi driver took them to the Hotel de Paris and, when Laxalt complained of the price-gouging fare, shrugged "*La vie est chere.*"

Before leaving home, Laxalt had arranged for purchase of a Volkswagen bus in Paris and, after a brief stay in the city, the family packed up the suitcases and trunks for the drive to the Basque Country in the South of France. But his heart pounded when he saw the mad traffic swirling around the roundabout at the Arc de Triomphe. It dashed in all directions like spokes from the hub of a wheel. Rather than risking their lives with him in the driver's seat, he quickly hired a driver to ferry them to the outer limits of the city.

The real adventure began as they headed south toward Bordeaux on National Route 10 a three-lane highway where cars heading each way darted in and out of the middle lane used for passing, which Laxalt thought was a recipe for head-on disasters. He compared it to an elongated cemetery marked by headstone memorials every five kilometers or so honoring travelers killed in roadway carnage. Things got worse as they headed the Volkswagen into the mountain passes where winding roads were dangerously unprotected—there were no guardrails—and speeding French drivers forced slower traffic to what Laxalt called "the edge of the abyss." Rarely did he take his eyes off the curving road to notice the small villages far below with their stone houses that seemed like miniatures.

Laxalt kept his humor intact as best he could by advising his family that the next time he drove in France he would have a "James Bond special car with six inch thick bumpers front and back adorned with three inch spikes for ramming" and "for extra protection I would have twin 50-caliber machine guns set in the bumpers which I could fire by pressing a button on the dashboard, disintegrating the errant French drivers."

He described the National Route 10 with little love for such drivers. "This notorious arterial is lined not only by gravestones, but by shocked survivors of head-on collisions. They stand shaking their heads as if to say, 'How could this have happened?' I could have told them, but wasted words are wasted words when it comes to the French." He surmised that there was a national conspiracy to decrease the population through "eagle-eyed French drivers" lurking near Auto Ecoles "waiting to run down students and slow-moving teachers" alike.

They finally safely arrived at the picturesque fishing village of Doni-bane Lohitzune (St. Jean de Luz) on the Atlantic's Bay of Biscay, which would be their home from September until March. There were, however no inexpensive cottages to rent, as they had hoped. With none available, they were lucky to find an unoccupied, three-story summer villa with a living room, dining room, and bedrooms for all as well as a maid's quarters which came in handy when they hired a fisherman's widow to help Joyce with housework, cooking, and shopping in the village and nearby city of Baiona (Bayonne).

Laxalt set up a study and started up work again on the new novel he had begun back home in Reno. Joyce enrolled the children in a French school where, speaking only English, they would have to adapt to the strange new language. Joyce, who had studied French in high school and college, was thorough in reading and writing the language and, when immersed in it on a daily basis, quickly became fluent. Bob was limited to his own college French and that which he heard his mother speak at home as a boy and the children remembered the French songs Joyce had taught them as infants. Within a month, however, all three children were conversationally fluent with their schoolmates and teachers none of whom spoke any English.

The story that Laxalt was writing involved the bloody attack of a bat sinking its fang-like teeth into the nose of a coyote. The coyote had paused to attack a Basque sheepherder's flock, but now, bleeding profusely and reeling in madness, it bit into a sheepdog and a ewe. An epidemic of rabies quickly swept through the Basques' herds in Northern Nevada afflicting madness and death on more coyotes, livestock, and human beings

Laxalt Family in Basque Country with relatives, from left, Kristin, Bruce, Robert, Monique, 1961.

The book was going well when Laxalt shifted to another medium, a short story unlike any he had written before that would reveal a Hemingway-like style and a glimpse into the complex nature of Bob and Joyce's marriage.

Ernest Hemingway was the acclaimed author of *A Farewell to Arms* about World War I and *The Sun Also Rises* about the Lost Generation of American writers and artists in the Paris of the 1930s who made forays into Spain to run at the deadly point of bulls' horns over the uneven cobblestones of Pamplona's narrow and winding streets. Hemingway's fascination with the medieval spectacle of the bullfight and Spanish culture would lead him to another book, *For Whom the Bell Tolls*. And it would create more opportunity for his journalism as he simultaneously shifted from the literature of books to the daily deadlines of the North American Newspaper Alliance (NANA) and weekly *Life* magazine coverage of the Spanish Civil War.

Hemingway had broken into writing as a reporter at the *Kansas City Star*. Laxalt, like Hemingway and many other journalist/authors, would shift his literary efforts and journalism back and forth in pursuit of storytelling. Unlike Hemingway, who was a writer but not a publisher, Laxalt would unfold a career not only as a journalist writing stories for the *National Geographic* magazine from datelines across the globe but also as the author of literature and, ultimately, the publisher of his own books and the works of hundreds of other authors—simultaneously. The Hemingway-like moment came in a short story he set in a dingy hotel room in Paris that he would eventually sell to *Cosmopolitan* magazine and that would appear in the August 1964 issue, is titled "From a Balcony in Paris." It must have captured some of the flavor and dynamics of the Laxalt's first arrival in Paris:

> The room was on the Fourth Floor, or *troisieme étage* in the French way of doing things, and it looked down on a narrow street that ran along the side of the hotel. The street was crowded with afternoon activity, but he had not come out to watch that.
>
> The room had suddenly become monstrous to him, and Clete had escaped by the simple device of stepping out on the balcony. Through the high, open doors behind him, he could hear his wife crying. He gripped the iron railing with both hands. "If there's one lesson I will one day get through my thick head," he said to the street, "it is that nobody has ever listened to anybody in the world, not even Christ."

The story continues exploring the couple's ill-fated romance with international travel and the friction in communication between husband and wife:

> He had not traveled much, but enough to have learned that places never turned out the way you thought they were going to. The travel posters and the postcards were all selective lies. They showed none of the poverty, and they didn't smell, like the Congo marketplace that had looked so colorful from a distance but was something else when he got inside. He had talked his head off trying to convince her of this. But how does one describe poverty in a foreign land without making it attractive?

The story takes the reader into the fictional couple's marriage of twenty years. It is, despite the trauma of the story, a continuing love affair sprinkled with good humor, much of it self-deprecating, along with the independent mindedness of mutually annoying, personal disagreements on matters of creativity. In this respect, it is not unlike Bob and Joyce's own eleven-year marriage at that time. Laxalt wrote of his fictional protagonist's reflections on his wife's difficulties:

She was a grown woman with her fair quota of shattered illusions. But not this one yet. In this one, she was a woman with a child's illusion carefully shaped from the time she had picked up her first Daphne du Maurier primer. As she kept up a pretense of conversation, he had watched the frantic lines that only he could recognize make their tiny appearance in her planed face. *Good,* he had thought in an instant's vindictiveness. Then, in remorse as quick, *Why does it always have to hurt you so much, and finally me?*

The story described the "rude and angry confusion" in a French railway depot "when he had gone a little insane himself trying to locate thirteen pieces of luggage filled mostly with party dresses he had told her she would never wear" and how their taxi ride to the hotel was filled with her stony silence. They made their way through "the dim and musty dungeons of corridors" that led to the room that shocked her to tears and caused him to escape from her trauma to the balcony.

Clete's wife implores him to come in from the balcony and they continue their discussion. Clete's wife makes this observation: "You *don't* know what it's like. . . . You never look at anything you don't want to see. You just pretend it isn't there, and it goes away. How very convenient. Like having a magic wand."

Laxalt took the reader through continued bickering with the protagonist Clete escaping again to the balcony from which he began studying the street scene below where prostitutes tried to lure men passing by. He returned to the room to have drinks sent up from the bar and, after reconciliation, she joined him on the balcony where they both studied the prostitutes at work, their spiked, high-heels clicking as they sauntered along the cobblestone street. They had more drinks sent up from the bar and began comparing notes on the prostitutes—a heavy-breasted mulatto showing off with a dark tilt of her head, a coquettish blonde with her hands on her hips and her hair tousled in calculated disorder, and another, older woman in a proper print dress who didn't appear to have many prospects.

After dinner of entrecôte and red wine at a restaurant sidewalk on the Champs-Elysées, they returned to the room for double brandies on the balcony where they again observed the prostitutes and speculated about their lives. After a while, they went to sleep. "He turned in bed and, quite by accident, touched her. It was like an electric shock between them. They made love then as they had not known it for many years. Long afterward, the clicking of heels wakened him, and he began to get out of bed and the story reaches its climax:

> "Are you going out on the balcony?"
> "Yes, just for a minute."
> "Clete," she mumbled. "Everything is going to be all right with me now. Will you thank them for me?"

Virginia City Poet Shaun Griffin, a long-time friend of Laxalt and a serious follower of his work, included the *Cosmopolitan* story in his book *The River Underground: An Anthology of Nevada Fiction* because he saw it as an unusual departure from most of Laxalt's writing. He knew Laxalt was an admirer of Hemingway's often blunt, to the point, dramatic prose, and many who read the story thought it to be a touch of Hemingway with the echo of Joyce's voice. The argument over thirteen "fictional" suitcases illustrated the biographical reality of Joyce's packing her party dresses in the many trunks and steamers that they had shipped to France.

Family and friends of Bob and Joyce saw their manner and heard their tone in the piece. Theirs was a complex marriage of deep love and loyalty intermixed with the frequent expressions of their individual artistic temperaments. Joyce had performed in plays through her high school and college years and had written plays in college. She established her own creative life of acting and writing before he began his college and subsequent professional newswriting. She would, in years to come, act as his editor and counselor and adapt his prose to screenplays. She always spoke her piece, eyes focused directly at him, in total candor with her creative insights that he respected however ruffling and challenging they could come across.

In Donibane Lohizune, as Bob worked on the novel about rabies spreading through Basque herds in Northern Nevada, Joyce bought a German camera and began taking photographs of the family treks through the Basque Country that could be used to illustrate his writing. After six months in the seaside village, the family packed the Volkswagen bus and prepared to drive the next day through the small villages and towns in the hills to a new home in Donibane Garazi (St. Jean Pied de Port) in the higher Pyrenees. Laxalt loaded their belongings in the trunk of the Volkswagen including a footlocker containing the unfinished manuscript of his novel. That evening, they drove to the village plaza to join in a festival of singing and folk dancing.

After watching the merriment, they returned to the vehicle to find it had been broken into and looted. Gone, with other belongings, was the footlocker containing the manuscript. Laxalt was unaware that a gang of black letter-jacketed robbers called *blousons noir* from Bordeaux regularly worked such village festivals. Instead, he had been assured that dishonesty simply did not exist in the Basque Country.

Laxalt deeply regretted not leaving the footlocker open, thinking that the manuscript would have been ignored and only things of value like cameras and souvenirs would have been taken. But since the trunk was locked, he realized, the thieves simply took the entire footlocker.

"To track down the French thieves and reclaim the footlocker would have been futile," he reflected years later about the most devastating misfortune that can afflict a writer with a creative work in progress and no backup copy. "My manuscript and a year and a half of my writing life had disappeared. I could not reword what I had written. I was left in a state of despair." He simply didn't know where to turn in his writing or what to do. It was March of 1961 and the family's plans and reservations to return to Reno and the final planning and inauguration of the university press were months away in June. He wanted to remain in the Basque Country to do research and his wife and children were adapting to the challenges of their cultural shift from their lives in America.

They settled into a small villa in Donibane Garazi, once the capital of the ancient kingdom of Navarre, where the children enrolled in the Citadel school building that had been built by Napoleon. The villa was centrally located with shops handy for Joyce and a plaza where men gathered to tell stories that Bob took down in his notes for future writing about the Basques. No one knew, he learned in a bit of a paradox, where they had come from. It was suspected the Basques had found their way into the Pyrenees centuries earlier and settled into an isolated, inward-looking culture that produced a people distinct in blood and language unrelated to the Indo-Europeans who were spread throughout the continent. Some claimed the Basques to be "pure descendants" of Cro-Magnon man, which Laxalt found to have the support of scholars examining archaeological, linguistic, and DNA evidence.

Laxalt established a small study in the villa's attic where he pondered what to do following the loss of his manuscript. There, he remembered the short story he had written about snakes that the editor of *Esquire* had turned down as an unwelcome magazine topic. Now, spurred by the success of *Sweet Promised Land* as a book and his effort at writing the new novel still on his mind, and with even more thoughts about actually publishing books through the new university press, he wondered if the snake story might be told as a book rather than magazine piece. He wasn't sure. But he remembered the detail he'd pitched to *Esquire*—about a man named Smale Calder who entered a wire mesh snake pen and charmed snakes as the public gathered around to watch in horror.

> The rattlesnakes, a dozen of them, all sprawled basking in the sun, their eyes eternally open and unblinking, had all coiled as one. They had arched their necks and cocked their spade heads low, the forked, black threads flickering out of their mouths, their tails buzzing together until the air was filled with a death-dry rattle.

Laxalt had described in the short story how Calder walked to the center of the pen, stood absolutely still and surveyed the snakes with his roving black eyes as the buzzing of their rattles rose to a roar; how, suddenly, the buzz decreased to a slight hum; how Calder didn't move but just stared at the snakes until the rattling ceased as onlookers watched in frightened disbelief; how Calder finally kneeled in the sand amid the snakes as they uncoiled and then slithered "like chicks to a mother hen. . . . They coiled on his arms, and his legs, and he twined them about his neck, and a woman screamed and fainted, but the snakes didn't buzz. Calder stroked their heads and their undersides with his short, square fingers, and they curled lazily and sensuously about him."

The more he thought about the snake story and how it represented good and evil, the more the idea developed. He thought the story could not be about Basques because they would be too restrained by their nature to react appropriately to the emotional situations he had in mind for the story.

Laxalt thought that Italians, whom he knew to be more open with their emotions, had the classic qualities for the story that was taking shape in his mind. He began to write, setting the story in a small town in the Nevada desert populated by Italian immigrants. He created the spirit of evil through the mind of Savio Lazzaroni, a priest who had an absolute belief that there was, in fact, a devil. Father Lazzaroni saw the devil in the arrival of the outsider Calder, a non-Italian whom the priest saw as an invader threatening the tight-knit community with his passion for rattlesnakes. Laxalt began to explore humankind's essences of *good, envy, ego, hypocrisy, innocence, symbol, myth*. He theorized that people use such words because they are taught them through their culture but, in fact, really don't know what they mean until they learn through personal experience.

The story involved two dreams—one of a child haunted by "an unknown and unseen presence of evil," the other of the child grown to be a young seminarian haunted by the child's nightmare presence taking on a shape.

Laxalt created a cast of characters whose lives were changed by the outsider who tried to live among them quietly with his snakes but instead became a catalyst bringing out the hidden emotions of the others. The snakes, in Laxalt's view, were not evil but represented a Christian symbol. In fact, he noted, the house snake was regarded as holy in Grecian times. The snakes and the stranger were conceived as the innocents in the story developed around the characters' fears: Father Lazzaroni's fear of the devil; Tony's fear of the larger world beyond his little town; Smale Calder's fear of the "brute snake"; and so on.

Laxalt populated the little town with farmers and tradesmen who as practical people couldn't understand the abstracts of evil as preached by Father Lazzaroni but who did react to the stranger and his snakes with suspicion. Laxalt pitted these characters in a conflict of righteousness confronting innocence creating the "same fate that Christ underwent in the Crucifixion." As the story moved toward surprise endings for the characters, Laxalt the writer explored the theme that mankind will always kill innocence, even if Laxalt the man wished the opposite were true.

The book, *A Man in the Wheatfield*, was Laxalt's own exploration of what Hemingway called "all the things you don't know." One reviewer described the book as "a stark and chilling tale of human nature and the ways in which people deal with fear and prejudice." *Time* magazine called it "a fascinating, ambiguous allegory of man's various ways of confronting fear." The book was published by Harper & Row in 1964, three years after the Laxalt family sojourn to the Basque Country. The American Library Association named it one of six notable works of American fiction that year including it with Saul Bellow's *Herzog* and Hemingway's *A Movable Feast*.

A writer for the *Cleveland Press* noted that Laxalt's book had been compared to Hemingway's *The Old Man and the Sea* "perhaps because Hemingway was so greatly concerned with a gigantic fish while one of Laxalt's chief interests is a superbly beautiful, equally gigantic reptile." There, however, "any resemblance ends. Above all else Robert Laxalt is an infinitely compassionate man with no brutality whatsoever in his style. If anyone, he reminds me a little of John Steinbeck. But he is strong enough an artist to stand alone on his own merits. And his 'Man in the Wheatfield' is as beautiful, searching and riveting a novel as I have read in many a year." *The New York Times* said: "The tale is quietly but chillingly told," a "short taut novel" which is a "deceptively straight forward story."

A Man in the Wheatfield was republished in England and distributed throughout the United Kingdom and translated into Spanish for distribution in Spain and Latin America. The acclaimed publication of *A Man in the Wheatfield* would coincide with the first books to be published in 1964 and 1965 by the University of Nevada Press that Laxalt founded upon his return to the Reno campus in 1961 paving the way for literary opportunity for others and distinction for the university.

Back Home to Challenges

Robert Laxalt was refreshed in mind and spirit when he returned in June 1961 to the University of Nevada from the family's nine months in the Basque Country. He would immediately face two major challenges that would alter his life forever. His brother Paul would enlist the family's support as he entered into what would become a lifetime of politics by running for lieutenant governor. Bob found politics repugnant having covered many untrustworthy, self-serving politicians during his UP reporting years. But he saw his brother as the exception, a man of his word, and, with his reporter's eye, he loyally served as a shrewd observer and confidant in the many campaigns to come that he would eventually address in a Special Edition of *Sweet Promised Land.*

At the same time, however, he faced his own personal and professional challenge of inaugurating and developing the University of Nevada Press. With one manuscript tragically lost, but another, *A Man in the Wheatfield,* well in progress, he settled into a university that had become, under Charles Armstrong's presidency, what Laxalt had always hoped for—a place to think, research, write, and now actually publish books. He balanced his brother's political campaign with his own foremost need of concentrating on the press.

During the Stout administration, when Laxalt first struggled to write *Sweet Promised Land,* there had been limited funds for research in the humanities and the sciences. Now, under Armstrong, funds were being raised on a broader, out-of-state, basis and scholarly programs including a university press were under way to give new and veteran authors opportunity to write serious books and see them published in hard cover.

Laxalt's success with *Sweet Promised Land* and his deep interest in the history of Nevada and the West had put him in good stead with the new administration to look favorably upon his bold idea to create a university press. In the late 1950s, most of the power in the Nevada legislature was in

Dominique and Robert at sheep camp on the Nevada range, circa 1969. Photograph by
Bill Belknap.

the rural counties and in Reno's Washoe County in the north (Las Vegas
in Clark County would change this balance of power in favor of southern
Nevada in the 1960s and the future). Many legislators appreciated *Sweet
Promised Land* for its truths about the state's rural strength of character.
Consequently, Laxalt was welcomed by most legislators as he lobbied for
creation and development of the University of Nevada Press.

Before his sabbatical to France, he had begun turning over much of
the work in his public information office to others so he could take time
to figure out how a university press might work. He knew about writing
but he had no experience in publishing. He turned to other universities
for ideas. He ran into mixed feelings including a contact at Stanford who
responded to Laxalt's enthusiasm with a shrug, "That's all we need, another
university press." Others were more helpful. Lloyd Lyman, assistant director of the prestigious University of California Press, provided tips on what
to do and, more importantly, what not to do. Savoie Lottinville who was
nationally known for his expertise at the University of Oklahoma Press,
visited Reno at Laxalt's request and influenced both campus administrators
and the Board of Regents.

Laxalt thought of three main motivations as the purpose of the press. One was to address the history of the state by researching and recording its many facets to serve both present and future generations. He reflected in a report some years later: "The state and its youth were deprived in large part of knowledge of the evolvement of their government, law, business, industry, natural resources, transportation, ethnic and religious groups, and most importantly, change in a period of meteoric growth."

Another motivation was the stimulation of research and writing by faculty members and authors in specialized fields which Laxalt saw as "an absolute requirement if a university is to become distinguished." A third was to help build the university's academic reputation on a nationally recognized basis.

His first steps were cautious. He formed an advisory editorial board made up of faculty members to approve manuscripts that had been edited by Laxalt and his limited staff. The first hard-cover book, *Biographies of Nevada Botanists,* by Olga Reifschneider, was published in 1964 and the second, *The Nevada Adventure: A History,* by James W. Hulse, followed a year later. The start-up moved slowly with the decision to concentrate on manuscripts of local interest, the limitations of a small budget, and the understanding that university presses, especially small ones, are not designed to make money. Rather they serve the public with important but limited-interest books that commercial publishers avoid for lack of a market.

Both Reifschneider's botany book and Hulse's history fit the startup plan and they reinforced each other according to Hulse. The botany book was completed first but Laxalt wanted to bring the two out together to show publishing breadth so he asked Hulse to rush toward completion of his manuscript. He did so at the risk of some error and, years later, reflected that his book would have been better off if more editing time had been devoted to it. He recalled a joint book signing for the authors was a bit of a "spectacle" as the public turned out to celebrate the first books for sale at the Grey Reid department store on North Virginia Street in Reno.

Laxalt set out to find public and private resources to fund the press and fulfill his vision. He went personally to the legislature and secured an appropriation of $7,500 to cover the cost of the first book. He stitched together gifts ranging from five hundred to three thousand dollars from private donors and businesses such as the Sierra Pacific Power Company, Bell of Nevada, Nevada National Bank, First National Bank of Nevada,

Reno Newspapers, Inc., and, eventually, he won a five hundred thousand dollar grant from the Max C. Fleischmann Foundation for a Great Basin Natural History Series.

The Great Basin Series would be one of an eventual lineup in a number of series including Environmental Arts and Humanities, Gambling Studies, Natural History, the Urban West, Vintage West, West Word Fiction and Western Literature and, of international interest, a Basque Books Series. Laxalt was instrumental in the acquistion of the Basque library of the scholar Philippe Veyrin while living in France and in the recruitment a young scholar from Reno, William A. Douglass, who was studying in the Basque Country, to help create a Basque Studies Program out of which the special series was born. Douglass would serve as editor as the series grew with many titles including Laxalt's own.

Laxalt's early vision would prove out from the formative days of the press through its first two decades with publication of forty-three original books and revised editions by faculty and another sixteen books by faculty in production. Addressing his third motivation, the development of the University of Nevada system's academic reputation on a national basis, Laxalt eventually could cite hundreds of "laudatory critical reviews not only from Nevada, but major newspapers and scholarly journals throughout the United States and other countries including England, France, Spain, Hungary, Mexico, Argentina and Venezuela."

By 1978, the press had published overall fifty-one books or revisions, by faculty or others, ranging from Don Driggs's *The Constitution of the State of Nevada* to John Folkes's *Nevada Newspapers: A Bibliography* to Elmer Rusco's *Voting Behavior in Nevada* and such works as Wilbur Shepperson's *Retreat to Nevada: A Socialist Colony of World War I,* Mary Ellen Glass's *Silver and Politics in Nevada: 1892–1902,* and Helen Carlson's *Nevada Place Names: A Geographical Dictionary.*

Five art portfolios published included Robert Caples's *The Desert People: A Portfolio of Nevada Indians* and *People of the Silent Land,* Craig Sheppard's *Landmarks on the Emigrant Trail,* Will James's *The West of Will James* and Tony Ko's *6 Impressions* (original lithographs by university art department members). Another thirty-three books were in the writing, editing, or production stages.

Laxalt produced this during a stormy period in 1978 and 1979 when the press came under fire in what a combined *Reno Evening Gazette* and *Nevada State Journal* editorial called a "witch-hunt" in the legislature.

Sparks assemblyman Don Mello, chairman of the powerful Ways and Means Committee that controlled budgets of state agencies, claimed Laxalt was "juggling funds" for the press to stay alive financially and called for the chancellor's office to investigate the press. This came in a fiery controversy involving Chancellor Donald Baepler's reported offer of a promotion for Mello's wife, Barbara, from a classified position of sales and promotion at the press to a professional position with similar duties. She turned down the offer of the reclassification category.

The controversy would be the biggest public challenge Laxalt faced personally in his development of the press and the most significant threat to the press itself over allegations of mismanagement and questionable use of state funds. It played out in a sort of culture war as supporters of Laxalt as the state's most celebrated literary icon fought for him in the legislative halls and on the front pages and editorial pages of Nevada's newspapers at the same time tight-fisted legislators were cheered by voters for controlling costs.

The university itself was frequently put on the budgetary chopping block as its officials had to defend their expenditures in line-by-line justifications of everything from salaries and professor work time to such cultural programs as its art galleries, theater, opera, and orchestra. But the press controversy drew the biggest headlines because of the bitter fight between Laxalt and Don Mello.

Questions were raised in the media by critics about whether Mello's committee approved an extra $7,500 for the press budget in connection with the chancellor's job offer for Mello's wife. Mello was quoted in the *Reno Evening Gazette*: "That $7,500 has already been earmarked for contractual services, and in no way would have involved giving an increase of salary to my wife."

The newspaper reported Mello asserting Laxalt made "untrue" public comments "that he was unaware of why his office received the extra $7,500 . . . I think it is incompetency that he (Laxalt) does not know or remember talking to chairman of the regents, Bob Cashell, about this extra money. If he doesn't know, he should know." Mello added: "Robert Laxalt sent me a message that the press had been juggling funds from one account to another to stay alive and would be grateful for any additional money they could receive."

Laxalt countered in a Reno-datelined UP International story that Mello's claim of juggled funds was "totally absurd." Laxalt said that he did, in fact, know about the funds but that Mello and Cashell had advised they were for promotion, advertising, "and whatever contractual editing we do. I think it is ridiculous for Mello to say this money was just earmarked for contractual editing, because we don't spend that much in 10 years of outside editing."

In the midst of the controversy, the newspaper reported Barbara Mello offered to resign from the press but, according to her husband, Laxalt declined her resignation and said she was doing a good job. As the plot thickened, Barbara Mello filed a grievance against the press which the university refused to discuss on the basis it was a personnel matter. And Mello was quoted in a UPI story saying "none of these budget additions are of any monetary benefit to my wife." The same story reported that neither Laxalt nor the Board of Regents had asked for the additional $7,500 that Mello's committee approved.

The fight heated up when Laxalt wrote an eleven-page memo to the chancellor that made bold headlines: "Mello Made Job threats, Says Laxalt."

The *Nevada State Journal* story reported that Laxalt claimed Mello threatened, in a heated phone call, to cut funds from the press and university system because of Barbara Mello's grievance and, on top of that, to get Laxalt fired. "This whole thing is ridiculous," Mello said of Laxalt's claim. "We did have a telephone conversation, but I never threatened Mr. Laxalt. Most of his remarks are trumped up because he wants to divert attention away from an investigation that's being done on possible mismanagement in the University Press." The newspaper reported Mello saying Laxalt phoned him to ask him to get his wife to drop her grievance and that he told Laxalt he could not because he had nothing to do with it.

Laxalt, offended that his integrity was questioned, responded that Mello's comment didn't "deserve the dignity of an answer. The University Press is an open book and he knows it. Any questions he would have about the Press are all on record and all he has to do is look at the record." Laxalt added that an editorial board of deans oversees the press "and the board has demonstrated total approval of what we've done. This is the first sustaining publishing venture of this type in the history of Nevada."

Meantime, the public watched the controversy widen when Chancellor Baepler said he began an "efficiency study" of the press after talking to Mello and regent chairman Bob Cashell to determine what the five employees in the office do on a typical day to determine if changes should be made. Mello had complained Laxalt was sending "part-time clerks on junkets to San Francisco and San Diego." Laxalt countered he had sent one clerk "but I told Mr. Mello when he accosted me that I was training this person for a technical-clerical position in our Great Basin Natural History series. She's a cum laude graduate from the University of Washington."

Laxalt told the chancellor Mello "subjected me to threats, abuse and coercion. I feel strongly he has usurped his position as a state assemblyman and as chairman of the Ways and Means Committee and has acted to the discredit of the Legislature." Laxalt added Mello "threatened to parade me and all of my staff in front of his committee to show why we shouldn't all be fired."

The chancellor said in press reports that the Mello/Laxalt fight seemed to be a personality conflict and pointed out that the press had been one of the beneficiaries of the $3 million given to the university system above and beyond the governor's recommendation. He also credited Mello and his committee with specifically helping the press by upgrading two positions to full time, obtaining funds for the Basque Studies Program, and providing the extra $7,500 for both editing and advertising.

However, the *Reno Evening Gazette* and *Nevada State Journal* reported that the chancellor's preliminary audit of the press showed that Mello's allegations of "fund juggling" were not true. "Right now, it appears that those charges are without foundation," the report said.

The newspapers ran an editorial summing up the conflict as having "the aura of a witch-hunt. And a witch-hunt is something that no university—no institution of any kind—can afford." The editorial commented on the complexity: "Beyond all the charges and countercharges ricocheting around the head of Assemblyman Don Mello lies one undeniable fact: Mello is chin-deep in conflict of interest. . . . It is indisputably clear that Mello has no business whatsoever getting involved with the University Press while his wife works there. During the Legislature, Mello should have stepped back when the University Press budget was discussed. And now he should immediately remove himself from the current argument over the internal functioning of the press. If he has complaints, he can convey them to another member of the Ways and Means Committee, who can take whatever actions he sees fit. But Mello, to put it bluntly, should bug out."

The editorial noted the chancellor's preliminary audit showed no indication of fund juggling and added "the Press has performed a distinguished job for many years in producing scholarly and general interest works about Nevada, and Laxalt himself has added greatly to its prestige and accomplishments." The editorial also noted that it had supported Mello in his reelection bids "because he has been a good—even a superb—watchdog over the public purse," that he "has been tireless in his dedication to duty. . . . If the state is in excellent financial shape today, a good deal of the credit must go to Mello. . . ."

But the editorial also noted Mello "has made enemies—needlessly and, it would seem, gratuitously. . . . There comes a time, at last, when the watchdogging and bullying do not even out, when even the most excellent budget controls do not begin to pay for the humiliation and fear and intimidation of human beings. If Mello does not find a way to mend his behavioral patterns, the day cannot be far off when the voters will say: Enough."

Joe Crowley, a professor of political science who found himself in rough-and-tough legislative battles as he lobbied the legislature in his nearly twenty-three years as president of the university, summed up the Laxalt/Mello controversy in interviews for this book: "Don Mello was a skilled and powerful legislator, sometimes quarrelsome in a public way. This was a quarrel he would have been wise to avoid. Bob Laxalt, likeable and widely respected, was cleared by the chancellor's inquiry. No surprise about that. No victory here for the chairman of Ways and Means."

Mello continued to serve in the Assembly, where he was first elected in 1963, through 1982 when he was elected to the Nevada State Senate. He retired in 1989 following twenty-six years of service that included strong leadership roles.

George Herman, a retired faculty member who served on the press editorial advisory board, wrote a letter to the editor saying it "would be a great pity were a misunderstanding between State Assemblyman Don Mello and the University of Nevada Press to have detrimental effects upon any of the persons concerned. In a very real sense . . . the University Press has earned the approval of the critical, conservative presses to which it belongs. A great portion of that success has come from the intelligent, conscientious and imaginative leadership of Robert Laxalt, its director. . . . Without Bob Laxalt's steady concern and careful guidance, the Press would, I believe, never have won the respect it receives throughout the country. Its publications are very carefully selected and are produced with every attention by a talented staff."

Herman rounded out his letter as a peacemaker amid the din of the strident controversy: "These persons are active in a number of specialties, all necessary to the production of informative and beautiful books: the reading and editing of manuscripts. The designing of page and text and whole volume, the management of accounts and other matters of business. The handling of sales and distribution, and the conduct of an involved correspondence inevitable to so complex an enterprise. None of the people on the Press staff are in any sense mere clerks, however, they may be classified."

Laxalt used the strong record of the press to counter the controversy that had stirred passion throughout the state. He cited the Great Basin Natural History Series aiming "at filling a serious vacuum in western publishing—the natural history of the Great Basin, of which Nevada comprises a major part." The series would embrace "books on climatology, life zones, rivers, lakes, geology and fossils, birds and fish, mammals, reptiles, insects, trees and shrubs, plants and wildflowers, and so on. Books in this series would be aimed at the general public, students in natural history, and scholars."

Laxalt pointed out the increasing responsibilities of the nation's university presses which, of course, included Nevada's own. It was dependent on state funding to augment the serious private funding that would be done through a new organization he founded called The Friends of the Press. In in the press's purpose outline, he wrote:

> In the past, eastern-based commercial publishing houses have helped share the responsibility of scholarly publishing. Recently, there has been a drastic change in this division of responsibility. The commercial publishing houses are abandoning the field of scholarly publishing, openly admitting that they are producing popularized books aimed solely at short-range entertainment value and high profits. . . . The heavy burden of publishing scholarly books that make a contribution to the future has fallen squarely upon the nation's university presses. The University of Nevada Press is no exception. We must count on bearing the main responsibility of preserving the heritage of our state for future generations.

Laxalt disclosed a new series being initiated by the press aimed at such heritage. The Vintage Nevada Book Series planned reprints of books about Nevada in territorial and early statehood days. "This series is aimed at making rare old books about Nevada available to the general public and the schools. Depending on finances, the frequency of this series will be two books a year."

Laxalt went into the 1979 legislative session where he would engage in the battle with Mello with what he called modest requests "to avoid imposing an undue burden upon state finances." He noted the press planned to hold itself to the governor's budget in 1979 "although it may cut back somewhat in our publishing schedule" just as the press had done with its "hold the line" posture in 1977. He pointed out staffing had remained static for the past twelve years with three professional positions and one-and-one-half classified positions. He reported that 20 percent of book production funds was provided by the Legislature and 80 percent from book sales amounting to over three hundred thousand dollars in the previous seven years. In the immediate past three years it had been fifty thousand dollars a year. And he predicted sales revenues would increase as the press expanded its books to new topics. He added: "We are also reappraising our sales price for books, which we have maintained at a reasonable profit level so as to perform our goal of public service."

Laxalt listed the staff with himself as director, Nicholas Cady as assistant director and editor, Kenneth Robbins as business and production manager, Barbara Mello as sales representative, and Cameron Sutherland as management assistant (half-time basis with clerical duties). He listed the Editorial Advisory Board with himself as director and a membership of UNR and UNLV deans and faculty members and representatives of Basque studies, oral history, and community colleges.

Cady served in a unique way. As an editor, he was deft in working with authors and their manuscripts. Most authors proposed manuscripts that were natural fits with the mission of the press since its purpose was well known as publisher of unique intellectually inclined topics serving the state and region. Occasionally, Cady recalled in an interview for this book, a friend of Laxalt might have an idea that didn't quite fit, a problem all publishing houses face. Laxalt would simply call the friend and explain the proposed book just didn't line up with the press mission and the friend, as a friend, would accept the verdict. Cady, in his quiet literary manner, also supported Laxalt by accompanying him on goodwill visits to the legislature to head off budget problems and shore up the many details in the line item revenues and expenses that were challenged. The press did not get a simple administrative budget to work with but had to defend every decision that might draw critical attention from thrift-minded legislators.

Laxalt provided the vision and leadership in developing the press but he turned to Cady's sure eye for detail in the actual editing. Hulse's history book got closer oversight as he worked with Cady to clean up the manuscript and bring out five subsequent editions over the next sixteen years. Hulse was a history professor on the Reno campus with a Ph.D from Stanford who came to see many sides of Laxalt as a friend and publisher. Years later, he wrote what he called a "diatribe" over the government's failure to provide proper services in the state. Laxalt was reluctant to publish such harsh criticism by the press and the editorial board split three to three with a seventh member abstaining. An outside reader recommended publication with some adjustments and, in 1986, the press brought out Hulse's *Forty Years in the Wilderness, Impressions of Nevada 1940–1980*. Hulse didn't blame Laxalt, whom he saw of as a nurturing leader, and, in fact, figured if he himself had run the press he probably wouldn't have wanted to publish such a scathingly critical book about the state.

Laxalt formed the Friends of the University of Nevada Press to raise private funding and, at occasionally difficult political times, serve as both a sword to fight for the press and a shield to protect it. The membership looked like a Who's Who of Nevada political, cultural, business, community, and media leadership including former Governor Mike O'Callaghan and attorneys who had held offices ranging from the Nevada State Senate and U.S. Congress.

Laxalt's own persona, tested by years of local and national writing and service in his brother's political campaigns, fit naturally with the many visitors who came by the press offices in the basement of the Victorian Morrill Hall that stood as a four-story brick anchor at the southern end of the massive grass quad. The offices had an air of friendly prestige rather than stuffiness. The mood was recalled by long-time press associate Cameron Sutherland : "I remember newly-elected Governor Richard Bryan dropping by one day for a visit to say hello. I've always appreciated that casual, friendly attitude of many Nevada politicians and other leaders in the community" who were welcomed by Laxalt and his staff.

Laxalt was encouraging when literary-minded members of the Friends of the Press produced their own manuscripts. Buck Wheeler and Bill Bliss turned to Laxalt after he had retired from the press in 1983 for a foreword for their book *Tahoe Heritage: The Bliss Family of Glenbrook, Nevada* which the press published in 1992. Laxalt guided the authors while Cady did the actual editing. Bliss was a friend of Laxalt's from their teen-aged days caddying at the Glenbrook golf course on the Nevada shore of Lake Tahoe. He found himself at ease with Laxalt who, as a professional, was a patient listener nurturing the story as the authors unfolded it. "I sensed his fine hand and encouragement in his quiet way," Bliss remembered when talking about Laxalt years later.

Laxalt continued to guide authors into publication. He called me one day to suggest there could be a book about a University of Nevada graduate who had been a hero in the Spanish Civil War. I was a long-time newspaper reporter, editor, and publisher but I knew nothing about writing books. Don't be afraid of it as a book, he counseled in that same soft voice others had noted. Just look at it as a bunch of chapters that basically are the kind of feature stories newspaper people know how to write. Get the story by doing the research reporters do and then write the chapters so they tie together as the story unfolds. It didn't seem that easy and, in fact, it was downright scary, but I followed his advice. Laxalt worked patiently with me and coauthor Marion Merriman Wachtel and, in 1986, the press published *American Commander in Spain: Robert Hale Merriman and the Abraham Lincoln Brigade.*

Both before and after Laxalt retired as founding director of the press, his efforts saw the publication of hundreds of books, launching writing careers for new authors and bringing international acclaim to the UNR campus and the expanded press program at UNLV. During his tenure as director of the press, only one of his books, *In a Hundred Graves,* was published by the press and that, in 1972, was in the unique Basque Book Series. His other five books in that timeframe were published elsewhere, four nationally and one locally in Reno.

Following his retirement, during his teaching years at the university, the press published his eleven remaining books. Of those, eight were in the Basque Book Series, two in the Western Literature Series and one simply as a general book on the press list.

This prompted some colleagues to speculate how Laxalt's writing career might have gone differently through wider national publication in New York and away from the University of Nevada Press that he had founded. Such discussion was prompted by the national acclaim he won with *A Man in the Wheatfield.* Friends often wondered if his concentration on Basque topical books diverted his writing attention from continuing on the literary path of *Wheatfield* toward other more unusual topics.

Publishing colleague Douglass recalled Laxalt expressing "frustration over being considered a regional and/or Basque writer. In a sense his first book was his most successful and *Sweet Promised Land* cast a long shadow over his entire career." Douglass noted in his own biography that

Laxalt's celebrated book was a nonfictional sort of oral history and that Laxalt regarded the novel *Wheatfield* as his most important work. When *Sweet Promised Land* went out of print Douglass advocated the book be reprinted by the University of Nevada Press but Laxalt was reluctant for two reasons: (1) He didn't want it to appear that the press would publish it simply because of their relationship, and (2) his New York agent was reserved because there had been talk of the book being made into a movie that could have spurred commercial sales. However, Douglass recalled in an interview for this book, Laxalt eventually grew tired of such a New York/Hollywood waiting game. When Douglass assured him that he, not Laxalt, would be the instigator of the press bringing out the book in a new edition, Laxalt finally agreed. Douglass wrote the foreword in the press 1986 reprint which, once again, sold briskly. Laxalt did continue to consult with his New York agent including possibility of a saga about the Laxalt family but that eventually materialized in a trilogy also published by the press.

Laxalt once described himself in an interview with scholar David Río. "I am not a Basque scholar or even a Basque writer; I am just a Basque who writes."

Throughout the University of Nevada Press years, Laxalt continued to feed sheets of paper into the Royal typewriter in pursuit of storytelling that alternated between magazine journalism and new books of fiction and nonfiction and the political career of his brother that would unfold in increasingly dramatic ways.

Writing and Family Adventures

The acclaim of *A Man in the Wheatfield* coming on top of reviews celebrating *Sweet Promised Land* was nothing short of the literary equivalent of a batter stepping up for the first time to the major leagues in Yankee Stadium and hitting home runs out of the park two times in a row. While contemplating a third book, once again to be researched in the Basque Country, Laxalt shifted his writing focus to a magazine where only star writers performed. He knew his topic—Basques.

The title in the June 1966 issue of the *National Geographic*, priced at eight dollars a year or one dollar a copy:

> *Basque Sheepherders: Lonely Sentinels of the American West*
>
> By Robert Laxalt
> Photographs by William Belknap Jr.
>
> The old sheep camp lay in a sheltered hollow. In this high place, the only thing above us was the shoulder of the Sierra Nevada, looming so near that its tattered fringe of wind-blasted trees stood out in clear relief against the skyline.
>
> My father spoke from where he knelt by the open campfire. He said in Basque that he could remember the day when these mountains were filled with sheep: "Oroitzen naiz mendi horiek ardiez betezielarik."
>
> "Bai," I said in assent, knowing what he really meant. In those days, we had our own sheep in these mountains, too. And here at his old campsite, he was recalling that time.

The first three paragraphs of the story took up 25 percent of page 871 of the magazine which devoted 75 percent of the page and almost all of the preceding page to a color photograph of a smiling, hearty sheepherder, Fermin Alzugaray, with rolled up sleeves and a well-worn, wide-brimmed cowboy hat sheltering his sun-bronzed face. The sheepherder, one of hundreds like Laxalt's father, Dominique, had come to the American West from the Pyrenees Mountains of France and Spain. He clutched a walking staff in his strong right hand and leaned his left elbow high on a saddle from which hung a gunny sack containing an orphaned lamb. The sheepherder was in search of a foster mother ewe that would adopt the lamb as her own and care for it.

Other photographs by Belknap dramatically illustrated the eighteen-page story layout showing in full color Laxalt wearing a battered cowboy hat and his father, with his iron-gray hair rolling in a thick natural curl on his forehead, leaning on a truck watching the nearby sheep-shearing. A map highlighted Basque settlements in California, Nevada, Washington, Oregon, Idaho, Wyoming, Colorado, Arizona, and New Mexico. Another map showed the tiny region of the Basque homeland straddling Southern France and Northern Spain from the Atlantic Bay of Biscay to the high Pyrenees. Still more photographs, for which *National Geographic* was acclaimed by professionals and its loyal subscribers, showed the majestic sweep of high country sagebrush and craggy mountain towers with thousands of sheep being guided by herders on foot and horseback as well as the ever present sheep dogs.

"Late spring had come, and the earth was still moist from the winter's snow. The wild canaries and jays had returned to the mountains," Laxalt wrote as he drew his own picture for the readers with his descriptive choice of words. "I found it hard to conceive that the bright glitter of Reno, Nevada, lay less than thirty miles away to the north."

Laxalt detailed the immigration of the remote, little known Basques to the harshness of the sheep camp settings.

> Their role in our history has gone nearly unrecorded. Yet, without their incredible capacity to endure hardship and solitude, the great era of western sheep raising would not have been what it was. Descendants of an ancient race whose origins and language still remain a mystery, the Basque sheepherders of America were urged here by the same restless spirit that lured their forebears around the world as sailors with Magellan and to South America as soldiers with conquistadors.

Still more photographs illustrated the gentleness of tough men helping lambs adapt and adjust to their mothers moments after the ewes gave birth. Laxalt chronicled in photograph captions how a herder finding a dead lamb quickly removes it from beneath the ewe, skins the lamb and fits the pelt like a sweater on a newly orphaned lamb, then nestles it to the side of the ewe who accepts the orphan as her own.

Laxalt's words and Belknap's photographs continued to tell the stories of sheepherders such as Isadora Aquirre and Peyo Garazi who arrived by ship in New York, traveled across the continent by train to settle in places with names as foreign as their own such as Winnemucca, Nevada, which was named for a Native American chief.

Laxalt got the assignment for the *Geographic* story because of a lack of understanding about the American West by other writers whom the magazine had asked to document the life of the sheepherders to accompany the photographs Belknap had already taken. The first was an easterner who turned in an unacceptable story and the second was a southern writer whose prose the editors also found lacking. Jim Cerutti, one of the editors, had mentioned in a conversation with Laxalt's magazine agent, Emilie Jacobson of Curtis Brown, how the magazine had spent a lot of money trying to develop the story and ended up with terrific photographs but no written copy it could use.

The agent asked the editor if he had read Laxalt's *Sweet Promised Land* and, learning that he had not, sent him a copy. The editor read it, phoned Laxalt, offered him the assignment and sent him a guide book on writing for the magazine which Laxalt surmised to be "a few thousand words of 'do's and 'don'ts.'" Laxalt once joked, "They sent me 5,000 words worth of instructions on how to write a 5,000-word story." Laxalt did his best to follow the guide and sent in the story which the editor thought lacking in the warmth of *Sweet Promised Land*. Laxalt told the editor he'd followed the guide but the warmth of the story didn't seem to fit in with the *Geographic's* rules. The editor told Laxalt to take another try and stick with his own instincts, which Laxalt did. The story was accepted for the June 1966 issue and launched a new career for Laxalt as a contract writer for the magazine.

Years later, when Laxalt taught magazine writing at the University of Nevada's Reynolds School of Journalism, he would share with students what he called the "the most demanding writing one could ask for," that being the rules and regulations of the *National Geographic* and how he modified them through his own experiences.

"First," he would say, "let me explain Mother Geo's process."

Writers got assignments in two ways. They came up with their own ideas and pitched them to editors, which was the usual way it happened, or they waited for assignments from editors, which Laxalt defined as having dismal chances. Editors typically pigeonholed writers' identities and personalities and in Laxalt's case they saw him as "a rugged mountain man type of writer." The consequence: when editors thought of deserts, mountains or horses, they called on Laxalt. He liked to joke with the editors that he was really the fragile type who ought to be assigned to stories on beaches or perhaps the bistros of the French Riviera but he confided they wouldn't buy such a notion and kept him heading into the rugged outdoors on assignments.

Once he was assigned a story, the magazine provided travel funds for him to go to the setting and spend a month to six weeks researching the topic and talking with potential sources. If he ran out of funds, he could send a wire or make a call and quickly receive more research money which he called a "boon and a blessing" because "writers nearly always are poor." After on-site research, he returned home to spend another month organizing his notes and writing a first draft. Up to six editors then read the draft and offered "decimating comments." Laxalt then had two choices. He could assimilate the comments into a second draft or he could "fight a lusty battle as to why they wouldn't work."

The editors were mainly worried about what they called the transitions writers used to hold the story together as they brought in and shifted around new developments. He explained a typical transition by citing a writer focusing on mountain trout streams but yearning for a steak dinner and moving to lower country to then write about cattle. Laxalt joked with the editors that they ought to rename the *Geographic* the National Transition Magazine. Laxalt said the rewriting process "can be normal or hideous . . . if the story is about an area that other *Geographic* types have been to . . . it will be hideous . . . each of them will come with an idea that he feels should be incorporated." When that happened, Laxalt said the writer could redo the draft four times and go through "a nervous breakdown."

Once approved, the story was sent to the research department where up to five fact checkers could tear the story apart and send the writer scurrying for more detail that would prove out. The secondary research could keep the writer on the hunt for up to six months with editors phoning the writer to discuss the new detail for hours. At the same time, the magazine's map-makers and illustrators were phoning to work out more detail.

The New York Times once summed it up: "Built into the editorial process at *National Geographic* is an unusual fact-checking cadre, the *researchers*. They do their work after the stories have been written and try to demolish facts and assumptions of the writers so that the end product conforms to the Geographic's rubric of absolute accuracy. They begin with the assumption that the writer is a *liar* and doesn't know what he's talking about."

"When it's all done," Laxalt liked to joke, "your story is scheduled and one day it appears . . . then you are in the position of defending what you have written to some 50 million readers around the globe."

With the founding of the University of Nevada Press begun, the *Geographic* learning process absorbed, and his political experiences assimilated in his brother Paul's successful campaign for the lieutenant governorship in 1962 and troublingly narrow loss in a U.S. Senate race in 1964, Laxalt needed time and space to think. He particularly wanted to get away from the intensity of politics that at a later date he would address in a special edition of *Sweet Promised Land.* For now, in September of 1965, it was time for Bob and Joyce to gather their children and head, once again, to France for a nine-month sabbatical to research and write in the Basque Country.

Everyone was five years older—and wiser—based on the first family sojourn when there had been visions of gay Parisian life requiring suitcases of party dresses. Before heading back to Donibane Garazi in the Pyrenees where he would continue his research for a new book about Basque life—and death—the family settled into the Atlantic coastal town of Arcachon in a cottage named *Bizi Gozua*—"The Good Life." Son Bruce, then fourteen, and daughters Monique, twelve, and Kristen, nine, had no language problems at school having learned French on the earlier trip and, now accustomed to French ways, all were more relaxed. They quickly became impassioned with the product that made Arcachon the oyster capital of France.

The summer cottage, owned by a cousin's wife and lent rent-free to the Laxalts, was cozy but not well equipped for winter visitors, warmed only by the fireplace. Eventually, they secured an electric heater to serve the main floor kitchen, living room, and dining room. The downstairs bedrooms and Laxalt's writing room were as cold as the arctic, Laxalt joked. To keep his typing fingers warm and agile, Joyce outfitted him with flannel gloves that she trimmed so his open fingertips could accurately make contact with the keys.

At Christmas time, Joyce decided to have dinner *a' la Américane* with cranberries she had brought from home in Reno, a tender turkey hen she bought in a poultry store, and pumpkin and apple pies. The family welcomed Laxalt's aunts, uncle, and cousins to come from Bordeaux and gather around a pine tree Laxalt retrieved from the woods and enjoy the "Anglo Saxon" dinner and a holiday show the children performed. Daughter Kristin proclaimed the title: "La Petite Chèvre de Monsieur Seguin."

Daughters Monique and Kristin recalled years later in interviews for this book how they and their older brother Bruce bonded so closely on the first trip when they were ushered into a French language school in sink-or-swim total immersion and then five years later when they had a better grasp of the language. "We learned to depend on each other as a family," Monique said. The family name for Monique was Nicky. Kristin, who was called Kris, was seen as the "second son" because she was a bit of a tomboy growing up. Laxalt's writing at home did not separate the family's life even though his work required deep concentration. "His writing never involved shutting himself away from us," Monique remembered. As he typed, the children romped in the combination family room/writer den of their Reno home as well as in various houses where they lived during their forays to the Basque Country. Laxalt's ability to concentrate as life went on around him was a common trait of journalists who worked amid the newsroom cacophony of teletypes, police radios, and endlessly intense, frequently argumentative, voices of reporters and challenging editors.

Bob and Joyce made family life sacrosanct despite the pressures of his writing and work at the university and her years as a school teacher. But there was a difference, Kristin thought. "Pop always seemed to be different from other dads," she told me in one of the interviews that peeled away the privacy so typical of traditional Basque-American immigration family life. "He wasn't the classic all-American Dad. And I was always proud of that. I think it had to do with being from an emigrant family." That, she felt, was important in her growing up years. It wasn't so much that they were Basque; rather it was that they were family. "He instilled in us a sense of family as a tangible entity, something that had a wall around it that I could see in my mind, a barrier to and from the outside world."

Having recovered from childhood rheumatic fever and grown into teenaged athletics, Bob knew exercise was critical not only for himself but also for his family. So as he broke away from his writing and university work, he led the children into outdoor recreation, riding them on the handlebars of his bike to Reno High School a few blocks from their home and jogging around the football field track. He hung a boxer's heavy punching bag from the rafters in the garage and shook the whole house as he banged away on it in the evenings. Bob and Joyce took the children into the Nevada wilderness on weekends to gather desert and mountain flowers and cattails and pinecones. Laxalt loved to tell stories, frequently embellishing through his own adventures, and when Joyce interrupted to straighten out the facts, he counseled her: "Joyce, you're ruining a good story." His admonition was born out of his love of fiction where he thought there was no sin in altering the truth, just the opposite of the absolute accuracy he required in his journalistic work for the *National Geographic* and the UP. Most of all, whether at home in Reno or during their extended life in the Basque Country, they came to know a spiritual honesty he instilled in them. They could see it in his eyes.

"He spoke to us through his dark eyes which so expressed deep emotion of every kind," Monique said. Kristin added: "His eyes held and expressed every emotion, mood, and even unspoken opinion more eloquently than words ever could. We all knew 'the look.' If he was angry with us, his eyes somehow changed color, became the blackest of black and looked right into your soul. It was impossible to hold his gaze. No words were necessary. His eyes also held a sadness that often came over him and seemed to come from somewhere so deep inside him. Just as often, though, his eyes expressed a deep well of joy and humor and love, and to have that gaze come upon me was like the warmth of the sun." The children saw and felt his moods immediately through his eyes, whether sparkling with merriment or focused in concern.

While Laxalt wrote at home, either in the Reno home or in quarters he set up during Basque Country sabbaticals, he did so quite naturally as far as his children were concerned. Monique described the click of the typewriter as the "background music" of their home and Kristin didn't think of her father as a famous writer, in a public sense. But, they knew, from their earliest consciousness, that he was a writer. "It felt somehow sacred, this art and craft of his," Kristin recalled. "But he didn't talk about it that way. He was humble and private in his writing. It was just something he had to do."

A result, however, was built into the home by both Bob through his writing and his and Joyce's constant reading. This was a respect for the books that were found in every room. Everyone, parents and children, constantly read and everyone wrote. "We wrote poetry, we wrote in our journals, we wrote stories," Kristin recalled. They did so privately, only sharing with each other by volunteering their written thoughts, never prying on what others were writing. "It was an unspoken rule that writings were not read unless invited. That was a trust we learned very early."

The love and discipline of reading and writing that Bob and Joyce had developed in their own childhoods inspired a lifetime of effort for their children as Bruce and Monique eventually developed careers as trial lawyers—he also became as a poet, she a novelist—and Kristin became a physician and sensitive thinker and writer. They thrived on their sense of family and heritage.

After three months, the family ventured to the "storybook village" of Donibane Garazi and took residence in a villa. Bob had been asked by the Desert Research Institute (DRI) in Reno to explore the possibility of a program to study Basque culture. The DRI had hired Joyce to photograph the areas to accompany Laxalt's research which she now did, capturing over a thousand images of life in the villages and countryside. In the process, Laxalt met a Basque scholar, Phillipe Veyrin, who was dying of cancer. Laxalt would eventually arrange for the university library to buy Veyrin's 750-book library for six thousand dollars from his widow that would become the core start-up of the university's Basque Studies Program. It would become unique to the western hemisphere and attract scholars from around the world.

During this time, Bob welcomed the visit of William A. Douglass, a young graduate student from Reno who was working on a Ph.D at the University of Chicago in social anthropology. He was conducting his dissertation field research in two Spanish Basques villages. Laxalt was intrigued and eventually coaxed Douglass to return to Reno upon completion of his doctoral studies, which included learning the mystifying Basque language, to develop the program out of which a university press Basque Books Series was born with Douglass as editor. Years later, Douglass recalled how Laxalt was able to get Nevada rancher and university regent Molly Knudtsen to loan the campus library the six thousand dollars to buy the Veyrin collection and he credited Laxalt's early fund-raising in paying off the loan. Douglass and Laxalt eventually built the program to include visiting scholars from the Basque Country as well as respected Americans of Basque descent such as Richard W. Etulain who brought National Endowment of the Humanities distinction as an academic in residence through a grant.

Laxalt continued his research and the writing of the new book that, one day, would be entitled *In a Hundred Graves: A Basque Portrait*. The village and rural countryside provided the Basque life that Laxalt created in forty-five stories and sketches and the villa provided a perfect place for him to write. He worked at a large wooden desk in a study with French doors through which he could look up and watch and listen to refreshing rain showers which fell on the white plaster villa's red tile roof.

Laxalt took lengthy notes not knowing whether each facet of Basque life he discovered would actually make a story. He was in many ways like a reporter on the prowl in a city hall or a court house or an athletic training site. You go to where you know news or stories exist and you try to find them. He had good intentions of writing a novel but no concrete ideas, no models to follow, just the instincts for finding material by exploring the traits and psyches and day after day, night after night experiences of the village and country-side people. Notes were important. "I have always been a taker of notes. Memory alone is inadequate. It becomes fuzzy with time. Notes are a blessing in recapturing dialogue and setting and subject matter," he commented when explaining the research for his writing. He began to realize he could not learn enough do a novel in an authentic way in the brief months he would be in the Basque Country.

"It was then that the idea of a mosaic on Basque life began to take form. The question of a point-of-view character was solved. And with it the concept of an American Basque seeing his ancestral land became valid. That in turn provided the key to the order of the stories." He decided to follow the American who was, in fact, himself through the reality of his own developing experiences which included family life with the children. He created fictional embellishments that provided opportunity for poignant storytelling.

For the first vignette, Laxalt created a village at dusk, stilled by the tolling of a deathbell. "Someone is dying in the village tonight." He described the taverns being quiet without their usual songs, the villagers eating their dinner in homes of silence, a deathbell ringing like a faltering heartbeat—the American awake feeling as though his own heart was pounding:

> But it was not my heart at all. It was the churchbell ringing out in a clamor. The angel of death had arrived.
>
> Now there is silence, absolute silence. And because I have come from a crowded place where death has lost its meaning, I lie awake in the dark and am filled with amazement.

Laxalt set the pace for the forty-four sketches and portraits that followed. On the single first page he established five terse paragraphs, 7 words in the first, then 49, 38, 34, and 32 for a total of 160 carefully chosen subjects, active verbs, and descriptions.

He created a "Grand House" for the American's family, and a "Fortress School" for the children, a "House of No Name" to represent a farmhouse where the American could be free to visit and see its typical Basque activities, a companion, Dominika, through whom the children could learn Basque life and pride, a "Perpetual Spring" for the women gossiping in the village while washing clothes, and a "Town Crier" to tell of village goings-on.

He added "Eyes of the Dove" to show an ancient practice of luring hundreds of the wild birds into nets for capture. This created opportunity for village and farm men to interact in a "breathtaking" drama that some might condemn as cruel but that the American accepted as ritual. "In a Basque Kitchen," he took the reader into the heart of a Basque house, a rarity for someone who wasn't a family member. Laxalt wrote a picture story of words describing oaken tables and chairs "scarred by the use of generations" and the fireplace mantle with its "copper and pewter pitchers and bowls and an embroidered covering."

The first thirteen sketches developed the characters and their settings and prepared the way for the reader to meet the American narrator involving himself in active farm life. He chose a family gathering on a gray wintry day of big men with "burly shoulders and thick chests," men in heavy sweaters and "baggy, blue cotton pants stuffed into black rubber boots." Each wore a beret and Laxalt noted that they were very much alike, that "the same blood ran through all of them." They had gathered from other farms to help in the annual slaughter of a pig that would provide the farm house with pork through the months of winter. Laxalt was there by invitation of his neighbor, the pig's owner, and he noted the others were distant to him at first because they were not used to being with strangers. But they warmed to him once he joined in the slaughter which he described in bloody, squealing detail to capture for the reader the graphic realities of Basque farm life.

The man chosen to be the butcher sharpened his knives and the others hauled out the slaughter block. Laxalt joined them as they went to the pig pen to confront the "brutish and unlovely pig" that the writer surmised had "the capacity for anticipation" of his fate. "Though he had been taken from his pen a hundred times before, he knew on this morning that we had come to fetch him to slaughter. From the moment we gathered around his pen in the gloom of the barn, he began to circle his wooded prison at a run, snuffling and grunting in panic."

Laxalt detailed how the rope snared the pig's hind foot, leaving him hobbling on three feet, the harsh binding of the pig's jaws with the loop of a cord, the grasping of men's hands on to the ears and tail of the squealing animal that twisted and turned and heaved the men into the barn's wooden stalls until, finally, they hauled it to the slaughter block which was "black with old stains." There, the butcher awaited the pig:

> With his black beret and a dark apron that covered him from neck to ankles, he resembled a patient executioner. The execution was done quickly. Hardly had the pig settled on the block than the knife stabbed down. The blade disappeared in his throat and made a quick circle, and a plug of skin and flesh popped out onto the ground. There was a mortal scream from the pig, and then black blood—turning to red as it touched the air—pumped out in a jet.

When it was done, the pig was covered with straw and set on fire to burn off the body hair. The men gathered around the flames and were greeted by a woman from the farm house who brought them glasses and a bottle of red wine. "Bruised and spattered with blood, we drank wine over the smoldering heap that had been our adversary, and grinned at each other like old friends." Laxalt was no longer a stranger. A participant in in the ordeal of the pig, Laxalt was now accepted among his fellow Basques.

He continued to capture the stories, moving on to the troubadour, *bertzolari* (singular) or *bertsolariak* (plural) in Basque. He described how on a rainy night he and his cousin found dueling troubadours in a tavern competing with songs. One took the role of a shepherd who thought a peasant's life was superior because of his warm home and family, but then looked through a window and saw a dirty house, an angry wife and fighting children. His song then mocked the peasant's life. The other, the peasant, sang praise for the life of the shepherd in the hills, then turned the story around by developing a dangerous battle with a smuggler who tried to steal the sheep. Each derided the other as the singing grew fierce in *melody and rhyme*. The drinkers at the bar took sides, cheering one onward when he seemed to have the upper hand, and shifting praise to the other when his story came out best. Who won? Laxalt wrote the cousin's answer.

"That matters little," he said. "If what they sang was important and beautiful enough, it will be remembered and sung again. If what they sang was unimportant," he shrugged, "it was at least a diversion on a rainy night."

More stories flowed:

The healer is the seventh son of seven sons, and he is called in Basque "jainko-ttipi," which is to say little god. . . . There was a funeral in the village that should not have been. It was that of an old man who had come home from America to spend his last years at ease. . . . Today was market day in the village. The men's livestock market began in the early morning, and the winding central street of the village was a scene of much confusion. . . . Last night while the valley was black with sleep, a giant came and planted the forests. . . . There was an auction of horses in the village today. . . . He had always wanted to be a monk. But monk he could not be because he was consumptive, and the rules of health are unyielding in monasteries. . . . Ramon is my cousin's domestique. In body, Ramon is a man. His chest is deep and his arms are strong and he has a constant beard that never seems to grow beyond a stubble. When Ramon was a child, he had meningitis, and it left him with the mind of a child. It left its mark in other ways, too.

Laxalt, now seasoned in journalism and literary books of fact and fiction, knew that the secret of writing is in building suspense that inspires the reader to turn the page and find out what happens next. He unfolded the stories of Basque life in such a way that readers who knew nothing about the rare culture that was spread over four provinces in Spain and three in France wanted to know more. The readers came upon the strange sounding word Euskal Herria that translates as "homeland of the Basques or "the Basque Country." It is not a country as in the sense of a nation with legal boundaries but, instead, a unique state of mind in a geographical region of two very unlike nationalities, the French and the Spanish.

Laxalt continued writing the book after his return to Reno from sabbatical in June of 1966. He included a chapter, 38, about a family day in the countryside—"The meadow slopes down to the stream, and from where I am lying I can see my wife and my children below me. I cannot see them distinctly, but as in a dream, because it is through a veil of waving grass." He described blonde-haired Bruce watching a stream flow over a bed of pebbles, Joyce and Monique making chains of golden buttercups and white marguerites and Kristin "chasing the ripples in the grass . . . her flaxen braids fly in the wind."

The University of Nevada Press, eleven years after its founding, would publish *In a Hundred Graves* in 1972, which Laxalt dedicated to his children, to commentary, both scholarly and in the popular press. David Río wrote that in this book, "Laxalt is fully conscious of the great relevance of oral tradition as a part of Basque tradition. Thus, in *In a Hundred Graves*, oral and vocal elements hold a privileged position, imposing their dominance over the written word. This can be seen clearly in the accepted importance of the words of the *bertsolaris* (Basque ad lib verse makers), which contrasts with the low prestige of poets in the same society. Indeed, poetry appears to be a second-class artistic endeavor, reserved for those who do not stand out for either their ability to sing or their ability to dance."

The Journal of Ethnic Studies described, "the poetic language of a man sensitive to his heritage and *Western American Literature* compared Laxalt to Sherwood Anderson, William Carlos Williams and Hemingway."

The New York Times, The New York Review of Books, American Anthropologist, and *Journal of American Folklore* carried notices and the American Library Association selected *In a Hundred Graves* as one of the outstanding books within five years of its publication.

In Idaho, home to a large population of Basque immigrants and their American-born next generations, *The Statesman* commented: "This is an expertly written, sparsely lyrical portrait of Basque life in the home provinces, shown in a series of vignettes as definitive as the brushstrokes of a master painter."

When it was time for Laxalt and his family to return to Nevada and the very mountains where he had grown up and where he and Joyce now raised their children, the Sierra, he grew poetic. He reflected on leaving the mountains and villages of the Basque Country where the family had come to live as if it were their own home. He would eventually try to put it in words.

Homeward Bound

On his return from France for the third time, the first with his father, then twice with his wife and children, Laxalt summed up his feelings in what would become an epilogue for still another book about his origins, *The Land of My Fathers: A Son's Return to the Basque Country.* He typed it in the working style of the wire service reporter almost totally in lower case.

Epilogue

Farewell

The time has come to say goodbye to:

—the sounds of morning, of cocks crowing in a nearby farmyard, of a multitude of birds filling the air with song, of sweet perfume from forever blooming trees, of air as soft and sensual as a child's caress, of white morning mists obscuring the mountains until the sun lifts the veil to reveal green mountains. . . .

—rainy mornings in winter when wreaths of blue smoke rise from a hundred chimneys into the clouds above, of the patter of rain on a dun-colored landscape. . . .

—summer days when the pressure of the coming storm begins to mount so that your heart is pounding in your ears, and then the sky cracks with the sound of artillery fire and the rains come down in torrents that hurt like arrows piercing your skin. . . .

—girls on the country lanes at night, singing in high soprano voices, a shepherd boy playing his flute on some mountain above, a *paysan* walking home to his farm alone, singing because he is happy with the world. . . .

—of village men singing melancholy songs in baritone voices over a bottle of red wine in a bistro, black berets planted on their heads and elbows firmly planted on a table. . . .

—to churches with balconies of warm brown wood rubbed soft with the oil of ten thousand hands, of men singing from the balconies in deep voices and soprano voices of women rising up from the nave below. . . .

—of valleys with whitewashed farmhouses and red tiled roofs, and in contrast the stone fortresses of homes and hawk-faced men with sturdy bodies in the high mountains where my father was born. . . .

—the thundering fury of Atlantic tempests on the Bay of Biscay, and the men who brave them, with scarred eyes from flying hooks and muscular arms developed from hauling in nets filled with fish. . . .

—to Mid-summer Night's Eve and the fire of Saint Jean, a huge bonfire burning at a crossroads and young men proving their manhood by leaping through the flames, as their warrior ancestors did in primitive times. . . .

—village feast days when townsmen and countrymen sit down together at long wooden tables in the shade of oak trees, drinking from bottles of red wine in tumblers. . . .

—to the kitchen in the house where my mother was born, and the chair at the corner of the fireplace where she loved to sit, watching the fire that burned behind the gray polished steel of andirons, shining brass candlesticks on the mantle, rafters overhead with glorious hams cured with red pepper hanging from them, and the manger next to the door, neat and clean, holding a gray cow and a pig with shoats sucking noisily away. . . .

—distant farmhouses of whitewashed stone bordered on one side by vineyards and on the other by tiny figures of grazing sheep. . . .

—schoolchildren going home at end of day with arms locked, dropping off one by one at the country lanes until there is one boy left who walks alone and sings to the sunset. . . .

—funeral corteges through the heart of the village, the priest in his white surplice leading the procession, acolytes with candles walking behind, of men in black suits carrying the casket, which is covered in macabre fashion with a black pall decorated by a skull and crossbones, women bringing up the rear of the procession, praying inaudible voices that make a monotone. . . .

—deep forests of oak and beech and chestnut, cascades of water flashing down to form green pools where the shadows of trout move like phantoms. . . .

—vineyards and gnarled vines straightened with stakes in orderly lines, resembling an army of wounded soldiers walking on crutches. . . .

—walking alone along a country lane at night under the uncertain light of a gauzy moon, past barns pungent with the country smell of cattle and sheep and pigs and a wind whining through bare branches, and coming upon a draft of warm wind that is familiar out of some forgotten memory of a hundred years ago, telling you that you have walked this country lane in a life gone by.

The Political Wars

While Bob disliked politics—"The guys in the three-piece suits, the politicians, their word isn't good 24 hours," he made one exception in his brother Paul.

Bob returned to Reno in June 1966, to find Paul deeply involved in an historic run against incumbent Democrat Grant Sawyer who was seeking an unprecedented third term for the Nevada governorship. He was compelled to help. His loyalty to Paul—and his expertise in news—made it not only mandatory but extremely useful for him to join into what was building to be a gut-wrenching political campaign. He had been involved in Paul's successful run for lieutenant governor in 1962 as well as the dramatic U. S. Senate race in 1964 when Paul lost by eighty-four votes to incumbent Democrat Howard Cannon in a tense contest that ended in a heavily monitored recount.

Bob's journalistic eye made him a keen political observer and, despite his antipolitics attitude, people close to him thought he thrived on politics as a quiet insider, not an ideologue, in the campaigns. His *Sweet Promised Land* had made the family iconic in Nevada and even though Paul's credentials as the son of a Basque sheepherder were well established in his own right, Bob would eventually allow a special edition of his celebrated book to be used as a political vote-getting instrument. He did so over the protest of a publishing colleague, William A. Douglass, who thought the book was a cultural classic, a deep part of Basque life that should not be turned into campaign lore.

In an epilogue, he summed up the political impact on the Laxalt family: In 1962, the handsome cowboy actor Rex Bell was a two-term Republican lieutenant governor, serving once under the GOP's Governor Charles Russell and a second time when he was elected to serve under Sawyer who had defeated Russell's reelection effort. Bell made it known that he intended to run for governor against Sawyer, who was well known throughout the state including, importantly, in voter-rich Las Vegas. Bob wrote in the epilogue that the family gathered in the childhood home in Carson City with mother Theresa. Paul, John, and Peter were settled into their law practices, Suzanne had established herself as a Holy Family nun, Marie was teaching school in California, and Bob was busy with his writing and developing the University of Nevada Press.

> We had settled into the Friday lunch habit easily because of the lure of my mother's French pancakes on a meatless day. But more than that, it was staying close to each other. Here, where we had done most of our growing up, the old family home had been a fortress against the world. This is something that the children of immigrants all know.

Paul had been popular in those growing up years as student body president at Carson High School, a handsome football and basketball star, and a respected honor student. So it came as no great surprise when Paul shared the news that Bell wanted him to join in the campaign as candidate for lieutenant governor. Bell was well known in Las Vegas where he had been in business after his Hollywood film days had faded. Paul's candidacy could balance the GOP ticket with his northern Nevada roots and Basque charisma, which *Sweet Promised Land* had established among the ranchers and farmers and small town citizenry in what were affectionately called the "cow counties" in rural Nevada.

> I think that we all knew it was going to happen sometime. Paul was a lawyer and a good one, the kind other lawyers come to for advice. So his success in law was assured. But the pull of public service was fermenting in him. The law meant money among other things, but money as an end was not that important to him. He was baffled by those to whom riches meant everything. Underneath it all, he was growing restless, and I think that more than anything else was the final trigger.

Bob wrote that Paul asked for the family's advice and, in turn, got it candidly and frankly. He quoted his mother: "Politics is such a dirty business, Paul." He quoted Paul's response: "I've been hearing that all my life. I don't happen to believe it." Bob reported in the epilogue, aimed at explaining Paul's virtues to voters, that as a potential candidate for state-wide office he saw more "disadvantages than advantages" but that he would make his own decision. "We haven't even touched on the biggest minus of all. If I run, life will never be the same for us again. It will mean the end of our privacy as a family."

(Paul would tell the story in a different way in his *Memoir*, published in 2000. He reported Bell phoned his home in Carson City and asked if he could join Paul and wife Jackie for dinner at which time he disclosed that he planned to run for governor and that he would like Paul to run with him for lieutenant governor. The *Memoir* reports Paul phoned him the next day with his decision to run.)

After Paul decided to run, his brothers and sisters and boyhood and college friends joined thousands of Nevadans who followed the handsome candidates as they traveled through sagebrush deserts and mountain passes to local communities, small towns, and Northern Nevada's largest city, Reno, before moving on to Las Vegas for a Fourth of July rally. Bell had a warm and friendly twinkle in his eye. He was an easy-going, gifted star from his Hollywood days. And as a two-time lieutenant governor, he was the head of the Republican Party in Nevada. Paul had an engaging smile that made him welcome with friends and strangers alike, particularly in a gathering of women. As Ormsby County district attorney, a seasoned trial attorney and prosecutor, he took as naturally to the campaign as if he were putting a jury at ease in a courtroom.

But a tragedy quickly developed that altered Nevada history and Paul Laxalt's life and that of his family forever. Bell and Laxalt campaigned together on a blistering hot Fourth of July, 1962, at an outdoor rally in a popular suburban park. After the rally, Bell drove Laxalt and political adviser George Abbott to the Desert Inn. They planned to meet for dinner later in the evening. But shortly after going to his room, the phone rang and Laxalt got the startling news from a distraught friend of Bell's who reported, in tears, that Bell had been stricken with a heart attack and died.

Republican leaders turned to Laxalt with hopes he would replace Bell as the gubernatorial candidate but he quickly declined after sizing up family and law office obligations and the realization he was simply not ready to move to the top of the ticket. Hank Greenspun, publisher of the powerhouse *Las Vegas Sun*, lost out in a Republican primary to Las Vegas Mayor Oran Gragson who, in turn, was defeated by Sawyer. While winning his second term, Sawyer also learned on election night that he would be saddled once again with a Republican lieutenant governor. Laxalt had won his race, defeating a well-known Las Vegas Mormon bishop, Berkeley Bunker, setting the stage for four years of political scuffling in Carson City and Laxalt's eventual challenge to Sawyer four years later.

Bob Laxalt's role in the highly contested and dramatic political races was best described by journalist Ed Allison whom he had employed in the university's information offices and would eventually work with side by side in the campaigns to come.

"The one thing he did like about being around politics was that it allowed him to be a first-hand witness, observer, of notable events. He did not want to participate in politics nor did he care for politics or get directly involved in policy—but liked the front row seat where he could quietly observe and record in whatever fashion he chose the event he witnessed," Allison told me in an interview.

One dramatic event was the clash between Lieutenant Governor Laxalt and Governor Sawyer over Nevada Highway Department procurement processes that Laxalt described as "if not fraudulent, extremely sloppy, costing the taxpayers millions of dollars." As second in command of the state, Laxalt would rise to acting governor when Sawyer traveled out of state. On one such occasion, Laxalt called for empanelment of a state grand jury to investigate the highway department. When Sawyer returned, the war was on—in the courts. Eventually, the Nevada Supreme Court ruled Laxalt lacked such authority and the controversy—which did result in some reforms—died. But it would be a harbinger of things to come when Laxalt would challenge Sawyer's bid for a third term.

Before that would unfold, two years into the lieutenant governor-ship, Paul rallied his family and inner circle campaign loyalists for another major event that would send Bob once again to his Royal typewriter keys as political observer and media expert turning out press releases and guiding his brother through the troublesome thickets of breaking and investigative news.

On July 3, 1964, Paul filed a last-minute candidacy to run against incumbent Democratic United States Senator Howard Cannon. In doing so, he surprised everyone—including virtually himself and no doubt Cannon—when no other candidate rose to the occasion causing Laxalt, out of loyalty as head if the party, to do so himself. Laxalt's close friend, the crusty Senator Barry Goldwater was running an uphill battle against President Lyndon Johnson. Johnson flew into Nevada to rally Cannon's votes and former Vice President Richard Nixon went to Las Vegas to support Laxalt.

The race was down to the wire on the weekend before the election when Goldwater, en route home to Arizona, decided to make a last-minute campaign stop at the Las Vegas airport. Laxalt's close friends and political observers advised him that he could lose the race if the newspapers ran photographs of Laxalt and Goldwater together. But Laxalt refused to duck out on his friend and greeted him on arrival. The newspapers ran the photos. It was a big story with predictions Goldwater was about to lose in a landslide for Johnson. Goldwater did just that. And Laxalt lost his race by forty-eight votes. A testy recount adjusted the loss to eighty-four votes. There were cries of fraud in the media and thoughts of a potential appeal to the Senate Rules Committee. Laxalt dismissed that idea when he evaluated a "stacked deck" in a Democratic-controlled Senate, a reelected Democratic president, and, if that weren't enough, the fact that Cannon was a member of the rules committee.

Bob lamented the meaning of losing in the epilogue he wrote for the *Sweet Promised Land*'s special edition:

> What children we were. Because we had known politicians, we thought we knew politics. But all we had really known was the outward face of politics . . . We had taken it for granted that a man in politics either wins or loses, but we had never considered the absoluteness of those extremes. To have almost won meant nothing but to have lost. There was no middle ground. We were in a game where there was a winner and a loser, and an awful nothing in between.

Paul analyzed where he stood with politics after the election and didn't want any more of it. After four years of being in the public eye in two elections, serving as lieutenant governor, family privacy gone, vast time on the road away from wife and children, he returned home. But by the summer of 1965, a good ten months after the Senate election, he received a visit from one of his most astute analysts and pollsters, Wayne (Peck) Pearson, who approached Paul about running for governor. Pearson did so curiously by saying Laxalt owed it to not only to the tens of thousands of Nevadans who had voted for him—including Pearson himself—but also to his family members who stood at his side through the endless hours, days, months, and even years with hard fought support.

So Paul turned again to his mother, brothers, and sisters with the question of whether he should enter the political fray one more time. Although opposed to politics the first time, Theresa now encouraged her son. "Paul, run. You should be governor. It will be hard but worth it. Who would have ever thought that the son of a Basque sheepherder could one day be governor?"

Bob went to work contributing to the campaign kickoff speech telecast September 22, 1966.

"Our theme . . . is a NEW LOOK FOR NEVADA," the speech declared. "But underlying this is another theme. We want to substitute a new look for a tired look in running the affairs of state." The speech hit hard at what would amount to twelve long years in office if Sawyer were to be reelected. "The by-products of one administration wanting to stay in power for twelve years have to be—and no doubt about it—a deterioration in leadership and too much attention to building up a political machine in the ranks of state government."

The speech zeroed in on various state commissions and boards having limited meetings inferring failure of accountability and responsibility, a prime example being those in charge of gaming control. "There is no public record of the gaming policy board even having met in the last three years." It called for conducting "our affairs openly and honestly—and not behind closed doors" to avoid making "ourselves open to national suspicion and distrust."

Meeting FBI Director J. Edgar Hoover, following Paul Laxalt 1966 election as Nevada Governor, from left, Robert, Hoover, Paul, Reno banker Art Smith.

Paul claimed the Sawyer administration had failed "to dig out the truth" about illegal skimming of cash from Las Vegas casinos. He said in a press release, typical of what Robert Laxalt and other wordsmiths were writing, that Nevada had to work with the FBI and its extensive crime resources to resolve their differences. He chided what he called Sawyer's "public admission on national television that he didn't know whether or not there was skimming in certain casinos." Paul laid plans to travel to Washington, D.C. with Bob and two of FBI Director J Edgar Hoover's personal friends, Art Smith, a Nevada banking leader, and Del Webb, a developer and gaming license holder. "We have to get to the bottom of these skimming accusations. The only way to accomplish this is to make sure that the state itself gets the first count. If there's any skimming going on, we'll find out in a hurry."

The Sawyer administration did, in fact, have an audit division within the operations of the Nevada Gaming Control Board and Commission that required official inspection in casino counting rooms. Agents were assigned to follow the money when it was taken from table games to the counting room. But the rumors of skimming were hard to combat, a Sawyer official, Guy Farmer, recalled.

The Laxalt/Sawyer/FBI war escalated amid rumors of federal eavesdropping or wire-tapping tied in with Attorney General Robert Kennedy's battling with Teamsters boss James Hoffa whose pension fund financed some Las Vegas Strip hotel construction. Laxalt saw it as Nevada distrusting the FBI as oppressive and the FBI feeling Nevada was coddling criminals.

Another Laxalt press release, on September 29, 1966, laid it on the line:

> Lt. Governor Paul Laxalt said today he was "dismayed and ashamed about charges likening J. Edgar Hoover to Hitler and the FBI to Nazism." Laxalt revealed that in his official capacity as lieutenant governor, he had sent a wire of apology to Hoover in Washington, D.C. for statements made against him in Nevada in recent days. He was referring first to a charge by Governor Grant Sawyer that "I'll be damned if I'll cooperate with J. Edgar Hoover," and that FBI activities "remind me of all I have read or heard about Nazism." The second charge was by Gambling Control Board chairman Edward Olsen that "appeasement is no more of an answer to federal invasion of state's rights than it was to Hitler." Both Sawyer and Olsen were criticizing Laxalt's stand that if elected governor, he would immediately ask for a meeting with Hoover to "mend our fences and end this childish war with the FBI."

The war went on with Hoover publicly rebuking Sawyer in a letter to a Las Vegas newspaper which Laxalt seized upon in another press release to claim the FBI had no confidence in the Sawyer administration and Sawyer ordering up Gaming Commission hearings to investigate possible skimming. Gaming control official Guy Farmer, who, like Bob, was a former wire service reporter, Farmer with the AP, later summed up the hearings in an oral history at the University of Nevada:

> I was there. What can you say about them? You bring in people that say skimming is taking place, and those that adamantly deny it, and the Gaming Control Board had very little specific evidence of skimming We never could really make the ultimate denial. "No, there's no skimming taking place." So there probably was some. I hope it was not of the proportions that some alleged, but we'll never have any way of knowing. As I recall, the governor finally told Keefer (Chairman Milt Keefer) to put an end to the hearings.

Laxalt won the election with 52.2 percent of the vote, 71,807 to 65,870, preserving the Nevada tradition of no governor winning a third term. He was the only Republican elected to a statewide office that year. He made good on his promise to patch up state and federal relations with a Washington visit to Hoover. He did so accompanied by Bob, banker Smith, and developer Webb who addressed the FBI chief as "Edgar" to the surprise of everyone including his staff who always addressed him formally as "Mr. Director." Bob saved his notes for another day of writing that would produce his 1994 novel *The Governor's Mansion*.

When Paul left the campaign trail to serve four years as Governor of Nevada, Bob left politics behind and concentrated on developing the University of Nevada Press. He turned to field research and his old Royal typewriter to produce "New Mexico: The Golden Land" in 1970 and "Golden Ghosts of the Lost Sierra" for the *National Geographic* in 1973. His acclaimed *In a Hundred Graves* came out in 1972. During this hiatus from the political wars he took on another assignment for *Geographic* to write about "The Other Nevada," which the magazine combined with "And the Other Yosemite" by another writer under the title "Unfamiliar Glories of the West."

Paul finished his term as governor in 1971 and chose not to run for reelection but to return to private life. The family put plans to work building a first-class hotel for Carson City. They made sure the ten-story Ormsby House would not exceed the dome of the state capitol in height and they created a grand ballroom which they named in honor of their mother, the Crown Thérèse.

But politics would not remain away from the Laxalt family for long. In 1973, veteran Democrat Senator Alan Bible surprised the state by announcing he planned to retire. Immediately, speculation spread through the state—and national political circles—that Laxalt would run as the Republican candidate against either Sawyer or Democrat Mike O'Callaghan who had succeeded Laxalt as governor. Neither was interested. Harry Reid, the thirty-three-year-old lieutenant governor, announced he would be a Democratic Party's candidate.

The pressure was on Paul. Even his law partners urged him to return to what they saw as his proper calling—and duty—public life. The clincher came in a phone call from his old friend Senator Barry Goldwater, who declared: "What's this crap I hear about your not running?" Paul tried to explain he was enjoying private life but the blunt Goldwater would not go along. "That's bullshit!" Goldwater added in no uncertain terms that Paul should view public service as "a high honor, not a burden" and added: ". . . if people like you and I check out of this business, what in the hell is going to happen to this country?" Paul's closest advisers, including his brothers, agreed with Goldwater, and in February 1974, Paul announced that he would run for the United States Senate.

As they planned the campaign's multiple strategies, Paul's team turned to Bob about the prospect of reissuing an earlier special edition of *Sweet Promised Land,* but this time with a unique epilogue that would chronicle every race from 1962 forward by reintroducing Paul's values in public and personal life including his growing up years as the son of a Basque sheepherder. Five thousand copies were printed in paperback at forty-five cents a copy. While some were sold at five dollars a copy, most were given away to help build the vote.

Bob's university publishing and Basque cultural programs colleague Douglass was stunned when he learned of plans to use the book in the political campaign. He tried to persuade Laxalt not to allow *Sweet Promised Land* to become a political instrument, declaring dramatically, "It doesn't belong to you anymore," that it had become, in effect, the property of the Basque people who revered it as their own story and that it would be inappropriate to use it in so blatantly in politics.

The book had been produced in the 1964 Laxalt/Cannon race in a small, nondescript paperback but this time, in 1974, it would be far more notable. Though the book was privately printed, it carried the name Harper & Row, the original publisher in 1957. A diagonal white stripe at the top right corner declared in bright yellow capital letters: SPECIAL EDITION. The cover was illustrated with an iconic color photograph of Dominique with his thick, iron-gray hair and Bob wearing his tan cowboy hat, sides of the brim furled upward showing vintage use, sitting on a rocky, grassy ridge at the Marlette sheep camp looking out at sprawling Lake Tahoe two thousand feet below.

Below the author's name and the title, the cover carried the description: "A true story, luminous and tender, of the author's father and the journey of discovery he made to his native Basque village," which was followed by a quote from the Chicago Sunday Tribune: "This is one to warm the cockles of your heart . . . It has humor, tenderness and adventure." The back cover carried a note printed in yellow type standing out in the photograph over deep blue Lake Tahoe. The message: "*Sweet Promised Land,* first published in 1957, is the story of the roots from which U.S. Senate candidate Paul Laxalt sprang. It is reprinted here in a special edition, with an epilogue by his brother on Paul Laxalt's career. In a different time and a different endeavor, Paul Laxalt's life is not unlike his father's." It goes on to tell of the candidate's rise "from political obscurity" to the top two offices in Nevada, how he retired to family and private life, then "made his own discovery as to where his duty lay in his lifetime"—". . . to become a candidate for U.S. Senate from Nevada."

The promotional words were created based upon the eloquent language in Bob's epilogue about his brother:

> Paul had time to think about his life. He did most of it at stolen intervals from law and business ventures at the mountain hide-away that had been our father's sheepcamp, surrounded by his kids and us and close friends. In that setting of pines and hot sun and mountain stillness, we talked only if we felt like it. Still, I can remember nights around the old campfire, when the world outside seemed a thousand miles away, that the conversation seemed almost weirdly to come back to politics.
>
> And I can remember Paul in the daytimes, sitting apart from us in faded jeans and boots on the same rock where our father had liked to sit, lost in his own thoughts. It was there he came slowly to the realization of where his commitment and his duty lay in his own lifetime.

The epilogue was signed "Robert Laxalt."

Bob had some misgivings about the literarily renowned *Sweet Promised Land* being used for political purposes, and they were captured years later when his daughter Monique, an attorney and author, wrote a reflectively sensitive novel entitled *The Deep Blue Memory*. In her book, she recalled how her father had presented the first copies of his book with its distinctive blue cover to the family in a joyous moment that she would come to see in a very different light in the political years.

She created a fictional Uncle Luke patterned after her Uncle Paul and tied the significance of *Sweet Promised Land* to the family in almost Biblical terms with a scene from her sheepherder grandfather's funeral in Carson City. "Uncle Luke, the eldest of them . . ." went to the podium and opened a book "that was deep blue in color, that bore the family name on its edge, the book that told the story of their father. He opened it, and turned the pages to the place which he had marked, and looked up to the sea of faces, and commenced reading the familiar words that were pure poetry, the words that sang of the boy born to the green hills, that sang of the hope and promise that lay in the desert hills of a new land. . . . Our uncle read the words in a voice that was one with the language of the deep blue book, and in the end . . . it was not certain which of the brothers had spoken to the crowd this morning, our father or our uncle, or rather, it was as if both had."

In a chapter entitled "The Sacrifice," Monique reported: "The flurry of the senatorial campaign beginning to gather itself" at the now ancestral Carson City home where the Laxalt children had grown up and the grand children frolicked as toddlers. "The dining room table was covered with boxes filled with thousands of communications that had poured in on the occasion of Grandpa's death" from public officials, family friends and associates who had known some or all of the Laxalts ". . . and from people who had never known them but who had long admired them, who had read the book that told the story of their father, or had voted for Uncle Luke, and usually both."

She described the politics that would eventually carry *Sweet Promised Land* into the heart of the campaign. "Late August, a Wednesday, and the look in my father's eyes as he came through the front door of our house in Reno. The afternoon of the debate telecast live to the entire state, and the opponent, and the uttering of the allegation that was black in color, as brutal and deadly as if the opponent had pulled a revolver and aimed and shot across the room filled with microphones and cameras. My father coming through the front door of our house in Reno with murder in his eyes."

Monique turned to the form of the novel to reach the greater truths that she felt fiction could capture, what she saw as the many hues of gray that avoided the pitfalls of simple black-and-white judgmental thinking. She zeroed in on the truths as she saw them with the campaign's nucleus or inner circle gathered, once again but now "stone silent," around the dining table covered with white lace in her grandmother's Carson City home which had become transformed from "a place of privilege" to "a place of protection." Monique placed her own generation of family members in the room—"The group of us lined up on the couch against the inner wall, and Grandma in the corner by the window, silent." The question of injecting *Sweet Promised Land* into the campaign was about to come up.

"Then our Uncle Luke speaking up, in a voice that we had never heard before, a voice that had lost its warm ring of optimism but which was trying for it, insisting on it, in the way the children of immigrants had once pulled themselves up by their bootstraps in the privacy of this very room." She described her Uncle Luke rallying the family to face the fact that when a family itself tried to do something good there was an inevitability that someone else "will try to turn all good things into bad. Asking how the hell they had come this far if they did not have the stuff of which fighters are made. Saying that they would counter it pure and simple, and put the opponent in his place."

Monique told of another uncle, Francis, who most people close to the Laxalts saw as the calm and reasoning Peter—known affectionately as Mick or Mickey—"speaking up, in his voice that was rational, incisive, crystal clear. Saying that which the rest of them knew but did not want to hear, saying that no matter how you looked at it, the fact remained that the family name had been tarnished. Saying that with little more than two months remaining before election day, in no sense could a simple refutation be counted on. Saying that it was going to have to be something greater than that, something major, something that would restore the name in the eyes of the voters."

Monique's novel bore into the heart of the matter as she saw it, pulling no punches, as she described *Sweet Promised Land* being bound for a new life that turned literature into campaign literature.

"We have no memory of who said it first, but suddenly it was there, amidst the steam of coffee and the smoke of cigarettes, the image of the deep blue book, the book that was the first to flow out of the lovely rhythm of the old Royal, the book for which we had been given champagne as small children, the book that you could hold under one arm as you escaped from a fire, the book that was part of what we were." The conversation moved quickly toward a mass printing of the special edition. "They were talking of the genius of the idea, the brilliance of it, and with each sentence the voices were regaining their ring, the crystalline ring that went with the top of the table."

Monique described her father quite differently from the others as the politically troubled gathering turned jubilant, "the look in my father's eyes as he walked out of the U-shaped house that day, the look of confusion so deep it swirled. And the broken, rhythm-less sound of the typewriter that began the next morning, stammering, invading the little subdivision house in Reno, filling it." At an earlier time she had described her father's typing as "the background rhythm of their home." Monique sensed the music was missing that day as her father began writing the epilogue.

In the end, Bob's love for his brother caused him to write the epilogue and allow use of the revered book as campaign literature with the hope it would help make a difference in Paul's uphill battle against Democrat Reid. And it did. The Republican Party was reeling from the aftermath of the Watergate scandals that resulted in the resignation of President Richard Nixon and his pardon by President Gerald Ford. Laxalt quickly turned off any effort to tie him to the Nixon scandal when he came up with a one-liner: "I had as much to do with Watergate as Harry Reid had to do with Chappaquiddick," referring to a scandalous car accident involving Democrat Senator Ted Kennedy that took the life of a young woman companion. Laxalt credited Reid's demand for financial disclosures by family members with actually helping his campaign, as he responded that his sister Suzanne was a Catholic nun who had taken a vow of poverty.

Laxalt won the election by a squeaky 624 votes. Stategist Jerry Dondero summed up use of *Sweet Promised Land* in the campaign in an interview for this book: "You can attribute the election win to that book. We used it well." Laxalt was the only Republican elected to a Senate seat held by a Democrat in the disastrous Watergate year. Senator Alan Bible put Nevada above politics by resigning early—on December 17, 1974—which enabled Laxalt to be sworn in the next day gaining a leg up in seniority that would not have come if Bible had finished his term and Laxalt had been sworn in after the first of the year with other freshmen senators. Laxalt served two terms, defeating Democrat Mary Gojack in 1980, and retired from the Senate six years later in 1986.

He briefly considered running for president in 1987, which drew the attention of national media because of his Nevada background and the Las Vegas Strip's notoriety in contributing to political campaigns but he withstood such focus through his record, fully explored during his terms as a governor and senator. By the summer of 1987, facing a crowded field of presidential candidates including the sitting vice president, George H. W. Bush, and having run several major costly campaigns, he analyzed his inability to meet fund-raising benchmarks he had set and told companions gathered at the old sheep camp at Marlette Lake to "pull the plug."

Being popular and well established in Washington because of his own experience and his close personal ties to President Ronald Reagan, he shifted his career to other public service and lobbying. That allowed a more relaxed life that included gathering with his brothers and sisters and extended family for occasional summertime rest and inspiration at the sheep camp that Robert Laxalt would use again and again as a pivot point for his storytelling.

The Other Nevada . . . The Enduring Pyrenees

The difficult political year aside, 1974 proved to be significant for Laxalt's professional journalism. He published two stories close to the heart and soul of his life's experiences in the *National Geographic,* one set in Nevada, the other in the Basque Country. And he set in motion plans for another book, a history of his state that would run into unexpected problems. The *Geographic* article about Nevada began in a storied gathering place:

> Whenever I am in Virginia City, I visit Gordon Lane, genial owner of the Union Brewery Saloon. It is a place I remember as a haven of warmth and good talk on cold winter nights. Few tourists notice its existence, because Gordon shuns notoriety and too much business. The tiny saloon with its well worn wooden floor and peeling wallpaper is a museum of what he calls "authentic junk," heaped in corners and on old card tables.

The descriptive lead paragraph was an perfect example of what Laxalt had learned early in his writing career and what he later advised other writers and aspirants to the craft: Write about what you know. If you know New England, write about New England, not Texas. If you know about hunting, write about hunting, not fishing. He knew Nevada inside and out and he knew how to write about its flavor and moods, its color and texture, its people and places. He knew a story about the other, or real, Nevada had to start a long way away from the post–World War II boom town of Las Vegas and, instead, in the territorial Nevada of 1863 and emerging statehood of 1864.

But that caused a problem in the eastern offices of the magazine. As Laxalt told the story: "I had to fight a battle with the editor in chief who didn't know how any one could write a story about Nevada without opening it in Las Vegas. I won . . . and Las Vegas was salted into the middle."

The *National Geographic* of June, 1974, nol. 145, no. 6, carried a title at the top of its front cover featuring: "Close-Up: U.S.A."—"California and Nevada" with the lead headline:

Unfamiliar Glories of the West

The subheads:

The Other Nevada . . . And the Other Yosemite

The credits on the Nevada story: Robert Laxalt.

And for the striking photographs that would follow on pages 733 through 757: J. Bruce Baumann.

Laxalt continued after his lead paragraph with the natural follow-up detail that brought his first-person life to the story:

> Gordon and I must go through a ritual. He maintains that he can pro-duce any potion I order. I come prepared to stump him, but I always lose. In my chagrin I ask him, "When are you going to clean up this place?" He points to a hand-painted cardboard sign that sums up the attitude typically Nevadan: "This is my house. I do what I damn please."

The story would be seen by the magazine's legendary worldwide read-ers. Importantly, it also could be seen by the hundreds of Northern Nevada locals who had lived the Union Brewery Saloon experience and knew—and loved—the dusty detail. So Laxalt had to get the story right, not only because of his author's pride in professionalism and accuracy but also because if he failed, proprietor Gordon Lane and his loyal if sometimes eccentric and always eclectic patrons would call him on it. He had to cap-ture the color as they (the author included) knew it: A bar so dusty that the cat of the house left paw prints as it meandered and sniffed among the cocktails in front of the drinkers perched on their bar stools. A Free French flag draped from the ceiling in a back corner so full of grime that it blended a brownish hue with the faded red, white, and blue weathered through years of indoor neglect. An upright piano with keys so dusty that players' fingers left indelicate prints on the worn and chipped ivory after knocking out an off key note that was ill-produced through years of lack of tuning. The iconic stool Lane placed in the partially open doorway blocking entrance of the tourists who peered over it from the wooden planked sidewalk, then, thinking it a barrier, turned away fearful of intruding which is exactly what the proprietor desired. He knew the locals would simply sweep past the barrier and take their rightful place at the bar.

Laxalt described Lane as "a perfect representative of the other Nevada," which he explained had been outshone by the neon flash of Las Vegas, the twenty-four-hour hotels-casinos of Reno, and the sometimes posh Sierra ski resorts that gained global fame when the Winter Olympics were held at Squaw Valley in 1960 near the north shore of Lake Tahoe. He cited the facts and figures of the state: highest elevation of scores of mountain ranges at Boundary Peak's 13,143 feet above sea level in lower central Nevada's Esmeralda County and the lowest point near the Colorado River at 490 feet in southern Clark County; temperatures ranging from 120-degree summer heat in the deserts to 40 below in the mountain winters; rivers and lakes bearing water in remote places, the Truckee, the Humboldt, the Carson, Tahoe, Walker, and Pyramid.

Laxalt personalized the story: "By jeep and horseback and on foot, I have traversed Nevada from the grasslands in the north to the parched deserts of the southland, from snowcapped Sierra to wrinkled old mountains of the east . . . where it is still possible to look for a hundred miles without any signs of habitation." He took the reader in search of wild horses called mustangs and found a mare nursing her colt and a stallion "with powerful neck arched" that, sensing human presence, "whistled a warning" to its harem of mares who obediently "lined up like a cavalry troop, all with ears cocked and nostrils flaring."

He described ruggedly lively buckaroos and a barely alive ghost town where an eighty-one-year-old woman "with severe blue eyes, white hair caught up in a net, and a .44-caliber pistol" mistook him for a scavenger but invited him into her house for coffee "after we had made peace and her stern demeanor melted." He told how Territorial Secretary Orion Clemens was visited by his brother Sam in Carson City who went up to Virginia City to work as a reporter for the famed *Territorial Enterprise* where he came up with a unique byline, Mark Twain. He recited the state's history from the Comstock Lode's silver mines that produced wealth for individual millionaires but also for the nation that welcomed Nevada as its thirty-sixth state in 1864 to get that wealth and finance the Union army to end the Civil War.

Laxalt took the history into the modern times of the 1960s when the Atomic Energy Agency blasted bombs in dazzlingly bright atmospheric tests that sent vast, potentially deadly pinkish purple plumes of billowing smoke high into the desert air at the Nevada Test Site north of Las Vegas. And he detailed how his brother Paul, when governor of Nevada, helped clean up the Las Vegas mob reputation through the transition to corporately owned, publicly traded hotel casino development citing the more respectable patronage of the elusive but welcome casino property buyer Howard Hughes and the legitimate business leadership of internationally known executives like hotelier Barron Hilton and developer Del E. Webb.

Laxalt saved up a poignant ending for the story, describing a strenuous day on a ranch rounding up for iron-hot, hide-scorching branding of "a kicking, biting stallion, skittish mares and colts." When the hard work of the day was over, Laxalt stripped along with the buckaroos and joined them in a pool dug out of the earth that was fed by a stream of steaming hot mineral water.

> I lay back to watch the great clouds of steam rising into the night sky in which stars shimmered like elongated crystals. From a distant ridge a coyote yipped mournfully, and from the ranch a dog answered. I might as well have been a thousand miles away from city lights and sounds, and a hundred years back in time, in the old, unspoiled land that is the other Nevada.

As a newspaper editor in Reno, I couldn't resist complimenting his "Other Nevada" story as "the real substance of the people of our state," then added: "A full-throated protest. Letting the word out to 40 million readers of the *National Geographic* about Gordon Lane's inimitable saloon could have catastrophic results, What if all these people come shuffling by and begin peering over that stool in the doorway? Let us hope that your writings, fine as they are, do not hasten the day that two stools would be required to keep this bastion secure from an encroaching world."

It was rare for a writer to have two of the lengthy, detailed stories, coupled with many pages of dramatic photographs, published in one year in the *National Geographic*. But in December 1974, the second of Laxalt's stories appeared under the title "The Enduring Pyrenees."

> He must have been tall in his youth. One could see that in the sweep of shoulders beneath his high-collared mountain jacket and the long-boned hands that clasped the rustic shepherd's staff. Age and hard work had shrunk him in body, but there was enduring strength in his weathered face.

Laxalt's word portrait filled a column of type on the left side of page 794 which was filled out with a dramatic photograph by Edwin Stuart Grosvenor that continued over the entire next page showing in deep blue and brown hues two elderly sheepherders in berets standing, one smoking, on a craggy stone ledge with three of their sheep dogs tentatively at their side. The story detailed how Bob and Joyce expanded in their 1967 assignment for the *Geographic* from their earlier travels in the Basque Country. They crossed the entire Pyrenees range from the French Bay of Biscay on the Atlantic through the principality of Andorra to the Spanish Aragon region and the Catalan shores of the Mediterranean Sea.

"In the low-lying part of Gascony they had warned me against the Aragonite shepherds who roam the high Pyrenees, saying they were a hostile lot. But I have found that mountain folk are much the same everywhere— and that flatland people are prone to confuse reticence with hostility." Just as the photographer captured the natural beauty of the Pyrenees through his camera's lens, Laxalt drew his own picture with his choice of words. "It was a green mountain sprinkled with the golden buttercups of June and gashed along its flank by a torrent of frothing water. Peaks jagged as primitive spearpoints surrounded us, and a profusion of waterfalls dropped in white plumes to the valley floor."

As he had done in the Nevada piece, Laxalt worked in his researched facts and figures and history of "the wild heart of the Pyrenees" that was "raised by shifting landmasses and shaped by Ice Age glaciers"—twenty-one thousand square miles of territory including forty peaks above 10,000 feet with the massive Pico de Aneto the highest at 11,168 feet above sea level. He described the contrast of the ancient, isolated mountains' "medieval hamlets with gray stone houses, guarded by turrets of fortified churches" and the modern ski resorts as their lifts civilized newly populated peaks with tourism and recreation. He described the industrial modernity of huge pipes snaking down hills to tie into hydroelectric plants and "once secluded meadows bloomed with the blue and yellow and red tents of campers."

And he told of the people once content in their quiet villages whose lives were now torn by the passing of their children into a new era of sought after prosperity. They spoke of their children seeing "shiny cars and fancy clothes" who were enticed by new expectations of life beyond the villages in the cities where they envisioned opportunity awaiting them. "I lost my two sons to progress. They went away to the big cities for money," one Aragonese shepherd lamented. "Times are changing. But I don't know why they should."

Laxalt, always the journalist, sought out the larger story when he met with historian and author Maurice Jeannel who was acclaimed for his knowledge of the vast Pyrenees. They met in the village of St. Lary, which was filled with tourists, including trout fishermen and vacationing families from cities who sought the fresh air of the mountains. Laxalt told the historian how he'd learned of the sadness among elderly village people whose sons and daughters had fled rural life for the adventures of the cities. But Jeannel said that trend, which had developed throughout the Pyrenees, was reversing itself. The young people of St. Lary were no longer leaving. While they forsook the farm life of their elders, they found new opportunity in the small towns that were now catering to tourists. New jobs were created in hotels and resorts, in construction, and in thriving small businesses. They served as mountain guides for summer hikers and instructors for winter skiers.

"Progress works changes, but it has its benefits, too" Jeannel observed. "There is prosperity here now."

The story was accompanied in typical *Geographic* style with a detailed color map showing St. Lary about midpoint from the Atlantic to the Mediterranean near the Pyrenees National Park at Gavarnie in France, a stone's throw from Spain. With Laxalt's vigorously descriptive, sometimes poetic, prose and Grosvenor's dramatically poignant landscapes and humanity-capturing portraiture, the reader would be right at home following the map back and forth over the boundaries of France and Spain.

Laxalt's expert source Jeannel explained how the two countries signed the Treaty of the Pyrenees in 1659 that created a "frontier" illogically dividing "ancient peoples of common stock and language who share both sides of these mountains. In this part of the Pyrenees, as an example," Jeannel told Laxalt, "we belong politically to France but have cultural ties with Aragon. After centuries of isolation, a recent thing like a boundary means very little. Even the advent of modernism will simply add another layer of civilization without erasing our old essence."

This kind of storytelling through detailed research with highly knowledgeable sources, which is the soul of accurate journalism, and excellence in writing and photography and painstakingly thorough maps and charts created steadfast loyalty among *Geographic* subscribers. They traditionally kept the yellow-bound past editions in a revered stack somewhere in the home to be gone over again and again in encyclopedic reference through the years. And it is the challenge the writers and photographers and mapmakers and illustrators must religiously adhere to under the hawk-eyed scrutiny of the magazine's troublesome fact checkers. Laxalt applied his journalistic credo of getting it first, not the breaking news of his UP years but the uniqueness of the depth assignment seeking out what no one else had reported. He attached that to the second half of the credo—getting it right. Absolutely right in defiance of the torturous eye of the fact checker.

He compared the bizarre uniqueness of his ancient Basque forbears' language that "mystified" philologists to that of the Catalans, rooted in Latin, and noted that both carry modern influences of French and Spanish, which serve as common denominators in conversation throughout the Pyrenees. He moved through the dramatic history of the mountains, citing the eras of the Celts, Hannibal and Caesar, the Vandals and the Visigoths and the Moors, which he knew, surely, would send the fact checkers into overtime. He explored the ski slopes of La Molina with its 80 miles of runs and lifts and the 190 square miles of the principality of Andorra with its massive traffic snarls, its twenty-five thousand population and 215 hotels. In Andorra, he took the reader into the maddening enclave of shoppers from around the world who bargain for the lowest prices and tariffs in everything from Brazilian cigars to Japanese cameras to Afghan peasant skirts.

The words and photographs described and showed Catholic masses in remote villages celebrated on feast days with overtures of pagan times in ceremonial dances. And the reader was taken to Lourdes as priests, nuns, common folk, and the inspired visited the Grotto of Massabielle where young Bernadette Soubirous saw the vision of the Blessed Virgin in 1858.

Laxalt explored both the culture and the business of the *contrabandista*, a romanticized name for smuggler who traditionally plied his trade by moving livestock and other goods across the Spanish and French border. He found such a smuggler and asked over drinks in a Spanish village bar how the process worked. Seeing that Laxalt was of Basque heritage and thus trustworthy, the smuggler explained. "To be a good smuggler, one must have these characteristics: strong legs and sound wind, the eyes and ears of a cat, and, of course, an elastic conscience. He told Laxalt how he and his "comrades" would smuggle fifty Spanish mules into France where there was a good market for them. They'd work at night in bad weather wearing dark clothes and picking difficult routes with one man four hundred yards out front to watch for and avoid the frontier authorities.

"But what if the frontier guards see you?" Laxalt asked the smuggler who replied that they had somewhat of an understanding wherein the guard would fire his pistol in the air as a signal alerting the smugglers to abandon their largess to the guards and slip away uncaught. "What if you try to fight them for possession of the contraband?" Laxalt asked. "He wagged his finger at me. 'That is bad, very bad. One hothead beat a guard nearly to death with his walking stick. We could not protect him because he had broken the accord. The guards had a right to shoot him.' He added laconically, 'Which they did.'"

The story took the reader to Iruña-Pamplona and the Festival of San Fermin, which was made famous by Hemingway's novel *The Sun Also Rises* about scores of Spaniards and chance-taking visitors from around the world dashing in front of wild bulls through the narrow, uneven cobblestone streets en route to the afternoon's deadly bullfight. Deadly for the bull, that is, though through the years many matadors were severely gored, some fatally, and in most years at least one of the daring "running of the bulls" participants would be caught by the sharp, powerful thrust of the horns and tossed like a bloody rag doll in the air.

The editors of the magazine had sent Laxalt on a broadly defined mission. "We want you to follow the spine of the Pyrenees Mountains from the Atlantic Ocean to the Mediterranean and tell us what you find there. I wasn't sure what I would find on the sinuous mountain roads that went for 270 miles from one end of the Pyrenean chain to the other, traversing forty peaks exceeding 10,000 feet," Laxalt recalled later. But he noted, after turning in the story, "They were satisfied."

The scope of Laxalt's repeated travels resulted not only in the 1974 *Geographic* story but another, "Land of the Ancient Basques," earlier in 1968, when he was accompanied by acclaimed photographer William Albert Allard. Out of that writer/photographer liaison would come a book, in 1990, *A Time We Knew: Images of Yesterday in the Basque Homeland*.

Laxalt kept the story of the smugglers in his mind. He would eventually tell it in the novel, *A Cup of Tea in Pamplona*, which would be entered in the Pulitzer Prize.

A Collision with History

I find myself reflecting whimsically on how very much like the sagebrush the people are, at least in the hinterland that makes up most of Nevada, setting down their roots and thriving in unlikely places, hardy and resilient, restrained by environment and yet able to grow free.

—Robert Laxalt, *Nevada: A Bicentennial History*

Three years after the well-received Nevada and Pyrenees stories appeared in the *National Geographic,* Laxalt ran into an experience far different from the acclaim almost all of his magazine and book writing had won. He went up front with the reader and advised in a preface for *Nevada: A Bicentennial History:*

In the writing of this book, I have departed—perhaps radically—from the conventional approaches to history. I really cannot explain why, except to say that it was right for me. I do not pretend to be a scholarly historian. In that, I must defer to the meticulous and definitive histories of such as Dr. Russell Elliott, Dr. Wilbur Shepperson, Dr. Eleanore Bushnell, Dr. James Hulse of the University of Nevada faculty at Reno, and the historians who went before them.

But I do pretend to know the Nevada in which I was reared and where it is possible to have intimate exposures to the diverse facets of its makeup—from range life to mining towns to the gambling scene and to politics.

Out of these exposures, I have attempted to shape a narrative history of my state as I have seen it and as I have learned about it. The reader will find no footnotes here, simply because they are to me obtrusive in a narrative treatment. Neither will he find an abundance of dates and statistics, which should properly be contained in the more formalized histories.

Laxalt advised that the reader "will find, however, liberal use of the language of the people, sometimes to introduce a chapter and sometimes to end it. This I have done purposely and also may be construed as unconventional." He added that the "pure language" of the people revealed their character, attitudes and environment and that such expression "speaks for itself in the said and unsaid."

The preface became important when the book was published in 1977 and subsequently examined by reviewers. He had written another Nevada historical book, entitled *Nevada,* which had been published in 1971 by Coward-McCann, Inc., and targeted for twelve- to sixteen-year-olds in grades seven through eleven.

Basque scholar David Río wrote in *Robert Laxalt: The Voice of the Basques* that the two Nevada books were similar in their "historical vision" with Laxalt distancing himself "from typical and conventional historical narration full of dates, statistics, and footnotes, and in which thoroughness and extreme precision are paramount." Río noted that Laxalt chose to offer "his own interpretation of the history of Nevada, selecting and judging the facts that he deems most important from his personal point of view." This, Río noted, "caused the work to become the object of considerable criticism by certain professional historians who particularly pointed out Laxalt's excessive emphasis on rural Nevada, the disproportionate prominence of historical facts of a violent nature and a certain tendency toward sentimentalism in his description of the frontier past of the state."

One such critic was Guy Louis Rocha of the Nevada Historical Society who would serve as the state's eagle-eyed archivist for twenty-eight years successfully proving many an alleged fact to be fiction. Rocha, who worked in the historical society's Reno offices, reviewed *Nevada: A Bicentennial History* in the neighboring state's publication *Idaho Yesterdays,* which was important because of Idaho's prominent Basque population that followed Laxalt's work closely. Both of Laxalt's histories traced the Basque contributions to Nevada life.

Rocha opened his review by questioning why Laxalt had been selected to write a Nevada history while praising him as a writer of creative prose. "In light of Robert Laxalt's literary reputation, some would observe that the American Association for State and Local History made a questionable decision when they chose Laxalt to write an interpretive monograph on Nevada's history." "On the one hand, his credentials as a creative writer are impeccable. One merely has to read *Sweet Promised Land* to know that

Laxalt has a special insight into the state in which he was reared, and a way with language which graphically conveys both the tangible and the intangible elements that make Nevada unique. As a literary artist, Laxalt ranks with Walter Van Tilburg Clark—Nevada's premiere writer."

Rocha added the inevitable "On other hand" that writers often cite when opening with "On the one hand. . . ."

Rocha zeroed in. "Laxalt is not a historian. Despite the fact that he openly admits the same in his preface, the book suffers from a lack not of style or insight, but rather a critical approach to the secondary works he consulted. Of course, *Nevada, A Bicentennial History* was not meant to be a scholarly study, and should not be judged on whether it is all-inclusive or offers new historical evidence. Yet the book is called a history, interpretive or otherwise, and if there is one cardinal rule among writers of history, it is accuracy of facts. Unfortunately, what the reader will discover throughout the work is a number of inaccurate facts and statements."

Rocha cited chapter 7, entitled "The Fortune Seekers," and claimed Laxalt "sets up what he believes is the standard pattern for the development of a Nevada mining camp following the Comstock discoveries in 1859." The reviewer granted that Laxalt's writing was "penetrating and highly descriptive and captures the flavor and excitement of a frontier mining town" but added critically that Laxalt "more often than not far overgeneralizes."

Rocha then faulted Laxalt for crediting singularly "the California bank crowd" as financing Nevada mining when, in fact, the reviewer pointed out "New York money built Austin and furnished capital for the Pahranagat mines and mill. English investors vied with San Francisco capitalists for the riches of Eureka's silver mines and English money kept Hamilton alive long after it should have faded into ghost town oblivion." Drilling in his point, Rocha cited a French investment capitalist joining in with San Franciscans to develop one remote mining camp which, in fact, was so appreciative of the Frenchman that it took his surname, F.L.A "Pioche," as its own. The reviewer granted Laxalt's notion of the Bank of California being a major contender in Nevada but stuck with his stickling citations that Laxalt had failed to note that the "bank crowd" was but one of "hundreds of major investors in the state."

Rocha quoted Laxalt as reporting on page 39 that by ". . . 1900, Virginia City, the Queen of the Comstock, was a shabby dowager stripped of her elegance and reduced from ten thousand courtiers to a few hundred faithful. . . ." The reviewer then pointed out that: "Although definitely on the decline, according to the 1900 census Virginia City was still the second largest city in the state with a population of 2,695."

The criticism continued.

> Laxalt's problem of accuracy does not end with "The Fortune Seekers." In Chapter Eight, "A State Is Born," we find federal troops involved in the 'Mormon War' of 1857–58 being dispersed to the Presidio in San Francisco and to Arizona (there was no Arizona Territory until 1863) when in fact the contingent established and manned Camp Floyd outside of Salt Lake City (p. 42). Later in the chapter, Laxalt states that Nevada in 1914 had "the dubious distinction of becoming one of the last states to approve the ballot for women" (p. 51). Not altogether true:" the reviewer wrote, "Nevada was one of the last states west of the Mississippi, but nationwide at least fifteen states had not given women the right to vote."

Rocha challenged the historical accuracy of Laxalt's report on politics, which was particularly sensitive because as a journalist who covered and then participated in modern political affairs, Laxalt should have been knowledgeable of the state's major election dramas, past and present. Such politics were tied together through decades of party loyalties and frequently were germane as newsworthy. "In Chapter Ten, 'Titans of Nevada Politics,' one finds that when Republican Senator George S. Nixon died in 1912, 'Key Pittman was selected by the state legislature to fill the vacancy' (p. 68.) William A. Massey, a Republican, was appointed to succeed Nixon on July 1, 1912. Pittman, a Democrat, defeated Massey for the U.S. Senate seat by eighty-nine votes in the November elections."

Rocha balanced his criticism with praise for Laxalt. "If historical accuracy is the weakness of the work, the overriding strength is Laxalt's ability to capture and convey the essence of Nevada, both rural and urban. The 'Other Nevada,' as Laxalt affectionately calls the state outside the greater Las Vegas and Reno areas, is vividly described not only in the author's eloquent language but in the moving words of its residents. Laxalt perceives the two worlds of Nevada as few can, or will, having shared the best of both."

The reviewer summed up Laxalt and *Nevada, A Bicentennial History* with both questions and praise, saying he provided the reader with a "feel" for the state that most historians fail to achieve in their writing. "There is a real question whether the book should be called a history, or if Laxalt was the best person for the task of writing a state history. But there is no question that Robert Laxalt is an important literary figure, and the state's foremost living creative writer."

Such detailed criticism was new for Laxalt and he didn't like it. He eventually confronted the reviewer over what amounted to a condemnation for failed accuracy, the very soul of the journalism that Laxalt had mastered which was even more vital in the historical record that Laxalt was writing.

A chance encounter provided Laxalt the opportunity to face the critic not long after the review was published. Rocha's desk was just inside the entry to the research room at the Nevada Historical Society building on the northern edge of the University of Nevada campus in Reno. Laxalt visited the historical society with visiting *National Geographic* staff members who were researching western buckaroos. Rocha knew Laxalt by sight because the author had become a celebrity on the campus but it became clear to Rocha that Laxalt did not know him as he passed by without acknowledgement and entered the research room.

Later, however, just after Laxalt's guests had left the research room and he was approaching the door to exit, he paused at Rocha's desk. Suddenly, it became glaringly apparent that Laxalt knew very well who Rocha was. As Rocha told the story: "He wheeled on the heel of his boot and he slammed his hand on my desk and he said, 'That was one hell of a review. You son of a bitch!' I've never forgot that. I've never encountered anybody like that before. I thought, he's pissed at me. And what's going to happen now?"

Rocha got his answer immediately. Laxalt, acknowledging in a friendly way that he did, in fact, know who the reviewer was, said, "Guy I want to talk to you. Do you have time to come by my office? Come by and see me I want to explain to you how I got into this project," Rocha recalled. "Two days later, I went over there and he made me feel very welcome. And then he thanked me and said, 'Look, I was the second choice for this project. The first choice turned it down." Laxalt said he agreed to write the book but asked other historians to check the record for details which, he told Rocha, they failed to do. "They let me down," Rocha quoted Laxalt. "They obviously didn't go through this."

Laxalt then invited Rocha to identify any other errors that he did not include in the review "and get those to me for future reference." At that point, the critic and the celebrated author became friends, a friendship they would value throughout their lives as their paths crossed again and again in their careers pursuing facts, truth, and the written word.

Other reviews equally praised and criticized the book. Loren B. Chan wrote in the *Pacific Historical Review* that Laxalt "paints vivid word pictures of the state's mountains, deserts, natural vegetation, and wildlife. Interspersed in his narrative are colorful, anecdotal quotations from and about his fellow Nevadans, reflecting an earlier stage in the state's history when many people knew each other on a first-name basis."

However, the reviewer cited Laxalt's "affinity for rural Nevada" as "the book's major fault . . . Laxalt seems unwilling to point out the negative aspects of life which have driven many young Nevadans away from the 'cow counties' to Reno, Las Vegas, and out of state in search of the high quality of life that he asserts already exists." The book's "most serious shortcoming, then, is its relative lack of an urban experience."

The reviewer also faulted Laxalt for "debatable and unsupported assertions" citing his report that Chinese immigrants "never caught the contagion of sudden wealth" and "whether conflict between the Mormons and Gentiles was inevitable" as well as his contention that Nevada's economy based on gambling was "one of the soundest in the nation."

Nonetheless, as reviewer Rocha balanced his criticism with praise for literary value, reviewer Chan noted: "To read *Nevada: A Bicentennial History,* however is a rewarding experience. For despite its shortcomings, the book comes closest to being an updated version of Richard G. Lillard's 1942 classic, *Desert Challenge: An Interpretation of Nevada.* That is no mean accomplishment."

Critics aside, both of Laxalt's books helped fill a storytelling void. Nevada, a sprawling and yet only partially populated state, was rarely recorded as the more mainstream states such as California and New York and the colonial states were.

Laxalt took the reader through chapters ranging from the brash territorial days to the honorable birth of the state in the nation's Civil War, to the mix of miners sweating in the steaming depths of the earth to the cowboys and sheepherders working the sometimes blistering, often freezing ranges and mountains. He took the reader from the world famous Reno Arch to the more infamous mob days of the Las Vegas Strip, and he took the reader to the people Laxalt knew so well and whose languages he could hear clearly and interpret for others to understand, the state's combined immigrant family of Yugoslav and Serb, Italian, German, Irish and Scot, Scandinavian and Chinese, Hispanic and African American, and Native American.

In the opening of chapters he described the sense and mood of Nevada as a place:

> It was one of those warm, golden days in the sagebrush desert of late summer, when the air was so bright that one's eyes had to draw to a squint to be able to support it. . . . The desert was quiet and the silence broken only by the scraping of our boots on bare ground, and occasional talk.

Laxalt interwove the mood with history:

> The Mormon poplars still stand, and the roses still bloom in the green valley that presses against the snowtipped peaks of the Sierra. Here it was, in 1851, that Mormon colonists established the first permanent settlement in what was to become Nevada.

And he brought history into modern focus through description:

> If you can't do it at home, go to Nevada .. . . Reno is a modern amalgamation of Sodom, Gomorrah, and Hell. . . . You cannot legislate morals into people, any more than you can legislate love into the hearts of some professed Christians. . . . I as mayor of Reno would place a barrel of whiskey on every corner, with a dipper, and a sign saying: "Help yourself, but don't be a hog"

He reached back to his reporter style when he had covered gangland Nevada with prose that defined the mobsters.

> Bugsy was a psychopathic murderer. He had gotten away with so many gangland executions that he felt murder was legal, as long as it was done by him. . . . Hell, he was the founder of Las Vegas.

And Laxalt added his personal feel for the state by sharing his own emotions with the reader:

> Sometimes on a winter's night when the wind moans through the trees and the snow spatters against the windowpanes, and the lights are low and the rustling fire in the grate suffuses the room with a warm glow, and home becomes a cave against the storm and I think about Nevada, I find that my mind veers away from what is considered to be important. I think instead of elusive moments and little memories. Invariably, they have to do with the enduring essence of land and seasons.

The University of Nevada Press summed up the book in a note: "In a gently sentimental style, Robert Laxalt's narrative history offers readers a highly personal review of the Silver State's past, combined with delightful anecdotes."

Tales of Three Continents

Laxalt did not turn out another book for eight years but the span from 1977 to 1985 was filled with three major *National Geographic* assignments on three continents and the writing of a book that would be entered in the Pulitzer Prize for literature. He found, among many discoveries, a "shroud of mystery" in the remote Sangre de Cristo Mountains of New Mexico. This fit right in with Laxalt's often expressed thoughts that writers should write about what they know. He knew about remote mountain villages from the Sierra Nevada to the Pyrenees.

Robert on horseback in Superstition Mountains, New Mexico for *National Geographic* story, 1977.

Under the title "New Mexico's Mountains of Mystery," accompanied by Craig Aurness's photographic portraits of people and landscapes, Laxalt introduced the reader to the unique languages he found among the villagers he encountered.

> He was working on his knees in the secluded flower garden of the Holy Family Church of Plaza Abajo in Chimayo. Although he wore an open-throated shirt and his sleeves were rolled up to his elbows, something about his demeanor told me he was a priest. In halting English, Father Jose Maria Blanch said he had but recently arrived from Spain. He was the latest in a long succession of priests who have come from their native Catalonia to serve the remote villages of the Sangre de Cristo Mountains of northern New Mexico. Touching soil-stained fingertips to his lips, Father Blanch threw a kiss toward the green peaks surrounding us. "Here they speak the language of Cervantes!"

The priest told Laxalt he had studied and taught the classics of the sixteenth century for thirty years in Spain and was surprised beyond his dreams to learn that such pure language was routinely spoken every day by the villagers as their native tongue. "Es muy bonito—it is very beautiful. But it is only one of the mysteries that are the locked in the Sangre de Cristo."

Laxalt saw a *land of sunshine and shadow* as a torrential rainstorm, accompanied by thunder and lightning, swept without warning through the green hillsides and adobe houses that minutes before were baked in brilliant sunshine. Suddenly all was gray and dreary. Mountain peaks, seen in their majesty moments before, disappeared behind dark, thick clouds. Laxalt began to sense the story he had come to discover and write. "A shroud of mystery does hang over the Sangre de Cristo Mountains, and I was to encounter things difficult of explanation."

Not only did he find a dialect as pure as that spoken three hundred years earlier in Spain but he also discovered "wise village elders, religious apparitions, a shrine with purportedly miraculous powers, and the secret Penitentes." He reported the sect practiced scourging and crucifixion and speculated this may have given the mountains their name—*Blood of Christ*.

Laxalt traced the region's history from sixteenth-century Conquistadores to 1912 when New Mexico became the forty-seventh state and noted that throughout the process, this mountainous region had remained isolated "freezing customs and language in a time frame long eclipsed in other parts of the Southwest." He reported the facts and figures of New Mexico required by *Geographic* editors and expected by readers: it is a mountain range that is part of the Rockies to the north, the Rio Grande on the west, the plains on the east; its highest peak is Mt. Wheeler at 13,161 feet; it contains forests of pine, fir, and spruce.

Laxalt took the reader into one of the most alluring and secret of the mountain range's mysteries, that of the Penitentes and their bloody rites. He explained years later when teaching writing at the University of Nevada's Reynolds School of Journalism how he was able to do so.

Laxalt wrote of hearing

> A rare admission of a man who had been a Penitente. "What I am telling you, I should not be telling you," he said, "because we were under the pain of expulsion never to reveal our secret. But I do not believe in them anymore." He paused, then plunged on. "When I was initiated, the *sangrador,* or bloodletter, cut three gashes along either side of my spine with the sharp edge of a flint. Then I had to crawl three miles through anthills, the ants biting at my cuts as I went.
>
> "Later I had a heavy sin to atone for, and the hermano mayor had me flogged for a day with yucca whips. Every time I fainted, they brought me back with a drink of boiled sage. That gives you strength, so that you can endure it.
>
> "You ask if there were crucifixions on Good Friday. Yes! It was not the worst man in the village; that would be an affront to our Lord Jesus. The one to be crucified was a good man, and he had to volunteer. In times before, some say he was nailed to the cross, but in my time, he was tied to the cross with horsehair ropes. This crucifixion has a name, 'Tres Horas'; that was the length of Christ's ordeal, three hours."

The source who led Laxalt to the secret-revealing Penitente, told how his family had come from Spain in the eighteenth century as colonizers of Chimayo and how he himself had become a weaver of rugs and blankets employing sixty weavers in the region's villages. Typically in the *Geographic*'s tradition of blending history with modern times, Laxalt asked his source about the impact of change in the Chimayo region and wrote about what he learned.

> "Some of the local people don't like it, because the weaving brings too many tourists. But tourism isn't really a bad thing. Tourists buy and then go home, and the money they spend goes to make life better for all of us. Work gives a man pride. No work plus poverty breeds anger."

Laxalt took the reader to many villages including "Todos Vigiles" or "All Vigils" where every person had, for centuries, the same family name—Vigil. The eight-three-year-old patriarch explained simply "From the time when our forebear Jose Antonio Vigil settled the land, we were all Vigils here."

Laxalt questioned how that could be for the village women who married outsiders who had his own family names. The patriarch, Norberto Vigil, responded: "It is very simple. If their men wanted to live here, they were politely requested to change their name to Vigil. Or leave." Then the old man shrugged and told Laxalt: "But now there are young men who don't want to give up their names. Times change, you know."

In the Chimayo plaza, Laxalt observed what he described for the reader as "probably the first European drama enacted in what is today the United States . . . *Los Moros y los Cristianos,* The Moors and the Christians." He reported that in 1598, "nine years before the English settled in Jamestown," soldiers in the command of Conquistador Juan de Onate staged the dramatic play in which horsemen clashed and swords clanged. The Christians were victorious, and this led to the sultan being converted from Islam. A priest told Laxalt the play had been passed from father to son for centuries.

Laxalt reported on still another mystery—the shrine of Santuario in the village Potrero where "ten thousand pilgrims—many bearing crosses on their shoulders—come to worship at the chapel and take sacred earth from a hole in a room beside the altar." There are varied stories about the origin of the shrine, including one about a six-foot-tall crucifix painted with golden leaves. All relate to the miracle of healing.

Laxalt found his way to the 495,000-acre Vermejo Park ranch where he saddled up and joined cowboys who spend weeks rounding up 3,500 head of Hereford cattle that graze on the high grassy plateaus. "The cowboys were a picturesque crew ranging in age from 19 to 64. The older ones wore long weathered chaps that hung on their hips as if they had been born in them. The young cowboys wore short chaps called 'chinks' and high boots into which they tucked their jeans. Big sweat-stained hats, colorful bandannas, and warm coats finished off their outfits."

Laxalt was, as the song goes, "Home on the Range."

> Digging in my own spurs, I helped comb the ridges and ravines, driving cattle to the point from which the trail drive would begin. I soon learned that Vermejo cowboys prefer to do everything at a dead run. . . .

The air was filled with the sound of bellowing cows and bawling calves, cut through with the staccato yelps and shrill whistles of the cowboys.

Laxalt saved something special and personal for the end of the story.

I left them at day's end, bone tired and dusty—and envious of these men who had turned their backs on town jobs and found freedom in the unpeopled reaches of the Sangre de Cristo.

Laxalt would saddle up again for the *National Geographic* to write about the "Last of a Breed, The Gauchos" of Argentina. His story, accompanied by the dramatic photographs of O. Louis Mazzatenta, got right to the very personal point in the opening paragraph.

I got up in the first light and pulled on cowboy boots and a warm jacket against the Argentine winter. It was early September, and the whitewashed ranch buildings of Estancia Aguay were shrouded in cold mist.

The gauchos were already up and about. They had wakened in the darkness to a breakfast of mate, the bitter Argentine tea that is said to dispel fatigue, and mbaipoi, porridge of cornmeal and meat. By the time Victor Carrillo, the ranch manager, and I had our warming coffee, they were already saddling their horses.

Accompanying the story was a dramatic photograph that showed, in dark colors of blue, brown and tan, strong, lean, muscled men in wide brimmed black hats dressing "tense as toreros before a bullfight" for a rodeo in Ituzaingo, Argentina. A caption added to the mood of the photograph that dominated the page and a half layout: "Once lawless nomads of the plains, then heroes of the wars against Spain, gauchos became symbols of freedom—and remain today a romantic evocation of skillful horsemanship and manly conduct."

Laxalt took the reader to his source.

Varjona, a gaucho I had gotten to know, touched the brim of his low-crowned hat and murmured, *"Buen dia."* He was a classic gaucho of Argentina, of mixed Spanish and Indian blood, with fierce black mustache and upward-tilting eyes against a copper skin. Though not yet 20, he had already gained a reputation as a superb horseman.

Laxalt described the gaucho in detail—spurs buckled to bare ankles and feet tucked into sandals rather than the traditional boots of a cowboy, a fourteen-inch knife called a *facón* tucked into his belt in a leather sheath, stiff lasso tied to the side of the saddle, his "horse's mane . . . roached except for one hank of hair at its withers," loping off with the other gauchos into the shadows of the grassland horizon where they "vanished into the mist, like phantoms of all their gaucho forebears who had ridden out into the rolling plain."

The ranch manager explained to Laxalt how the lasso replaced the now ceremonially symbolic *boleadora* which was a sling made up of three leather thongs bearing tightly wrapped stones that, a century earlier, gauchos whirled and hurled at the legs of wild cows and horses to trip and capture them for their hides. They also used the *boleadoras* to capture rheas, the long-legged ostrich-like animals that dashed on springy legs through the deep grass, for their feathers. The practice eventually was banned to protect the rare creatures.

Laxalt told how the gauchos, in a "blur of bright sashes and bandannas and striped outer pants that served as chaps," headed off stampedes by ramming their horses with such great impact into runaway lead cows that the cows "flew into the air in a near summersault." That caused the other cows following the leader to halt, mill about, and be rounded up and guided back to the herd.

> I asked Varjona where he had learned the trick of ramming. "From my grandfather," he said. "It is rarely done now. It is dangerous. If you miss by a hair, then you and your horse will be the ones who will go down." He shrugged. "But I am a gaucho, and danger is part of a gaucho's life."

Laxalt explained how the gauchos took immaculate care of their horses including fitting saddles with several layers of fleece and soft leather to protect the animal's back during the many hours of hard-charged riding in the cattle drives. Laxalt complimented a gaucho for such considerate care and reported the horseman's response: "A gaucho without a sound horse is no gaucho at all," he said. "We say only three things are sacred to a gaucho. His horse, which is his freedom from the earth. His *facon,* which is his companion and protector in a fight. And his china, his woman."

Laxalt added in his report: "I was tempted to ask him which came first in a gaucho's life, but decided that that question had already been answered."

He explained the significance of the *facón* or long knife the gauchos kept sheathed and tucked in their belt. After a long day on horseback, a group of gauchos gathered at their cabins to rest. Laxalt and the ranch foreman approached to visit and Laxalt asked if he could examine one of the gaucho's knife. The foreman, without thinking, reached for the knife. Laxalt wrote:

> In an instant the figures of the gauchos became taut, their tension almost palpable. The foreman's hand stopped in midair. He murmured, "¿Permiso?" The gaucho, whose *facon* it was, considered for a moment and then nodded. When the *facon* was handed to me, I drew the long blade from its scabbard, tested its razor-sharp edges, and quickly replaced it. As we were walking away, the foreman said with chagrin, "That was stupid of me. I just forgot. It is forbidden ever to touch a gaucho's *facon*."

The writer learned more about use of the knives in deadly fights when one gaucho explained how the first movement is a quick unsheathing and slashing of an opponent's face to illustrate seriousness. "If it does not end there, you must fight to kill. Then your knife must wave in your hand like a snake. And when you strike, it must be like a snake—once, and mortal."

Laxalt took the reader into the family life of a gaucho's woman or *china*. At the *puesto*, or camp, of a gaucho named Baez, he interviewed Catalina, whom he described as a lively young woman with dancing black eyes. What was her routine? He reported her reply:

> "Cook, sweep, wash clothes, take care of the garden, take care of my children. That is my day, every day." She said the little family had not been to a town in many years. "In fact, I have never been to a church." "Not even for your wedding?" "Weddings are for rich people," she said. "Anyway, many gaucho women do not get married to their men." She laughed at my puzzlement. "If I were married, and he," she said, pointing to her husband, "turned out to be lazy or a drunkard or a wanderer, I would not be free to leave him."

Laxalt shared the conversation with ranch manager Victor Carrillo's wife Mary Ann. She advised him that in earlier times gauchos were nomads, always on a wandering run, with no time for families, and that the women preferred it that way in their own pride of independence. In fact, he found, in the northwestern province of Salta, independent horsewomen called *amazonas* or *gauchas* who were respected as equals to the gaucho horsemen. Laxalt reported: "To see them riding over a brutal mountain, clad in low-crowned black hats and the brilliant red-and-black ponchos of Salta, is a sight not easily forgotten." He learned that such *gauchas* lived only in the Salta region of Argentina and that the gauchos, themselves, were different in their fierce ways from the cowboy in Chile who was known as *huaso* or "man of the country," the *llanero* or "plainsman" of Venezuela and Columbia and the *vaquero* of Paraguay.

He explained how the uniqueness of the gaucho Spanish and Indian bloodline gave way to immigration as Scots, Irish, English, Italian, and Basque horsemen took to the saddle in the grassy lands of their new world. "The Basques were the most readily accepted of all. They were austere, strong in body and mind, and good with horses—all qualities that the gaucho admired. They were called *acriollado*—one of us." The bloodlines of the cattle were changed by the same immigration as the original Spanish *criollo* was joined by shorthorn, Aberdeen Angus, Hereford, Holando-Argentino, Brahman, zebu, and Charolais.

Laxalt wrapped up the story by reporting that the last bastion of the gaucho was the great interior of Argentina where ranches or *estancias* continued to spread over one hundred thousand acres and people were remotely settled even though roads were being developed to tie communities together. "The beginning of the end," ranch owner Jose Antonio Ansola told me in Corrientes Province. "When the roads are here, the old gaucho way of life will be gone. No longer can we live untouched by the corruption of outside influences."

Laxalt wrote about another old gaucho, "his face . . . creased with age and a lifetime of exposure to the sun and wind," who told of still riding with the trail drives, sleeping on the ground, eating beef cooked over open fire. "'All this must change when outsiders come with their modern ways,' he said with an overpowering sadness in his eyes. 'Adios, gaucho.'" Laxalt used the thought to finish the story that "Here at least, in this land of lonely plains and few people, it has managed to hold on longer than most good things."

Years later, Laxalt would tell his magazine writing students about the gauchos using his typical sly humor. "They all carried 14-inch knives in their belts . . . so I smiled a lot. . . ." He also noted that because of Argentina's distrust of the United States and their broken relationships, he was greeted with government suspicion that the *Geographic* assignment was really a front for political fact-finding. He drew such scrutiny, including posting of a guard at his hotel room on arrival in Buenos Aires, partly because his brother Paul was high profile serving as a U.S. senator. He described a stop in Paraguay as being "like a reunion of extras from all the Nazi war movies . . . never looked down the barrel of so many guns in my life." Flying home out of Rio de Janeiro in Brazil, he recalled for the students, drinks were "$150 a bottle . . . so we settled on sherry which was a steal at $70 a bottle. . . . I had two vodkas and wine and sang God Bless America." Once home, he learned the *Geographic* editors had been concerned for his safety to which he said, "Thanks a hell of a lot" as he held out hopes that his next assignment might be to seek out the charms of the French Riviera.

The editors didn't accommodate Laxalt's glamorous desires but they did ask him to write about the Basque historical angle in a massive thirty-one-page cover story entitled "16th Century Basque Whaling in America" that employed two scientific archaeologist writers, James A. Tuck and Robert Grenier, artist Richard Schlecht, and photographer Bill Currtsinger. Two other photographers, Stephanie Maze and Robert S. Patton, also contributed for a team-produced total layout of seven descriptive stories accompanied by twenty photographs, six paintings, and three maps in dramatic color.

Laxalt's piece, entitled "The Indomitable Basques," took the reader to the scene.

> For days on end the fearsome tempests had raged in the Bay of Biscay. Gigantic waves had roared in from the Atlantic, leaping the breakwater barriers to pound against the stone seawalls of the French port of St.-Jean-de-Luz. The Basque tuna fleet of 24 ships, manned by ruddy seamen bound for the coasts of Africa, lay helpless in the harbor.

He then described how the weather shifted enabling the ships to put to sea where great waves still bounced them about like toys, almost swamping them. He used the modern scene to take the reader into the history of Basque whaling which the other writers, photographers, and artists had described or shown in the pages that preceded Laxalt's feature, which was displayed over three pages in a specially lined typographical box.

"The scene I was witnessing must not have been unlike a day centuries before, when *atalayas,* signal towers perched on promontories overlooking the bay, had smoked with burning wetted straw, announcing that whales had been sighted." He proceeded to outline how the Basque seamen hunted the whales along the shorelines of Europe into the deeper seas and across the Atlantic where researchers had established their presence in what would become Canada's Labrador Peninsula. The magazine reported separately from the Laxalt story in an introduction to its overall coverage of whaling that French explorer Jacques Cartier had met a French fishing boat there in 1534 and that the remnants of three Basque galleons had been discovered at the southern coastal harbor of Red Bay.

Who, Laxalt asked in his story, are the mysterious Basques "whose presence keeps popping up in old chronicles and in remote corners of the world?" He answered his question with the sometimes proven, frequently elusive, facts and figures he'd been gathering for years in his book and magazine research. He described the Basque people and their unique language and culture in their ancient territory along the Pyrenees' borders of France and Spain. He cited a traditional story that Columbus had learned "of land to the west from a Basque whaler." He reported that Juan de la Cosa, the owner of the *Santa Maria,* Columbus's flagship, "may have been Basque himself; her boatswain and at least four other crewmen certainly were." He noted that when Magellan was killed in the Philippines, Juan Sebastian Elcano, a master of one of the ships in the 1519–1521 expedition, took command of the *Victoria* and proceeded to be the "first master mariner to circumnavigate the globe."

Laxalt produced a long line of Basque seamen who explored the waters of the New World and Basque soldiers who were afoot in the conquests of North and South America. He explained how the Basque St. Ignatius of Loyola established the Jesuit order of the Catholic Church and sent missionaries to the Americas and how the Basque St. Francis Xavier did the same in the Orient.

Laxalt brought the story full circle from his description of modern times in the storm-tossed port of Donibane Lohitzune (St. Jean de Luz) that he had seen personally through the ancient tales and reports of whaling and conquistador histories to today's continuing seagoing traditions of ship building in the industrial city and port of Bilbao. "The freighters produced in Basque shipyards today are but a natural progression from the olden time when whalers learned to build sturdy vessels that could brave the perils of unknown seas."

His descriptive prose took the reader to the scene of the Basque experience.

The Teacher

In 1983, Laxalt decided, at age sixty, to retire from the University of Nevada Press that he had founded twenty-two years earlier. He had started the press with a dream of grounded research and inspired writing by enlisting the vitally important support of President Charles Armstrong. He developed it with the support of successive presidents, regents, chancellors, faculty, students, legislators, and the general public. He put together a team of dedicated scholars, writers, and entrepreneurial friends who served as fund-raisers as well as the sword and shield he needed in frequent legislative budget battles and critical economic times. Together, they had enabled scores of writers, some just beginning their careers, to become authors of published books that appeared in diversified and unique groupings such as the Great Basin, History and Political Science, and Basque Book Series.

Among Laxalt's most celebrated work was the hundred thousand dollar legislative-funded 1975 publishing venture of *The Journals of Alfred Doten*, which were edited by Walter Van Tilburg Clark, the acclaimed western author whom Laxalt had visited on a snowy day in Virginia City to get advice on writing. Twenty-five years later, the one-time neophyte Laxalt became the publisher of Clark's work. Clark had given up his once fabled creative writing career but had been retained by the university through state funds to edit the epic 2,381-page diaries of Comstock Lode newspaperman Doten, who had captured the daily color and drama of Virginia City in the 1860s.

But now, Laxalt wanted to move on from his publishing executive duties to focus on his own writing. Very quickly, he would be encouraged by me as a longtime friend and others to concentrate on an entirely new career, that of the master teacher. As a former Reno newspaper editor and publisher, I had begun teaching journalism at the university and was working with President Joe Crowley to elevate the Department of Journalism into a full-fledged School of Journalism with its own dean and eventual building. The idea was to have journalism stand independently as a peer with other schools such as Medicine, Mining, and the Colleges of Education and Agriculture. We were developing, with the financial support of national media company owner Donald W. Reynolds and his leading executive Fred W. Smith, a visiting professor program to attract highly acclaimed national journalists and media executives into the classroom to bring their wealth of experience to students.

I thought Laxalt fit that bill, called him and asked if he'd like to teach. At first, he was uncertain. Writing, not teaching, was what he had planned for the years to come. Laxalt had been designated the university's Writer in Residence, a distinction also given earlier to Clark. Laxalt analyzed the teaching possibilities and came up with a plan for two classes, magazine writing during one semester and literary journalism in the other. He could teach writing through his extensive national magazine experience and he could develop a literary journalism course by tracing the evolution from early newspaper writing to fiction by the likes of Ernest Hemingway, John Steinbeck, Stephen Crane, Jack London, and many others who had broken in as journalists and moved on to book authorship. Laxalt would teach the very path that he had personally followed.

However, he could not be hired by the university with State of Nevada funds because he was drawing retirement from the state system. So, what universities call "soft" or privately raised money, was needed. The funding came through the Donald W. Reynolds Foundation which sponsored four Distinguished Visiting Professional Professors in that program's inauguration. The others were nationally successful advertising executive Bourne Morris, former *Life Magazine* and documentary film writer John Frook, and UP International foreign correspondent William Wright. Eventually, when the Reynolds Foundation interest turned toward becoming the major funder of a building for the journalism school, three of the Reynolds professors were brought into regular state-funded faculty positions. But Laxalt still needed private funding because of the retirement conflict.

The journalism program turned to Laxalt's longtime personal friend, E. W. (Ted) Scripps II, who had worked with him in the UP bureau in Reno while attending the university, and was the grandson of legendary Scripps Howard newspapers and UP founder E. W. Scripps. Scripps had great respect for the entire Laxalt family, considering them genuine Nevadans with the "independent minded spirit" that was the hallmark of Nevadans. He agreed to sponsor Laxalt's teaching with a stipend that covered salary for two courses, one each semester.

Donald W. Reynolds Professional Professors, from left, John Frook, Robert, Bourne Morris, Bill Wright, 1983. Photo courtesy of UNR Archives, University of Nevada, Reno.

Laxalt's classes were an immediate hit in the journalism program. They attracted a wide range of young undergraduate students, older students who had returned to the campus to complete their education and both aspiring and professional writers in the community who were media, cultural, and business leaders. The classes were so sought after that Laxalt could not accept all the applicants. He created a system of reviewing their work to determine who was most apt to learn from the class and contribute to the learning of others.

One such talented student in 1988 was twenty-three-year old John Evan Frook, a theater major with a minor in journalism who had met Laxalt through his father John Ellard Frook, the former *Life* magazine writer who was teaching in the journalism school as a colleague with Laxalt. "I'd written consistently for the *Sagebrush*, UNR's student newspaper, for three of my five undergraduate years," young Frook recalled. "I'd placed (maybe fourth) in the Hearst College Journalism Awards one year, and maybe, Laxalt liked my pluck." Laxalt actually recruited Frook through his father and asked him to take the literary journalism class. "When I said yes," Frook recalled, "I didn't know what I was in for." He was to be the only undergraduate among twelve graduate students who met at on a weekday evening for the three-hour class.

Laxalt opened each class by discussing how writers struggle with their work, asked the students about their struggles and then shared his own struggles. "Always, the theme was how difficult it was to put words on paper. How tiring it was to write well. And, his habits, which included writing first thing in the morning and putting at the bottom of each page before he started writing a phrase that said something like 'what in the hell is it that you want to say,'" Frook recalled years later in a career that took him to writing positions and assignments ranging from the *Los Angeles Daily News* to *The New York Times Syndicate, Daily Variety, Advertising Age*, and *QuinStreet* where his work was published on a dozen websites.

He recalled how the class "went methodically through Stephen Crane's *Red Badge of Courage* and looked extensively at Crane's background as a journalist for clues to the way he told his Civil War story. Laxalt was interested in the symbolism pervasive in *Red Badge* but he also took interest in dialogue and word choice. He was always prepared with questions, but it was a meandering kind of mentoring. He was always looking for an inspired moment of insight, and if it didn't come, so be it."

In another session, on John Steinbeck's *The Red Pony,* Laxalt told the class that one line in the book told the entire story and he challenged the students to find it. One student did, Frook recalled. "He said, 'It was the boy loved the horse and the horse loved him for it.' Laxalt said it was the first time in his entire tenure of teaching *The Red Pony* that someone had found it. And he never let that student forget it."

Laxalt's demeanor as a teacher was noted by Basque scholar David Río who had come to the university to research Basque-American literature that had been written in English. Río was apprehensive when first meeting the celebrated Laxalt and, out of respect, wore a coat and tie. He was surprised at Laxalt's informality in casual clothes including tennis shoes. Río greeted the author with a formal: "It's a pleasure to meet you, Mr. Laxalt." The response: "Please call me Bob." Laxalt invited the scholar to visit one of his literary journalism classes and Rio noted:

> Once Laxalt started the class, whose topic was an analysis of Hemingway's *The Old Man and the Sea,* I had the opportunity to see that same sincerity and friendliness with which he had greeted me were not merely a question of appearances. I was also able to admire his capacity for versatility, since the three-hour class was an interesting combina-

tion of serene reflection, humor, poetic emotion, and critical debate. . . . fundamental features of his character: his generosity and especially his modesty.

Laxalt usually limited the class to eight to ten students because he wanted an intimacy that would achieve full discussion for and by all and be the exact opposite of a lecture. When he taught about the writings of Crane and London, he developed an outline with topical headlines followed by discussion points. He wrote it as an outline in his own kind of shorthand code to serve as a tip sheet with some of his questions followed by his own potential answers. He underlined (changed here to italics) some points for emphasis.

—*"To Build a Fire" has been called almost a perfect short story. Do you agree? Why?*

—Story is stripped to bare essentials . . . man, dog and cold. Objective view of man or protagonist. Sustaining action, broken at perfect places so that ending is not surely telegraphed. Man against antagonists (nature and cold) (himself.) Differ?

—*2. The believability of a character in fiction has to be drawn from the author himself . . . if it is going to ring true. Do you believe this statement to be valid? Why?*

—Because it comes from personal knowledge. A person knows himself or herself, if one is honest. Strengths and weaknesses. If he or she draws upon these, then his characters must be believable. Because they are real.

—*3. What techniques or attributes distinguishes the two Jack London stories when it comes to description?*

—Particular attention to detail. Almost flawless in accuracy . . .

—*4. Do you believe Jack London learned more about himself before he died?*

—Yes. But he was not that concerned with self. I would say he learned more about other people. He was not particularly an ego-centered man. Perhaps he learned those lessons through experiences.

—*5. How about Stephen Crane? Did he learn more about himself through his writing?*

—Yes. Definitely. He imagined himself in a myriad of situations and asked himself how he would react. In *The Red Badge of Courage*, his writing was almost a classic example of that. Stephen Crane inserted himself profoundly into the character of the young Yankee soldier— Henry Fleming. Asking himself how he himself would feel before a battle, during a battle, would he fight or run, would he return to his regiment after running, living under the lie of "The Red Badge of Courage," his wound, could he act with courage if the situation were right, how would he handle being thought of as a hero. Like a jewel from every facet. The same in *ONE DASH-HORSES*. He examined Richardson every step of the way, an alien in an alien land, fear, decision, courage, fatalism. In *THE OPEN BOAT,* I think he was still puzzled and would remain so the rest of his life, as to how he really did respond. Except for occasional outbursts of injustice, we really didn't learn that much about the soul workings of Stephen Crane, the correspondent. What do you think?

Laxalt explored human character and writer detachment in point 6 and then, in point 7, zeroed in on "why do writers write?" by explaining: "Many reasons. To say something. To be read. To share an experience with others. Money. Fame. Satisfaction of ego. That is worthwhile and real, too. But there is one basic need that is satisfied in writing. Or should be. TO KNOW MORE ABOUT ONE'S SELF. Creative urge. Therapy. Compulsion. To inform."

And then he asked his students: "Other?"

Laxalt's transition into teaching was enormously satisfying not only because he loved working with students, who, in turn thrived in his classes, but also because the schedule allowed quality time for his own writing. But, suddenly, on June 15, 1987, his world was jolted with the news that his long-time friend and newly established benefactor Ted Scripps had died in his sleep during a flight from Hawaii to Australia. Deeply saddened by the personal loss, and concerned that his teaching might have to cease for lack of funding, he reached out in near panic to friends as he had done in other crises moments in his life when he was unable to join the armed forces because of a childhood disease heart murmur and when he found himself jobless after leaving the UP. He called me at the journalism school for help and, I, in turn, contacted Crowley, who had been a political science professor and was then in his eighth year as president of the university.

Crowley moved swiftly after a quick meeting with Laxalt at which the writer emotionally explained that while the salary was important to him so was the teaching that he hoped he could continue. Crowley established a plan for the University of Nevada Foundation to provide Laxalt's salary through donated funds, and, in the process, created the Distinguished Nevada Author Chair that would honor Laxalt. He called upon a small group of community leaders, both civic and academic, to establish the chair program and they chose Laxalt for the honor. "My feeling was that Bob was the obvious choice," he told a reporter. Crowley had read *Sweet Promised Land* and admired Laxalt as a writer.

Crowley saw Laxalt's distinction as a writer and teacher as a natural fit in the school of journalism. "My view was to look at parts of the campus where we had significant history and future promise," Crowley recalled. Combining a distinguished writer as a teacher with a journalism school that had achieved national acclaim "was one of those marriages made in heaven."

The "marriage" was celebrated by Laxalt's students, those young like Frook and others who were older. John Metzker, self-described as a "sylph-like, 48-year-old, well-monied, well-familied" chairman of the board of the Fitzgerald's Hotel-Casino in downtown Reno and a seasoned commercial property developer, signed up for Laxalt's literary journalism class as well as the course in magazine writing in that same year, 1987. Metzker had heard it was difficult to impossible to get into the classes limited to ten students. But he checked with me as a long-time friend and learned that, as Metzker put it: "Bob could be wheedled into three more students . . . and I was one of the wheedlers."

"Hemingway, Hart, Steinbeck, Crane, London were our subjects of study, Laxalt the interlocutor," Metzker noted. "For anyone who loves to read and is interested in writing, nothing could be sweeter. Invariably, I began staying after class to spend more time with Bob, and I had read most of his published books. I simply didn't want the conversation to end." Metzker saw Laxalt as "a very rare combination of shy and retiring mixed with egocentric, and he would switch from one mode to the other. A lot of what we did in that class was written—or read aloud to the class —to be critiqued by Bob. And, oh, how gentle and nourishing were those cri-tiques—nothing that might send a student running to the door, face bur-ied in hands. I pictured Bob, nodding and smiling, as the gentle gardener, pouring a light drizzle from his watering can on the emerging sprout that was his student. How we all revered him."

Metzker became personal friends with Laxalt, as did many of the students, so much so that Laxalt phoned one day in a raspy, hoarse voice and asked Metzker if he would read the syllabus to the class when the new semester began. Metzker arrived early and took a chair near Laxalt at the front of the class to do his reading duty. "He rasped his thanks at me and pulled conspiratorially close. 'I have a family treatment for this damned throat,' he breathily wheezed. 'It's honey and crushed garlic. Two to three times a day.' His breath made my eyes water."

Metzker so revered the teacher who had become his friend that, years later, he and his wife Lorie would name their adopted baby Zachary Christian Laxalt Metzker. "We wanted to provide our baby with a strong and meaningful Nevada name . . . We chose Laxalt. . . ." They thought the name "epitomized the greatness of Northern Nevada" based upon Laxalt's strength as a writer and teacher and Dominique Laxalt's work in the sheep industry as well as Paul Laxalt's leadership in politics and statesmanship.

Metzker also took the magazine writing class and, being a business executive as well as an appreciator of good writing, marveled at how Laxalt organized the class. As he did with the literary journalism course, Laxalt prepared a detailed but crisp and to the point outline (again with underline reproduced in italics) that introduced both himself and the teaching concept:

—II. My name is Robert Laxalt—will serve as both *professor* and *moderator.* By that I mean guiding discussions as we progress, in dissection of comment by class members of ind. stories by students.

—WORDS ARE TOOLS OF WRITER'S TRADE—REMBRANDT.

—III. In this class, we are going to use an *Editorial board concept*—judging *progress* of everyone's stories including my comments along the way.

—This I think, is a *good concept*—because it going to expose you to what you can expect along the writing way from a magazine *editor* or *BOARD OF EDITORS.*

—And out of this, hopefully—you will begin to develop the tough skin you will need in the writing game. Difficult but not impossible.

—Not *all* editors are cruel—some *kind*—but they are all always *exacting* in their job of meeting a publication's *demands—editorial policy* set by them + *publisher.*

—As an aside I *must* emphasize that each magazine or newspaper has own particular demands in *type of story—how written—attitude—length—and most import. audience targeted.*

—But at same time—*all* mags or newspaprs *use* essentially same story structure.

—By that—*structure*—I mean *framework* on which a story is built. That's one of things we're here to examine.

—Story may be *entertaining, informative, serious, humorous—or satirical but FRAMEWORK REMAINS CONSTANT.*

Laxalt continued to outline story "length, quality, quantity, balance, feel." He told the students they would serve as each other's peers:

> as we go through the process of discussing:
> —one–a story idea and its appeal.
> —two–a *preliminary outline* of what the story will be about—and I mean preliminary—because it will *probably* change—*revision.*
> —three–*structure*–how a story *should* be built on its *particular tack.*
> —four–research of *preliminary* nature—by that—I mean the *necessary background a magazine and reader want*—and what *story needs.*

Laxalt's outline ran twelve detailed pages through point 12 that included twelve story ideas. He wrapped up the first session of the class with an assignment for the following week. He told the students that he would discuss his *National Geographic* story "The Other Nevada" and that they should be attentive to thirteen major themes ranging from ghost towns to hoodlums, industries, and recreation. He emphasized in all his classes that students should draw ideas from their own life experiences just as he did with the Nevada story starting out in Virginia City's Union Brewery Saloon.

Verita Black was one such student. She had earned her bachelor's degree in journalism in 1986 and was, in 1996, a thirty-two-year-old graduate student in education who had dreams of becoming a writer. She shared with Laxalt how her African-American parents had come to Reno in the 1950s, her mother, from Arkansas, to find work at a nearby military base and her father, from Texas, to be a carpenter in Reno's hotel-casino construction development. They had experienced that era's Jim Crow racial prejudice in Reno and built their lives around their church and the civil rights movement then active in Northern Nevada. The student shared with Laxalt her experience in growing up within the culture of the family Baptist church as time wore down much of the earlier rampant racial bias in her emerging generation. Laxalt, whose own emigrant family experiences in Carson City helped shape his writing life, told Black that she surely had stories, including books, to write.

"Write about what you know," Laxalt told her. "I knew about going to church," she recalled, not only on Sunday but several times a week. "The church was so much a part of the African American culture."

Black had heard about a Laxalt class and signed up for it "pretty sure that a teaching assistant would actually instruct the course. To my surprise,

Mr. Laxalt was sitting there the first day with his warm, shy smile and open demeanor. He made a few things clear right away. He wanted to be called Bob, he would be teaching the class and that his goal was that we learn and enjoy his course. He did not disappoint." Black thought of him "as a legend in the state, a Nevadan with books on *The New York Times* best-seller list. I could not believe he was instructing this Nevadan who hoped one day to have a book on the same list."

Black noted his patience with the students, how he "thoroughly read everything we wrote. He had us read our pieces aloud. He assigned reading from inspired writers. He encouraged us to write at different times of the day. 'Set your alarm and get up early to see if that ignites a fire,' he said. 'If that doesn't work,' he suggested trying late at night. He told us to keep trying different times and places until we had a comfort level and all we wanted to do in that time and space was write. I believe he said: 'a time to get lost in your writing.'"

Laxalt told Black she was holding something back and that she needed to be more "authentic." "He sensed 'hesitation' in my pieces. After I turned in an assignment following those instructions, he sat me down and said, 'You have at least a few books in you.' He suggested I write a page a day for a year to complete the first book. I haven't followed that advice but it dances in my mind periodically and I know one day I will. To be encouraged by someone so great is the most precious gift."

Black put her writing skills to work in a short story entitled "Porched Suitcases" about the African-American cultural experiences in church life that was published in an anthology of Nevada fiction, *The River Underground.* She went on to edit the National Judicial College alumni magazine and serve as Northern Nevada and Reno director for Nevada Senator John Ensign and Congressman Dean Heller.

Nevada poet Shaun Griffin joined Black and other writers and artists in the class, noting that Laxalt's wife Joyce helped create and present questions for the students. "Bob didn't teach the class per se; he had a notebook of questions about the stories," Griffin recalled. "Slowly, he asked them after long silences. They were penetrating, deeply felt questions that wrestled with 'the soft' and 'hard' parts of the stories, in his words. I remember all of us leaving the room and wondering how the hours had just passed—because the discussion ensued almost without interruption until we woke from the dream and walked to our cars." "Bob had all of us write an original piece of fiction for the class. I turned in a very short, poetic narrative about the immigrants who died of suffocation in a boxcar in Texas. Bob wrote one word on my piece: 'artist.' I was humbled to my depths."

Griffin shared a story that illustrated Laxalt's demeanor. "One day in class, I blurted out, 'How did you write *A Man in the Wheatfield*? It is a seamless story. How did you do it?' In his characteristically understated manner, he looked up and said, 'I don't know.'"

Griffin, like others, became a close personal friend of Laxalt who later worked with him in development of *The River Underground,* which Griffin edited, that published the work of some classmates but also that of established writers including their short stories and excerpts from their novels. The anthology included, as we have already seen, a piece by Laxalt, "From a Balcony in Paris."

Laxalt developed a third course, "Special Topics—A Novel," that he taught with Joyce at his side during times of illness in later years. The students would visit his home in the piney woods off picturesque Franktown Road a few miles north of his boyhood home in Carson City. He had suffered physical ailments throughout his life going back to his boxing days as a teenager. And he developed a chronic cough and shortness of breath that required his use of a special nebulizer machine to deliver bronchodilator medications to his lungs.

As he had done with his other classes, he developed an outline to provide exact detail for the four students who took the class individually. "The tutorial class—Novel—is patterned after the tradition set in England and select universities in the United States," he wrote in the outline. "The aim of the course is to provide guidance and a one-to-one basis between professor and student in the writing of a novel." Laxalt met with the students once every two weeks for two hours or more. He advised the students that the home setting would "insure privacy and concentrated time for discussions."

Discussions were centered on "story thrust, characters, setting, time frame, beginning conflict." He limited the class to students who were recommended by faculty and had graduate student status. To be admitted to the class, prospective students were required to submit a sample of writing for his approval.

Chuck Alvey, the forty-eight-year-old general manager of KOLO-TV in Reno, had taken a novel writing class from Laxalt colleague Myrick (Mike) Land who had come to the Reynolds School of Journalism with a background as book editor for *Look* magazine in New York City and was author of many books, some cowritten with his wife Barbara, an accomplished journalist. Alvey had written a murder mystery entitled "Late Breaking News" that was published with Land's guidance in a special student-produced book, the *Nevada Sampler*. Alvey's short biography in the book reported his goal "is to be the best husband, father, friend, television general manager, community volunteer and driveway basketball player he can be. And in his spare time he wants to be the best writer he can be."

Land praised Alvey's work. "At one point, as I was piling up rejection slips from agents, he quietly asked if I would mind if he submitted a sample of my work to Robert Laxalt" who was working with a limited number of graduate students in the writing of novels. "Would I mind? I'd be honored," Alvey replied. When his telephone rang one cold winter Sunday, Alvey was greeted by a quiet voice, "Hello, this Bob Laxalt." Alvey was caught off guard. "I don't recall what I said but I was quite surprised when I realized that Bob was THE 'Robert' Laxalt."

Alvey soon joined Bob and Joyce at their home and marveled how they worked as a team asking him questions about choices of reading and storytelling processes. "They were building the foundation of a clear understanding of storytelling without the crass presentation of formats or outlines," Alvey recalled. "Bob and Joyce were thoughtful and incisive. They never really critiqued me as a writer but their curiosity about where I was letting the characters take the story helped me write with an unbridled enthusiasm. Normally, I was so excited when I arrived at home from our afternoon session that I wrote at least a chapter or more that evening."

Alvey contacted agents about two of his novels. "My query letters were always well received—far better than my manuscripts—probably from thirty years of writing tight television promotional copy." He mentioned in one letter that he had been working under the tutelage of Robert Laxalt. An agent who had rejected one of Alvey's novels suddenly telephoned him and asked that he rush a second manuscript to him, asking during the call what it was like working with Robert Laxalt. "I told him it was amazing, invigorating and inspirational. He said I was lucky and I agreed but I'm fairly certain Bob and Joyce would have told him that luck had nothing to do with it. They helped nurture a nascent talent that has served me well and one I hope to resume one day."

Both of Alvey's novels were rejected but he continued his writing as he developed into one of Nevada's leading business executives, and he never forgot how he was "cloaked with excitement" at each meeting at the Laxalt home where he joined with Bob and Joyce at the dining room table to discuss his work.

Laxalt's own work as a teacher was celebrated when Dean Travis Linn and the faculty invited him to be the Twenty-fourth Distinguished Scripps Lecturer in 1988 at the annual dinner hosted by the Scripps Howard Foundation and Scripps family honoring his long-time friend and benefactor, the late journalist and news executive Ted Scripps, who had died a year earlier. Laxalt was the only faculty member ever so honored. He was introduced through the citation of eloquent words expressed by colleagues such as Guy Shipler Jr., who had once noted in *The New York Times* that Laxalt was a writer of poetic beauty, and Mike Land, who had described Laxalt, in a Pulitzer Prize entry, as a master in the economy of words for his lean and clean style of storytelling.

Laxalt rose to the occasion by describing 1952 Nevada journalism graduate Scripps as carrying his legendary "family name and tradition with an easy pride whether at a board of directors meeting or as a lowly intern at the Reno bureau of the United Press." In his speech, Laxalt traced Nevada's sometimes dramatically humorous news history ranging from Las Vegas mobsters running amuck to state government trying to control them. The audience roared with laughter when he cited gangster Benjamin "Bugsy" Siegel's entry into the Las Vegas scene with a quote: "Bugsy was a psychopathic murderer. He had gotten away with so many gangland executions that he felt murder was legal . . . as long as it was done by him."

Laxalt held the audience of students, faculty, Scripps family, and foundation members, benefactors, and veteran journalists at rapt attention as he reported Nevada's flirting, mostly for economic not moralistic reasons, with everything from easy divorce to controversial prostitution to legalized prize fighting and gambling. He cited Nevada as being thirty-seventh among the states in legal gambling revenues, alluding to the claim, often cited by Nevada governors, that New York, Florida, California, and other states' race track–betting dwarfed the cash flow of Reno and Las Vegas slot machines and blackjack and craps tables.

Being honored in front of his own students as a Distinguished Scripps Lecturer, a designation reserved for the most prominent of the nation's journalists, was a high point in Laxalt's teaching career that included guiding beginning writers into the craft and inspiring veteran authors toward greater fulfillment in their already successful careers.

Laxalt even nurtured those who had no idea how to write a book and weren't particularly inclined toward finding out, typically journalists who wrote all day in their jobs and didn't have Laxalt's passion for working all night on a book. He tried, without success, to talk a local columnist who had been a boxer in college into taking the time to research and write a book on the rich history of prize fighting in Nevada. And he turned to me, a veteran newspaperman who had never written a book, with a story idea for a book that developed into a five-year struggle, multiple rejections, but ultimately successful publication by the University of Nevada Press. The book was entitled *American Commander in Spain: Robert Hale Merriman and the Abraham Lincoln Brigade* and told the story of a University of Nevada 1932 graduate who led international volunteers and was lost in battle during the Spanish Civil War.

Perhaps the most acclaimed tribute to Laxalt as a teacher came when CBS network television special "On the Road" storytelling correspondent Charles Kuralt, who had read many of Laxalt's books, told students at another Scripps memorial dinner: If you want to be a fine writer, do not emulate me on television, but go to the mountain. When you reach the top of the mountain, Robert Laxalt will be there for you.

A Cup of Tea in Pamplona

One year after Laxalt's seventh book, *A Cup of Tea in Pamplona*, was published, he confided to his students in the literary journalism class on April 30, 1986:

> "Today . . . I am going to break some rules and lead a discussion on the elements at play when a writer . . . in this case I . . . writes a book . . . in this case *A Cup of Tea in Pamplona*. In the material I am handing out to you . . . on Ernest Hemingway . . . he stresses that a writer should never talk about his own work . . . but then, he proceeds to do just that . . . in guarded form . . . or snidely . . . or smugly . . . whatever.
>
> I feel that a writer should share his experiences with potential writers and those who just like literature. So . . . I am going to take the gloves off today . . . and tell you what really went into this novella . . . and show you . . . in part . . . what I was trying to accomplish."

Laxalt chose the word "Tea" for the title because it had a more literary "feel" than "coffee," which was more commonly consumed in the Basque Country, to represent a code used by smugglers. When the book was republished in Basque, the title was changed to *Kafea Hartzea Irunean* or "A Cup of Coffee in Pamplona."

The students were well aware of *A Cup of Tea in Pamplona*. It had been entered for the Pulitzer Prize in Literature and reviewed in *The New York Times Book Review*, which reported the story involved

> Gregorio, an aging Basque smuggler, and Nikolas, his chosen successor. The plot focuses on Nikolas's rite of passage from long-suffering peasant to successful businessman. Although Nikolas's new business is illegal, it is redeemed by the notion that the smuggler's "only victim" is the government and by the observance—by French and Spanish police as well as Nikolas—of various time-honored 'codes' of killing and revenge. Besides, Nikolas has "dignity," a quality familiar to Hemingway readers,

that is not exactly demonstrated in the novel but is stuck onto certain characters as a kind of magic label, along with portentous words like "fateful" and "inscrutable."

The *Times* reviewer noted somewhat critically: "Mr. Laxalt's characters are so stoic and quietly suffering that their big symbolic moments must be explained, often with breathtaking literalness. When Nikolas's son drops a coin into a crack in the floor, we are told that "the wife of Nikolas let out a cry of rage and loss and scrambled from her chair in hopeless pursuit of the coin . . . Nikolas raised his eyes from the scene that had unfolded itself before him, destroying forever any illusion of the true circumstances of his life." The *Times* review noted that Laxalt was the author of "numerous books on Basque and southwestern American culture" and added that *A Cup of Tea in Pamplona* was "handsomely illustrated by George Carlson" whose black-and-white drawings were hauntingly poetic.

A *Reno-Gazette-Journal* review said the book "traces the midnight journey of Nickolas, a poor Basque peasant, who crosses two lines that fateful night. One is the geographical French-Spanish border; the other is the invisible border of morality." The review reported Laxalt describing the book as similar to people anywhere who live on the edge of the law with the quote: "What they gain in money they lose in conscience." The review reported Laxalt had done the research and written the story years before only to see it rejected for lack of a market for novellas. Then, years later, as he was going through his papers for the University of Nevada Archives and Special Collections, "I stumbled across it." He submitted the manuscript to the University of Nevada Press that he had earlier directed and it was accepted and published.

Laxalt reviewed the processes he used in writing the book to his literary journalism students. He explained that he wrote the novel on "three levels of comprehension." He cited "the surface level" as being how Basque smugglers live along "the frontier between France and Spain . . . in what is known as the Basque Country . . . or Eskual Herria as the Basques call it . . . the land of the Basques." He said he needed to tell how the smuggling worked, its traditions, its mechanics and the "accords" between smugglers and "guards through centuries of confrontation." He explained how the "surface level" included description of the countryside and the people and the setting which he captured "in glimpses . . . never in one large package." He said he liked to establish the setting "so that it is absorbed almost unconsciously by the reader."

Laxalt used "journalistic or curiosity devices" to dig into the detail of the story through personal observation and an important source—an "uncle-in-law" police commissar "who provided me all the intricacies and mechanics to tell the interior story of smuggling ... that had never been told before." The smugglers themselves were close-mouthed so he had to go to fringe sources for detail. He explained why the story had to be told through fiction.

"I could have used this material in an article about smuggling. I chose not to ... partially at least in the sense that in an article ... I could use no names or come too close to the facts in a factual story. With fiction ... I had the liberty of using what I wanted ... and even the smugglers could say that it was fiction ... and not fact."

The "second level" of comprehension dealt with "a plot line for an adventure story." He created "the first aura of suspense" by having the older smuggler alerting guards through "an accident of recognition" as he crossed over the border, then telling another smuggler in conversation in a café that he was growing weary and wanted to retire. That scenario opened the way for Nickolas to be recruited to become chief smuggler. "Nickolas neither accepts nor refuses the offer ... which creates an element of personal choice ... and suspense ... in the plot line." Laxalt added to the suspense when Nickolas eventually decided to go ahead and recruit helpers for a smuggling mission one of whom was his unpredictable short-tempered brother in law Luis. The reader was set up for trouble and confrontation, adding more suspense, when Luis got into a fight with another peasant over price fixing.

Laxalt took the reader step by step through the violent clash of the smugglers to an ending in family tragedy and death. "The smuggling team ... as we expected ... runs into the frontier guards. A shot is fired ... Nikolas is knocked down by a dog ... Luis uses his knife to commit the unpardonable crime ... that of killing a frontier guard. This is the actual crisis or climax of the story. Nickolas realizes that the code between smuggler and frontier guard has been broken ... violated. He hands Luis the guard's gun and abandons him to face the vengeance of the other frontier guards. He ... Nickolas ... has in effect executed Luis ... a member of his own family."

The "third level," he explained to the class, was the "real story of *A Cup of Tea in Pamplona*"—"This is the story of humans whose conduct is circumscribed by the irons of tradition and Basque mores ... by a society that is itself hypocritical . . . and a society that equates 'a good name' with no name at all . . . a grinding society that withers all hope by its collective inscrutable scrutiny. To avoid individual scrutiny . . . is to protect one's life in that society . . . to break 'the code' of appearance is death." Laxalt also explained the element of hypocrisy—"that a man cannot properly see himself . . . in terms of a morality higher than that of his peers . . . On this level . . . the internal level . . . it is an examination of the human element . . . individuals in rapport or conflict with the mores of the closed society."

Laxalt posed a battery of thirty questions for his students ranging from the character of the protagonist to turmoil in his conscience to what a "good name" means in the Basque society. Laxalt guided discussion of the questions with his own thoughts, answering the thirtieth and final question, "Is it written bitterly?" with the answer "No. With compassion."

Laxalt elaborated on his analysis of *A Cup of Tea in Pamplona* in *Travels with My Royal*:

> I left it to the reader to judge for himself whether Nikolas is a moral man when we first meet him, and why or why not. We must remember that, having made smuggling trips for Gregorio, Nikolas is, as the saying goes, a little bit pregnant. Still, he has made these trips against his better judgment for the welfare of his family.

Laxalt described Nikolas's wife as slovenly and pleading poverty while envious for unearned wealth, yearning for the riches that might come if one of her children would emigrate to the New World as other Basques had done. The author suggested that Nikolas was influenced by his wife's desire for the kind of money he could not earn in his peasant life.

> Nikolas is left to think over his options. He rationalizes being a smuggler's man by the fact that he has so little money and that the only victim is the government, for which the Basques care little.

Laxalt shared with the reader that Nikolas did, in fact, wrestle with his decision:

> From a secretly immoral man, Nikolas will become a publicly immoral man. We are left to wonder if Nikolas will be able to accept the consequences of that.
>
> In conclusion, we must ask whether this story has a hero. As author, I must say not really. Then why did I write this story?

I set out to reveal what can happen to a good person prevented by society from bettering himself. Though it may seem so, the story is not one of morality, but rather of immorality. The tone is not bitter. It is written with compassion for an individual whose adversary is a world of no hope, of grinding poverty. He takes a choice offered to him, not to be ground under any longer.

Professor Myrick (Mike) Land, author of some twenty books and the former book editor of *Look* magazine, and I joined forces to enter *A Cup of Tea in Pamplona* in the competition for the 1985 Pulitzer Prize in Fiction. I had served on seven Pulitzer juries in the journalism categories and Mike was expert on literary work and familiar with the Pulitzer processes. While any book may be entered in the competition, the process is serious and involves exceptional books.

"At first *A Cup of Tea in Pamplona* may seem a simple story," Land wrote in his letter to the offices of the Pulitzer Prize at the School of Journalism, Columbia University, in New York City. "Five Basques set out to smuggle 50 gaunt Spanish horses across the border into France. If they succeed, they will be rewarded with a few coins—not much, but a sum of great value to poor men. If they blunder and the frontier guards discover them, they are to abandon the horses and flee.

"But this assignment is not destined to be that easy. Before the night is over, one of the guards and one of the Basque smugglers will die, the others will be endangered, and a peasant named Nikolas will make a decision that will change his life.

"Mr. Laxalt tells this story with extraordinary economy and in 84 pages offers a remarkable portrait of an entire society. I have marked the passages I would like to quote, but will limit myself to three brief excerpts that demonstrate his style and give some sense of the achievement in this book."

Land cited Laxalt's poignant writing: "No one seemed to hold it against a poor peasant for being a smuggler's man . . . It was so little money, anyway . . . The rich drink with me because I am rich, too . . . And the poor drink with me because it is good to know a man with money . . . What we call respectability is a foolish game the poor must play in order to hold themselves equal to the rich who are seldom respectable . . . He revealed nothing to his wife, but his trips in the night were never discussed between them . . . He simply went, and sometime before dawn, he came back . . . The next day there was extra money in the brass pot on the mantelpiece . . . In this way, he imagined she was at least spared the burden of knowing exactly where the money had come from . . . It was a thin subterfuge, but for a woman whose good name was about the only thing in which she could have pride, it was better than no subterfuge at all . . ."

Land's entry letter added: "As you know, Melville, Henry James, Stephen Crane and Ernest Hemingway have all written short novels that have long been recognized as masterpieces. After you have read *A Cup of Tea in Pamplona,* I believe you will understand why I think it deserves a place on the same shelf with those works."

A second entry letter (by this writer) described Laxalt as a west-erner who wrote with "sensitivity and grace about the land and the rug-ged people who live in it. A Basque American, he writes from an ethnic background nurtured at his father's side in the lonely Sierra Nevada." The letter cited Laxalt's extensive experiences in the West and in the numerous visits to the Basque Country to research and understand his generational roots. The letter added: "The story tells of motivation to honor and conse-quences of betrayal, traits common to all humanity. The eloquence of the work speaks for itself."

In 1985, the year of Laxalt's entry, the prize went to Alison Lurie for her book *Foreign Affairs,* published by Random House.

Laxalt would be entered two more times for fiction, *The Basque Hotel,* 1990, and *The Governor's Mansion,* 1995, and once for biography, *Travels with My Royal,* 2001 but, in that competitive selectivity, winning the Pulitzer eluded him.

The Basque Monument

The title was enticing. "Only a Shepherd"

Carmelo Urza chose it for the opening page of *Solitude,* a book he wrote about the creation of a twenty-two-foot bronze monument in a project Laxalt and others organized to pay homage to the immigrant Basque sheepherder. Just as *Sweet Promised Land* came to speak for immigrants of many nationalities, the idea of such a statue was seen as a potential tribute to all who chose their destiny by braving life in the New World.

The title was originally published above a story from the April 8, 1910 edition of the Nevada mining town newspaper *Goldfield Tribune* that reported: "Back in the frigid hills of Humboldt County the remains of a shepherd were found the other day. He was only a Basque or common shepherd whose services were at the command of the big sheep companies for a nominal monthly stipend. The poor boy undaunted by inclement weather had insisted on venturing back to the range in spite of a blizzard and set forth with a couple of packhorses to reach his destination."

The newspaper story reported in graphic detail how "the shriveled remains denuded of flesh by mountain varmints were found. They could only be identified by the shreds of documents held in leash by the pockets of the faded clothing. . . . Only a Basque shepherd found in the snow lifeless and sodden in the clasp of an inexorable winter but true to duty and as consistent in his faith as the soldier who harks forth to the wars inspired by the blare of trumpets and the cheers of multitudes."

The story ended in a tribute that would decades later be similarly captured in a bronze plaque at the base of the monument in Reno. The *Goldfield Tribune* commented: "When the last roll is called and the spirit of the humble Basque shepherd shall respond to the trumpet his soul shall appear wreathed in all the glory of heroism to claim his reward at the throne."

It was a far time and distance from the early twentieth century mountains and mining towns of Nevada to the modern-day bustle of a Chicago

Navy Pier art exhibition where the Basque government was invited in 1984 to show the sculpture of current artists. But the spirit was the same, and it was contagious. Nestor Basterretxea of Donostia-San Sebastián on the Bay of Biscay in Spain just south of the French border, Remigio Mendiburu of the Spanish Basque town Hondarribia (Fuenterrabía) in Gipuzkoa, and Vicente Larrea of the major seaport Bilbao, all veteran sculptors, attended the exhibition to display their works. Each was a modern, abstract artist who revered the traditional culture of the Basque Country.

Jose Ramon Cengotitabengoa, president of the Society of Basque Studies in America and a Chicago steel industry executive, invited Laxalt and William A. Douglass of the Basque Studies Program at the university in Reno as well other experts to join the artists and present information. This cultural and artistic gathering gave birth to the idea of creating a national monument in homage to the Basque sheepherder whom Laxalt had written about in the June, 1966, edition of the *National Geographic* as the "lonely sentinel of the American West."

Laxalt decided to pull together a group of friends and colleagues to advance the idea of the memorial statue that would stand amid the grassy lands and sagebrush in Northern Nevada where sheepherders and their dogs once guided their flocks beneath sweltering sunshine, twinkling stars, and pelting rain and snowstorms. He started with Preston Q. Hale, a major Reno businessman who knew and loved the West and its people from his days as a government trapper in Idaho and administrator in Utah. Hale had widespread contacts in business and cultural circles and served as a strong private sector supporter of Laxalt in the development of the University of Nevada Press. Douglass added his expertise in the leadership of the committee. So did Janet Inda whose family had emigrated from the French side of the Basque Country and herded sheep in the hills above Reno and across the region. She had wide contacts in Basque heritage clubs based upon her presidency of the North American Basque Organizations, the Reno Basque Club, and her involvement in the Basque Studies Program.

More Basque expertise came from *Solitude* author Urza who frequently traveled to the Basque Country as director of the University Studies Abroad Consortium with campuses in the Basque Country that enabled him to manage the monument project between Europe, Reno, the sculptor, and Mexico (where the statue was cast). Nekane Oiarbide, who was primary coordinator for the European fund-raising efforts, brought a Basque nationalist point of view to the project from her home in Donostia-San Sebastián. She was fiercely independent in her devotion to the Basque culture, which the Spanish dictator Francisco Franco had threatened with deadly restrictions following his own "nationalist" victory in the Spanish Civil War (1937–39). He had so totally banned the unique Basque language from being written or spoken that the mere singing of a Basque song could put the traditional troubadours at serious risk.

Laxalt liked to tell the story about a moment long after the Civil War in a Spanish Basque tavern when a cousin, tipsy from red wine, began to sing about the same time a uniformed member of the Franco's Spanish Civil Guard entered, typically armed with pistol and short-barreled burp or machine gun. The civil guard waved a finger at the singer to shush him. Laxalt's cousin defied the odds. "You may stop my Basque song but you cannot stop my Basque heart," he said to the civil guard who stared at him for a long moment, then shrugged and left. All knew that in the tension of the moment he had full authority to arrest the singer and cast him into a Franco jail.

Others involved with the committee included Douglas County attorney George Abbott, a sophisticated former Republican operative in Washington, D.C. whose wife's family ran a typical Basque hotel and was prominent in the Western Nevada community, and this writer, as a longtime Laxalt friend and veteran journalist.

Laxalt enlisted his brother Paul to serve as honorary chairman of the project. His high profile as a United States senator and former governor helped the committee get the support of the governors of Nevada, Idaho, and California, which was important in fund-raising among the Basque Americans in their states.

In turn, Jose Antonio Ardanza Garro, president of the Basque government in Vitoria-Gasteiz, the capital of the Basque Autonomous Community, which encompasses the provinces of Araba, Bizkaia, and Gipuzkoa, gave his blessing with a rousing resolution that proclaimed: "Whereas, from time immemorial Basques have left their native shore to add the names of men like Elcano, Ignatius of Loyola and Francis Xavier to the annals of mankind, other Basque emigrants have been less famous but no less significant.... Nowhere has this been more true than in the history of the Americas, where many Basques appear in the rosters of illustrious Americans ... others quietly played an important, although largely unrecognized role in developing the unsettled Argentine pampas and the American West, most notably in the sheep industry, and they did so with strength of character, courage and dedication." He noted that "their descendants and fellow American countrymen wish to honor the contribution of these men and to maintain the vitality of Basque culture in the United States." He added: "their accomplishments should be recorded for future generations" and he urged "my countrymen to join me in supporting this tribute to our heritage."

In the summer of 1985, Cengotitabengoa brought the three sculptors who had been at the Chicago exhibition to Reno to meet with the committee and share ideas on the artistic approach of the statue as well as look for the proper site to display it including the location chosen on the lower slopes of Peavine Mountain, in Rancho San Rafael Park overlooking Reno and the Truckee Meadows. The sagebrush hills and natural grassy land had been home to Basque sheepherders and their flocks. Aspen trees bore the carvings sheepherders traditionally left as an artistic mark of their lonely presence.

The committee solicited help from notable figures in the city's arts community in setting up a competition from which a sculptor could be chosen. This included Peter Stremmel, owner of a prestigious art gallery; Yolande Sheppard, a noted sculptress; and Jim McCormick, chairman of the university's art department and himself an accomplished artist. Twelve distinguished artists, the three Basques and nine Americans, were asked to provide concepts. Peter Goin, a photography professor at the university, was asked to photograph the site to familiarize the contenders with its unique terrain. After narrowing the field to three, including George Carlson of Idaho and Gordon Newell of California, the committee's art advisers selected Basterretxea's proposed *Bakardade/Solitude* concept from meta! maquette he had prepared.

Solitude was an abstract conception of a sheepherder, standing tall on disproportionately long legs with abnormally dissimilar arms and shoulders and a significantly smaller head above which appeared a round plate representing the sun or the moon. But there were no sheep, no dogs, no walking staff, and no beret. That immediately set off a controversy among potential donors who were traditionally minded Basques and wanted the statue to look like the sheepherders their deeply respected immigrant forebears had been.

The controversy came as no surprise, for the Chicago exhibition had revealed the nature of Basterretxea's background and abstract art. He was born in Bermeo, Bizkaia on the Spanish side of the Basque Country but was forced into exile with his family in Argentina for seventeen years because of the Francoist persecution following the Civil War. In Argentina, he rose to prominence as a sculptor, painter, designer, and film director and was honored by the Salón Nacional of Buenos Aires with the Premio Único a Extranjeros or Single Prize for Foreigners for his painting. He returned to the Basque Country in 1952 where he continued to sculpt and paint as well as develop careers in writing and cinematography.

Committee member Urza described the controversy: "From the very outset, when the three Basque sculptors were visiting cultural centers around the United States with miniatures of their projects, the designs were received with enthusiasm by some and with an equal amount of dismay by others. The same perceptions continued throughout the competition phase and the inauguration, and thrive to this day. . . . The issue became the artistic design through which the herder symbol would be expressed."

Laxalt entered the fray with a letter on March 20, 1984 to Cengotitabengoa: "Although everyone (on the committee) appreciates abstract sculpture, there are worries that neither the general Nevada public nor the average Basque will be as appreciative. There is a strong possibility that a totally impressionistic group of sculptures may well touch off controversy here in Nevada with the political entities we are going to have to deal with. Nevada is a traditional state, and there have been occasions in the past when abstract sculpture—not the best—has aroused quite a public furor. We do not want to be put in that position."

Laxalt advised that Basques "who do not pretend to understand abstract sculpture" could rise in opposition and refuse to support the project which was essential for raising the potential $250,000 cost of the statue itself and upward of another $50,000 for supporting materials in the park. Laxalt's letter noted that one committee member suggested modifying the pure abstract with touches of tradition to bring in elements such as a walking staff or sheep. The committee agreed and the thoughts were shared with Cengotitabengoa with hopes he would, in turn, communicate the feelings to Basterretxea.

Meantime, the controversy continued, as Urza reported: "Proponents of modern, abstract medium had their own rationale. The monument was not intended to be an exact replica of how the Basque sheepherders dressed. . . . In fact, the monument was not intended for sheepherders at all! They of all people didn't need anyone telling them who they were . . . Indeed, the organizers not only understood that the monument was being built for people who may not know anything about Basques, but also largely for future generations. As such, it would be senseless to try to communicate with the twenty first century with language from the nineteenth."

Basterretxea listened and began to consider some interpretive developments for the work. He would eventually offer an eloquent explanation for his artistic choices.

As the controversy swirled in traditional and abstract circles, the committee put together a fund-raising plan that extended from the Reno base out to the Basque communities of the American West and to national Basque organizations. The committee decided that Laxalt, who had achieved celebrity status in the Basque Country through his extensive writing in books and the *National Geographic,* should take the fund-raising program in May of 1988 to Europe and meet with government, cultural, and business leaders in all seven Basque provinces, three in France and four in Spain. The committee decided I should accompany Laxalt because of my journalism background and ability to explain the project. As a descendant of Norwegian, Scottish, Irish, English, and German immigrants, I could spell out a message that memorialized, yet broadened, the Basque example to embrace all immigrants to America:

> We decided to honor the finest attributes of what we in America value for people everywhere—integrity, hard work, skill, compassion, courage, intelligence. . . . I speak of Americans of Italian descent, of Greek descent, of French, Yugoslav, Russian, Hungarian and a host of other ethnic and religious backgrounds ranging from Chinese-Americans to Jewish-Americans. . . . From the rich texture of global peoples who call themselves Americans, we formed a committee to explore a special honor for the Basque sheepherder whom we so admire . . . and in honor of the people of your Basque homeland. . . . Our Monument to the Basque Sheepherder of the American West will tell that story to new generations who hold high the long-proved values of human character for peoples of all nations.

We were joined on the fund-raising team by the fierce Basque identity advocate Nekane Oiarbide, which made a curious grouping for the mission. Laxalt, of course, was the most appropriate as the celebrity all the Basque leaders admired and wanted to meet. But I was a non-Basque and Oiarbide was female. Females did not traditionally attend the long lunches that we would be joining since such gatherings were reserved for Basque men only. The men showed great respect for Oiarbide, however, because she had widespread acclaim for her Basque cultural work and interpreter assignments in high government programs.

Among the oddities was the fact that Laxalt could, on occasion, grow sleepy and momentarily nod off during the long hours of banquet style meals with their rich food and richer wines and brandies, leaving the non-Basque and female members of the team to carry on with the executives.

Monument fund-raising in spiritual heart of Basque Country, Gernika, with officials including, third from left, Mayor Juan Luis Zuzaeta, Robert, Warren Lerude, circa 1988.

Oiarbide was notably helpful in Gernika (Guernica), which Franco had asked the German Luftwaffe to bomb in punishment for being the spiritual home city of the Basques who had stood against his fascism. She arranged for us to have lunch with the mayor and visit the museum memorial to the bombing that had inspired Picasso to create his horrifying painting of war. The mayor explained that the German pilots attacked in various kinds of bombing—strafing, lobbing from on high, and diving—of the city square full of civilians on market day. He told Laxalt the pilots repeatedly flew back to German bases in Franco-held territory in Spain to refuel and then return with more murderous fire as they developed their skills in deadly but real practice for the eventual World War II. The mayor explained the reign of fire devastated the city and killed multitudes of civilians but missed the fabled Tree of Gernika which was the symbol of Basque life. It was apparent to Laxalt that Basque pride would come naturally to a monument that paid tribute to their home country strength and New World courage.

It seemed odd to Laxalt when Oiarbide encouraged him to use the word Navarra rather than Basque in our visit to the province of Navarre which was widely known for Iruña-Pamplona's San Fermin festival and the running of the bulls made famous in Ernest Hemingway's novel *The Sun Also Rises*. Despite the fact that many sheepherder immigrants came from Navarre to America as Basques, she explained Navarre was its own kingdom of Iberia and had its own identity. And in the Spanish Civil War, Navarre, deeply Catholic, split with the other three Basque provinces and sided with Franco who was supported by the church, the army, and the aristocracy and opposed by an amalgam of the democratically elected Spanish Republic's "loyalists." They ranged from the Republican government itself to anarchists, communists, the navy, Catalonians, Basques, provinces of Andalucía in the south, and international brigade volunteers who rallied for democracy over fascism from fifty-two countries. After Franco's death, the Basque provinces united with their own autonomous government that exists within the scope of the democratic monarchy of King Juan Carlos who, with the elected prime minister, leads Spain.

Laxalt met with Navarre's prosperous banking, industrial, government, and cultural leaders who welcomed the news of the monument project and pledged their support. Basterretxea joined in several of the provincial visits. His presence was legendary for the many venues of his art including sculptures that stood centrally in several Basque cites and his iconic sculpture grace the Basque Parliament in Vitoria-Gasteiz.

The project was played up in newspapers that ran photographs and stories of Laxalt and Basterretxea in the many meetings with leaders who responded to the urging of Basque Country President Ardanza that his countrymen support the program with enthusiasm. After more than a week moving through the Basque provinces, where officials indicated strong financial support would be forthcoming, Laxalt returned to Reno to learn the fund-raising was going well as the May 1, 1989 deadline approached.

In the United States, donations tended to come from individuals and families, unlike the larger institutional support given in the Basque Country by governmental and financial entities. Many Americans sent letters of support even while commenting with curiosity about the abstract design.

"This contribution is from the sheepherders I knew in the 1920's," wrote one donor. "When I was a child my family occasionally visited my maternal aunt at her Basque Hotel in Fresno, California. The sheepherders who boarded there enjoyed seeing and talking to my brothers, sisters and I. This seems a fitting way to repay the many silver dollars that were pressed into our hands with warm smiles. . . . The monument sculpture is interesting but I don't see the herder's faithful servant—his dog. Good luck with the project."

Another: "A friend gave me your address and told me of your noble purpose. While I am not Basque myself, I am a Professor of Law at Hastings College of Law and have studied the Basque people. Theirs is truly an outstanding contribution to American History."

Some turned to Laxalt personally with contributions in remembrance of family. "Dear Mr. Laxalt: I am writing this letter to express the gratitude I and my entire family share for your efforts to enlighten the nation as to our Basque heritage through the erection of a monument to the Basque Sheepherder. It is through the efforts of dedicated persons like yourself that the Basque people have been able to overcome all obstacles and maintain pride and honor in our heritage." The donor asked that the father of the family be honored with his name engraved on a plaque citing the importance "to the people and culture he so truly loved."

Some donors chose to note both family honor and artistic commentary: "We would like to have the name of our father engraved on a permanent plaque at the site of the monument. We wish to honor our beloved deceased dad. . . . We think the idea of a national monument to the Basque Sheepherder is just great." The contributor added: "The drawing of the entire monument looks very impressive, but many of us can't exactly make out the sculpture of the shepherd. Where is the shepherd's head? Hope the finished project will appear better than it does in the drawing. Good luck to you."

Nestor Basterretxea was busy in his studio in Donostia-San Sebastián adding touches, incorporating ideas from the feedback that had come his way from the traditionalists including the suggestion of a sheep that found its way as an abstract outline of a lamb carried over the shoulder of the elusive sheepherder figure. But he was sticking with the integrity of design that was inspired in his heart and soul and motivated in his brain. He began to plan an explanation (and defense) for presentation at the dedication of the statue. He was also busy preparing for a complex process of casting the bronze work in Mexico, where artisans had expertise and which would be closer to Reno than Europe for shipping the statue to the inaugural site.

The sun rose in typical summer fashion August 27, 1989 with a glare that illuminated the mineralized color schemes of the rocky Virginia Range to the east and southeast of Reno where silver and gold had been discovered in Virginia City's famous Comstock Lode. By midday, the temperature soared above ninety degrees. Anticipating an inaugural attendance of several thousand who came from Europe and throughout the United States, the committee arranged for tents to provide shade from the intense heat. The festival opened with red wine and traditional cheese sent to Reno from the Spanish Basque Country.

Newspaper coverage captured the moment. Basque Country journalists and television crews reported the story in Basque, French, and Spanish. Reporter Mike Norris wrote in the *Reno Gazette-Journal:* "With smiles beaming as brightly as the sun above, Basques from around the world gathered in Reno on Sunday to dedicate a sculpture considered the first formal recognition of their cultural, economic and political achievements."

The reporter quoted export merchant Josean Lizarribar, who had come to the dedication with sixty business, cultural, and political leaders from the Basque Country provinces in France and Spain: "It's the dedication to a man who contributed significantly to the development of the American West." The story reported the joyful reaction of Ainhoa Arteta, a twenty-five-year-old opera singer whose great-grandfather, Tomas Foruria, had immigrated to Nevada at the turn of the century. Arteta declared: "When I look at that, I see the big effort to unify the Basque and American peoples."

Preston Hale, chairman of our committee, moderated the speeches from Nevada Governor Bob Miller, Senator Richard Bryan, and a multitude of speakers from other western states and the governments of several Basque provinces. Dancers from Donostia-San Sebastián were led by Iñaki Arregi dressed in white trousers and long-sleeved white shirt inside a red vest with traditional red sash who performed the ceremonial dance *Auresku*. Arregi, white shoes tied in red laces pointed downward tightly together, rose into the air in a flash of color before the massive bronze green statue and the deep blue Nevada sky.

Amid the festivity, the crowd awaited the word from the sculptor. Basterretxea towered over the lineup of dignitaries in a short-sleeved white shirt with his six and a half foot, wide-shouldered frame, sun-bronzed face, and prominent forehead highlighted by his carefully trimmed white beard and moustache. He knew all about the controversy surrounding his art.

Dedication of Basque Monument at Rancho San Rafael Park in Reno, sculptor Nestor Basterretxea, 1989.

Basterretxea spoke softly but with conviction in Basque as an interpreter turned his words into English for the anticipatory throng of observers many of whom stood beneath the hot sun with him while others, a few feet away, listened from the shaded tents. He asked that the audience indulge his need of an interpreter due to his limited English and thanked all who had made the monument possible. He praised his fellow sculptors and noted the greatness of choosing the site in Reno as representing the beloved Basque West and all of America. He said he was aware of the possible difficulty that could exist over the sculptural work of his choice. He spoke to his massive audience on an individually personal basis.

> Through your background and personal tastes, many of you would have preferred, without doubt, an image closer to the physical appearance of the herder. At this time I would like to shorten the distance which separates me from those who believe that.
>
> In order to establish a principle of understanding, one has to accept that most valuable artistic creations have always been those which have been produced from originality, that is from a personal vision of the artist which, because it is different from any other results, over time, in our contribution to that large and vital inherited body which is the History of Arts. If to create is above all, to be original, it is certain as well, that which is original does not usually benefit from public acceptance. It has always been that way.

He explained that while the masters of the arts through the ages are revered, their "luminous wealth" should not simply be imitated by other artists in their own creativity:

> To do so would be to renounce the search for personal expression and to renounce renovative imagination, which constitutes the foundation and passion of art. Each culture constructs itself and develops because of individual and different reasons, each of which is testament to the ideas of the epoch in which it is produced. Each culture defines itself through an accumulation of new ideas which reveal renovated forms of spiritual conduct.
>
> We are in the last years of the twentieth century, and no matter how archaic and rustic the character of the shepherd, I don't see a reason to abandon our own artistic form of expression as modern men. It would, in fact, be unjust to reduce the personality of the sheepherder to a portrait determined by the simple sum of external appearances, for example, by his manner of dress. In the end, a beret or hat on his head and the boots on his feet, do not make a herder. A herder is much more than a man dressed as a herder.
>
> The dress of a herder does not record the complexities of the uncommon existences of these men who acquired a mythical and religious conscience in these magical and startling silences of the nights, full of stars. We imagine them overcoming the sieges of solitude, the demands of an almost superhuman patience and an awareness of their physical

smallness before the ridges of the mountains through which they guide their herds. They were men whose existence was played out along the nomadic route of their herds, suffering the most extreme hardships of weather. They were dreaming stubbornly of making a better future for themselves.

A commemorative and allegorical sculpture of one of the most representative archetypes of our Basque heritage cannot give in to the superficial anecdotes of details.

A commemorative Monument is a solemn act, erected so that the concept it represents may live on in our collective memory. It is in these terms that I have understood the objective of the homage which we dedicate to our herders.

Basterretxea's thoughts were engraved on plaques in both Basque and English and hundreds of the tongue-twistingly long names of Basque families and donors were placed on walls around the statue that stood above the ground on a three-foot pedestal. An adjoining pedestal carried engraved guidance to show visitors how the Basque Americans are distributed throughout the United States. Tragically, some twenty years later, thieves stole many of the engraved tablets to sell the bronze illegally. The committee restored the names through newer processes that would continue the Basque celebration but not be susceptible to vandalism.

The controversy over the art continued. After Urza provided the monument's definitive story of record in his book *Solitude,* one protestor who signed his or her letter "A Nevada Basque" wrote: "I think the title of the book . . . 'Solitude' . . . is entirely appropriate, because *that disaster has been in Solitude since the unveiling ceremony!* With all respect for Mr. Urza, why in the world would anyone want to plunk down $21.95 for a book containing pictures of that repugnant eyesore? Nestor Basterrextea (sp) should be 'de-chiseled' for creating this insult to the Basque people. . . . Why couldn't we have had . . . a simple traditional statue of a Basque sheepherder in his beret with a walking stick and a dog?"

Other Basques disagreed and paid tribute.

Carmen Pascual, looked up at the monument and exclaimed: "It's absolutely great!" Pascual came from Miami to Reno for the dedication. Thirty-four years earlier, at age fourteen, she had come to America from Donostia-San Sebastián to see her aunt in New York. "It shows how Basques and Americans share the pioneering, exploratory spirit. . . . We feel very much like the American people."

The Trilogy

Laxalt's teaching schedule allowed him time to shift to another major project, the writing of a sum total of the Laxalt family experience, a saga of sorts. The University of Nevada Press suggested a memoir that would pull together all of the heritage and detailed drama of the immigrant family that had found the American way of opportunity and success through hard work, integrity, creativity, and initiative.

But Laxalt was perplexed, just as he had been many times when engaging in new writing efforts including his many false starts with *Sweet Promised Land.* He wasn't sure he was built in such a way as a writer to meet the "BIG novel" kind of challenge. He had tried years earlier to write a major novel about the Basques but he gave up on it after turning out hundreds of pages that just didn't work. He was left stranded with the fear he would never finish it. "My approach was wrong," he told an interviewer. "I started going into the minds of all the characters and the manuscript was getting longer and longer. I knew something was wrong. That's not my style. I don't like wordiness in writing." Laxalt turned to his trusted colleague, the veteran author, editor, and journalist Mike Land. "They want me to write a big memoir about the family. But I don't write big books. I write short books," he told Land.

"Why don't you split it up?" Land suggested. "You could write three short books." Laxalt thought over his colleague's advice. He asked himself: Well, what about a trilogy? But he wondered where it should begin and where should it end?" He pondered what he thought of as a lifetime of immigrant family aspirations that included achieving power and even having a son become president. Two such families came to mind, the factual Kennedys and the fictional Corleones, the Italian family that made up the film *The Godfather.* He leaned toward fiction based upon fact for the trilogy but didn't know what the mix of personally influenced fact might be or how much would come in the art of character development through fictional technique.

Robert at Royal typewriter as writer and teacher, circa 1989. Photograph by Marilyn Newton.

Laxalt thought the series of three books ideally would start with his mother and father being born in the Basque Country and then move on with their immigration to America. So he established his mother's story, *The Child of the Holy Ghost,* would be volume 1; the marriage and children settling into the New World, *The Basque Hotel,* or growing up, volume 2; and the family's rise to prominence and power, *The Governor's Mansion,* volume 3. That would be the ultimate presentation. But that would not be the way he would write it. He would, instead, begin writing with *The Basque Hotel* and it, though number two in the series, would become the first to be published, in 1989, to be followed by his mother's story in 1992 and, finally the political power story completing the trilogy in 1994. There was a reason why he did it that way.

> I chose instead to start the trilogy by introducing the point-of-view character in America. I chose to make him a youth so that there would be freshness in the people and things encountered. The story is mostly autobiographical and the narrator is a boy named Pete, whose experiences and emotions are mine. Most important, the story is already in motion, and hopefully, the reader is caught up in the emotion. Immediacy is inherent, and the authenticity of the trilogy is founded.

The reviewers loved the approach and one compared Laxalt's story of small town Carson City with Clark's celebrated tale of Reno, *The City of Trembling Leaves*. K. J. Evans wrote in the *Las Vegas Review-Journal*: "Robert Laxalt is generally regarded as *one* of the most significant Nevada fiction writers of all time. The generally regarded heavyweight was the late Walter Van Tilburg Clark.... But with the publication this year of "The Basque Hotel," Laxalt's stature as a man of letters has risen considerably. In other words, if he keeps this up, he's sure to be known as *the* greatest Nevada writer."

The reviewer elaborated by saying, "And we're not comparing lug bolts and cupcakes here, either. *The Basque Hotel* is of the same literary stripe as Clark's *The City of Trembling Leaves*. It's a tale of coming of age in a small Nevada town, and thus Nevada literature. Both are broad enough to have more than regional interest, to be described as works of Americana. And both deal with broader moral, social and historical issues and so qualify as serious literature.

"But, where *The City of Trembling Leaves* is slow-moving, and not much fun to read, *The Basque Hotel* snaps open like a hot chorizo sausage, drawing in the reader at once. It's entertaining, nostalgic, sentimental, funny and sad. And it's technically a delight."

Laxalt described in his memoir how he developed the characters who the reviewer praised as "well-defined, sympathetic and believable." Laxalt explained setting the scene in Carson City and with its symbolic silver-domed state Capitol as an "actual presence for a good part of the action." He talked about the town's main street as not being unlike that of any small town in America with "shops and stores and poolroom." But he brought life to the town with unique characters who added "color and humor to the story. Our story has Buckshot Dooney and George Washington Lopez, the town drunks." He added his brothers and sisters to be part of a typical immigrant family.

The reviewer found fault with some character development while appreciating how others emerged. "The peripheral characters . . . are a little vague. I would like to have become better acquainted with Hallelujah Bob, the drunken fanatic who blasts imaginary demons with a very real shotgun. A better-defined character is Buckshot Dooney, town drunk and small-time hustler. Dooney's ilk are traditionally tolerated in small towns, but Dooney's status as an outcast intensifies in proportion to the growth of the town."

Laxalt tells the story through the bittersweet adventures and perils of the autobiographical Pete. The reader follows the young Pete in search of a Christmas tree in the deep snow of the forest where he becomes lost. He struggles to survive and barely makes it home to his immigrant parents who have no concept of an Americanized Christmas tree to be tinseled and adorned with colorful, twinkling light bulbs. As Laxalt himself suffered rheumatic fever, so, too, is Pete afflicted with the crippling disease that restricts him to his home where family, friends, and town characters visit with books and the breath of life from beyond his bedroom window.

Like the young Laxalt, Pete sought recovery from physical illness by accompanying his father into the rugged wilderness of the Sierra sheep camps. The reviewer saw the Pete character developing through the kind of allegory Laxalt mastered in *A Man in the Wheatfield*. He described Pete falling in love with and losing his virginity to a tomboy, an outsider in the community, who then cast him aside. "Pretty simple," the reviewer observed. "On one level, we have a wonderfully Steinbeckish earthiness, full of images of Indian summer, haylofts and old leather, and adolescent randiness. We also have the economic history of Nevada—a place where outsiders grab the goodies, spit on the ground and run." The reviewer saw a bit of a Laxalt telltale motive. "The best use of the allegorical device seems to reveal some of Laxalt's sentiments toward the mining industry."

Hidden motives, real or unreal, aside, *The Basque Hotel* captured the sense of place for generations of visitors of all nationalities who found and favored the little, two-story, frame, sometimes brick, rooming houses that were central to Basque communities throughout the American West from Eastern Oregon to Wyoming and Montana, from Boise, Idaho, to Bakersfield, California, with stops in Elko, Winnemucca, Reno, and Gardnerville, Nevada, along the way. The hotels, with their beckoning family style hearty lunches and dinners of six, seven, and eight courses, also dotted the North Beach Italian neighborhoods of San Francisco. Many sheepherders found their way there from the Basque Country by train from New York en route to their ultimate destinations back in the hinterland mountains and deserts.

As had his other books, *The Basque Hotel* won overall acclaim in *The New York Times* despite some negative observations. "A quiet lyricism suffuses this semiautographical novel about growing up in Nevada during Prohibition and Depression years," the reviewer writes:

Robert with first book in family trilogy novels, *The Basque Hotel.*

The Basque Hotel is an episodic story focused on Pete, a teen-ager whose parents operate a boarding house in Carson City ("the smallest capital in the United States"), enjoy brief prosperity, the return to the family's traditional work of sheepherding. We observe the crucial and formative events of two years: Pete's mercurial relationships with siblings, comrades and local ne'er-do-wells (including his parents' boarders) and also such traumas as his experience of ethnic prejudice and his nearly fatal bout with rheumatic fever. Robert Laxalt, a former journalist who now teaches writing and literature at the University of Nevada-Reno, skillfully combines a Tom Sawyer-like evocation of adolescence with unpredictable flurries of ribaldry and violence; tall tales and shaggy-dog stories mingle with delicately understated passages, signifying Pete's bumpy progress toward maturity. Nor is this likable youngster prettified: he's introspective to the point of moroseness, has a troublesome "mean streak" and eventually recognizes that "vengeance was a part of his makeup." Mr. Laxalt's expository prose tends to plod, but he displays a talent for descriptive sequences that pack together conflicting sensory impressions. The wisdom of perspective also graces this book. It's a knowing, affectionate backward look at an earlier America. The story does not escape sentimentality, but Mr. Laxalt's painterly eye for detail and amused empathy with his young protagonist endow it with authentic charm.

Western American Literature, which had compared Laxalt with Sherwood Anderson and Ernest Hemingway in its review of *In a Hundred Graves,* called *The Basque Hotel* "a pleasant, even charming, book with a great integrity not intruded upon by people or events outside itself. Robert Laxalt's latest book holds a sense of place, a sense of youth, a sense of growth and a sense of change."

The *Northeastern Nevada Historical Society Quarterly* described the book as "another excellent story about Basques" and noted that Basque hotels were the gathering places for Basque families in Nevada communities.

The *Publishers Weekly* said the book was "a small gem, a perfect example of a childhood tranquility recollected." Its review called Laxalt "a rare find, a totally genuine, unaffected voice." Jim Kobak's *Kirkus Reviews* said it was an "ethnic exploration with an authentic feel to it." *The Washington Post* commented: "This shapely, small novel is as weightless and peaceful as cranes in the moment they break for the sky."

The acclaim from such Nevada and national reviews was a joy for Laxalt, his family, friends, and colleagues at the University of Nevada Press to celebrate. But as the reviews were praising and *The Basque Hotel* was selling, Laxalt was busy writing the second book in the trilogy. It was about his mother and would be entitled, *The Child of the Holy Ghost.* Laxalt explained in the memoir that despite it being logical to start the trilogy with her roots in the Basque Country, including the illegitimate birth that would shape her life and eventually that of her family's own values in America, he chose a different beginning for the book. He explained he was "writing for an American audience and attempting to show the emotional experiences of my generation of the immigrant story."

With Pete's existence, adventures, and attitudes as a child already established in *The Basque Hotel,* he was introduced as an adult in the new book. He had gone to the Basque Country in search of his heritage, just as Laxalt had done, and thus became the narrator of the story of Maitia, the fictional personification of Laxalt's mother Theresa. He would tell the story of his mother's birth and "unravel the mystery of what happened in the Old Country and provide the reader with the resolution of her life."

The book got right to the point.

Maitia was born a Child of the Holy Ghost. That was the way the saying went then, and one can still hear it in the remote pockets of Basse Navarre where language does not change quickly. She did not become aware of the designation until well after she had started school in the village, and even then she did not comprehend what it meant. For a while, she imagined it to be a special sort of compliment having something to do with the fact that she loved God, went to vespers, and said her prayers every morning and night.

Laxalt told David Río:

I tried to be honest when writing about the Basque Country. Well, *Child of the Holy Ghost,* was written because I was really triggered by what happened to my mother there. I genuinely felt it. I didn't try to portray the village as cruel. It was just the way things were. In a way it was good for me because it gave me objectivity. I could see that there could also be cruelty and I remembered all those wonderful movies about incidents in England and Ireland and the cruelty of village life.

Laxalt took the fictional Maitia to America by the same course his mother Theresa had taken, to aid her French Army brother who was being treated in a Reno hospital for poisonous gas wounds suffered in combat in World War I. This positioned her to meet the figure who would emerge in real life as Dominique.

Laxalt created a character named Petya to represent Dominique and a deadly set of circumstances that forced him to leave the Basque Country and strike out as a youth for America where he would eventually meet Maitia. Petya, a young shepherd in the misted Pyrenees, inadvertently came across a smuggler's dispute and watched in horror as a chieftain murdered another smuggler by forcing him off a cliff. The chieftain had identified the boy who escaped from the mountains and fled to his family in the village. They decided quickly that as a witness to murder his own life was at risk. He had to leave the Basque Country immediately. He made his way from France to New York and eventually, followed the path of other Basque immigrants to Reno.

It made for dramatic fiction, harkening back to the purported deadly circumstances of smugglers' disputes in his celebrated book *A Cup of Tea in Pamplona.* Laxalt had, of course, told the factual story of his father's departure from the Basque Country in *Sweet Promised Land* when he reported Dominique left his Pyrenees home because his family did not own the property on which they lived and he had a strong desire for the opportunity to own land and livestock in America as other Basque immigrants had proved could be done.

As Laxalt labored over the story of his mother's life, his own was severely disrupted when he was caught up in an academic dispute between two other professors when one accused the other of having undue influence over his students. The journalism faculty became embroiled in the controversy and professors split their allegiances with Laxalt's strong sense of loyalty binding him to one of the two professors. The argumentative atmosphere grew intense. Laxalt's span of attention for his own work was distracted. Then, in the ensuing strife, his concentration was broken altogether as the two embattled professors involved almost everyone on the faculty in a fight for their academic standing.

Laxalt reacted, not untypically, with emotion. He saw, because of his support of a friend, his prominent name being besmirched in a public controversy. He was shaken. He called me as a colleague to say he could not continue to write in such a fierce atmosphere, that, in fact, he thought he was losing the story through his inability to concentrate. He said he thought he would have to abandon the second book and give up the trilogy. Colleagues, more attuned to the rigors—and sometimes viciousness— of academic infighting, consoled him and attempted to steer him away from the drama.

The controversy ran out of energy and wound down with the accuser winning an academic point and both sides remaining adamant. The halls continued to blossom with student and professor collegiality and Laxalt returned to his Royal typewriter and finished the book about his mother and father in the New World.

The *Literary Journal* reported the *Child of the Holy Ghost*:

> explores the effect of cultural taboos (in this case illegitimacy) in a family and its descendants. The Basque American narrator, who uncovers his mother's long-kept secret shame (her illegitimate birth) . . . is spurred to discover the truth of this secret when he is introduced by one of his cousins as an American friend instead of a blood relation. The story unfolds like a collapsed telescope into a past connected to the present. The language is simple, the story poignant and dignified. Recommended for literary collections.

Laxalt discussed the fictional nature of the book in two interviews. "Fiction is a marriage between actuality and invention," he told Christine Akinaga for a story in the *Reno Gazette-Journal* shortly after the book came out. "I want the reader to understand that my new book is a novel. As with any creative work of fiction, it is drawn from what I know." And he reported to Kathy Trissell of the *Nevada Appeal* in Carson City that a New York publisher offered him an opportunity for considerable financial gain if he would alter his approach. "They wanted me to change a work of fiction to a work of non-fiction. I absolutely refused. It is a fiction book."

The New York Public Library liked the book as it was and selected it for its 1993 List of Books for the Teen Age. Emilie Jacobson, Laxalt's long-time periodical's agent at Curtis Brown in New York, wrote to him: "That's a very nice honor and will, we hope, be responsible for more sales. I seriously doubt that you'll want to come east to share the punch and cookies with hundreds of teenagers . . . but if I get a chance to pop in for a few minutes I'll give you a report."

An old friend from Laxalt's growing up years in Carson City was moved personally and deeply.

> Dear French:
> I just finished *Child of the Holy Ghost,* and want you to know that of all the books you have written this is my favorite. My heart goes out to your mom and grandmother, realizing the ridicule they endured because of the times and beliefs of their neighbors—beliefs that were carved in stone. I can still see your mom watering the hedge and front lawn at your home on Minnesota St. with that "far-away-look" probably still remembering the taunts she received as a young girl. Your description of "POP" at the sheep camps was great and brought back long forgotten memories. French, I consider this a literary masterpiece and thank you for writing such a great book and giving me an autographed copy.
> My best to Joyce and God Bless.

The letter was signed by Mike Horan who lived at Mountain and Telegraph streets five houses away from the Laxalt's Minnesota Street home in Carson City and went from kindergarten through high school as best friend of Laxalt's younger brother Mick. The families remained close friends through adulthood as Horan developed his career in education and served as a long-time teacher and principal at Reno's neighboring Sparks High School. Horan watched his Laxalt childhood friends develop their own careers including Paul Laxalt's rise to Nevada political power with his brothers and sisters assisting in the campaigns.

Laxalt addressed politics in the trilogy's final book, *The Governor's Mansion.* The eldest sibling, Laxalt's brother Paul, was characterized in the persona of Leon Indart. While Laxalt wrote it as fiction it was clear to readers who followed the Laxalt family that the unfolding events were very real. Leon called his brothers together at their mother's home to discuss his potential political fortunes and what the experiences would mean as the family emerged into public life with its total lack of privacy. Laxalt explained to the reader:

> The family luncheon is exactly as it happened in actuality. There is no need for heightening the drama. It was inherent in the scene. Even the dialogue was as it is related in the book.

The "scene" was covered over several dialogue-filled pages of the book in which Leon informed his brothers that Tex Maynard, a hero in silent screen western movies who was leading the Nevada Republican party as lieutenant governor, planned to run against popular Democratic governor Dean Cooper. In fact, Hollywood star Rex Bell had wrapped up his acting career and become a well-known business and political leader in Las Vegas and announced he would run against Governor Grant Sawyer who was seeking reelection to a second term.   '

"How does he figure he's got a chance of being elected governor?" one brother asked Leon who replied: "Don't underestimate that smiling cowboy. He's got a personal following that cuts across party lines." Leon turned to another brother and asked how he sized up the race. The response: "I think Dean Cooper would have to belt his wife in front of Harolds Club to lose this one." The conversation continued with another brother questioning Leon, something they were not accustomed to doing since he'd been almost a father figure to the family as the eldest child when Dominique was away in his long absences in the sheep camps. The blunt question: "If Tex Maynard thinks he's so strong, why does he need you?"

> "He's not that strong. All of us know that. He feels he can hold his own in the south, in Las Vegas, where the big votes are. But he needs an edge from the north to win, from Reno and the rural counties. He's convinced I can give it to him. I should be able to. The family's been here fifty years. We haven't welshed on any debts yet. Our family name is good. If we haven't made friends by now, then we've been living in a dream world."

The book brought to life the inside story and colorful characters in Paul Laxalt's political career with its many tosses and turns including Rex Bell's sudden death, Laxalt declining to step up to the governor's race in

1962 against Sawyer who won a second term and learned on election night that he would have a Republican lieutenant governor with Laxalt's victory in that race, and Laxalt's eventual victory over Sawyer's attempt at a third term in 1966. The book covered his loss in the 1964 U.S. Senate race, which he ran in midterm of his lieutenant governorship to incumbent Howard Cannon by 84 votes, his victory in the 1974 Senate race over Harry Reid by 624 votes, and his reelection in 1980.

Throughout, author Laxalt took the reader of *The Governor's Mansion* into the private lives of the four brothers who bonded together through the many trials and tribulations that would come their way. With Suzanne away as a nun and Marie teaching school in California, it remained for the brothers to stick close together.

> It became our custom to gather for lunch nearly every Friday at the old family home in Carson City. We pretended that it was the lure of our mother's French brandy pancakes that drew us, but actually it was a way of staying close to each other. As Leon said, "It's like going back to the womb." There, where we had done most of our growing up, the house had been a fortress against the world. This is something the children of immigrants all know, or at least knew then when it was not fashionable to be the children of immigrants.
>
> But it was something more than that. It came down to the fact that we four brothers could not live without each other. We did not enjoy anybody's company as much as our own. We never bored each other. If one of us was having a problem, he could count on honest advice from the others.
>
> Yet, there was a restraint that went with it. The word love was never spoken between us and none of us would ever have admitted that we needed each other . . . But in the end, the ties that bound us prevailed and what emerged was tempered and so better. It was also beautiful, and I know that those who have not known this kind of love have missed very much.

The trilogy was complete. Many who knew Laxalt well were aware of the penchant for privacy common to most Basques. They are not given to bragadoccio nor to opening their homes to other than family and close friends. Yet, his family, friends, and colleagues understood the paradox of Laxalt's need to tell vital stories even when the topics were so personally private they would be taboo in formal or even casual conversation. That storytelling need had taken him as a deadline journalist from a secret mob shotgun assassination hit to public gas chamber executions, from the depth of reporting cultural conflicts and fulfillments of humanity on four continents as a magazine writer and author of books to his own family's poignant stories in their ancestral homes. In so doing, he wrote with dignity about a mother's secret and shameful illegitimate birth and with gusto about a brother's public calamities in the wide open political corridors of Nevada and Washington, D.C. Throughout, his writing reflected the concise style he had developed as a journalist but the expansiveness he allowed himself in the blend of fact and creative fiction. The three short books also followed his succinct style that may have been lost if he had tried to bind all the stories in one massive saga covering the intense complexities of the family's varied journeys from emigrant roots to national prominence.

The Governor's Mansion had more mixed and critical reviews than its predecessors in the trilogy. It won acclaim in the *Publishers Weekly:*

> Pete, a journalist . . . narrates the story, providing a witty, devastating look at a political process rife with voter apathy and ignorance, patronage, favor-swapping, dirty tricks and slick packaging of candidates.

But scholar Richard W. Etulain found Laxalt's characters to be lacking in psychological depth, a criticism David Río believed well-founded. Río supported Etulain's criticism particularly in Laxalt's fictional character based upon the political career of Paul Laxalt. Río also cited commentary by scholar William A. Douglass in a letter to Laxalt about the work. "He has expressed his disappointment that the book clearly does not fulfill the expectations it creates, ones that are largely related to the variety of situations experienced by Robert Laxalt in the land of politics, both when he was a journalist and during his participation in several of his brother Paul's electoral campaigns. Douglass points out Laxalt's reticence to deal extensively with the negative effects of politics on the protagonist's family."

Río, on the other hand, noted "similarities between Leon Indart and Paul Laxalt are also very significant" in the timeframe of the 1960s which the book portrayed. "We see that the novel is a fairly faithful portrait of Paul Laxalt's first steps in the world of politics."

Still another scholar, Cheryll Glotfelty, called *The Governor's Mansion* "exceptional in Laxalt's canon" and

> a fitting conclusion to the Basque-family trilogy, since the campaign is a family effort. Leon's brothers, two of whom were Democrats, both become Republicans in order to help with the campaign. The family house in Carson City becomes an informal election headquarters and

is wired with extra phone lines to receive fast-breaking election returns. With Leon's visibility, the privacy of this immigrant family is forever shattered. From Dominique's humble beginning as a Basque sheepherder and within his lifetime, the Laxalts have become prominent Americans.

In the midst of publishing the trilogy, after *The Basque Hotel* and before the other two books, Laxalt reached once again to the setting of family roots with the 1990 publication of *A Time We Knew: Images of the Basque Homeland*. This book was a joint venture with photographer William Albert Allard and it was well received.

But Laxalt did not have time to linger in the limelight. His health was slowly failing from old injuries and new ailments and he had three, maybe four, more books he thought he should write.

The "Pure Love" of Writing

By the mid-1990s, as he turned seventy-two, Laxalt's health had deteriorated to the point that he had to move his classes from the Reynolds School of Journalism on the Nevada campus, where he had spent five highly productive decades, to his home in the Washoe Valley about twenty-five miles south of Reno and five miles north of Carson City. He was no longer driving and the years of smoking, an occupational hazard for journalists of his generation, and the wear and tear of traveling to remote places around the world were taking a serious toll. He began to require oxygen at night instead of just during the daytime, a health aide he had been using for two years now.

Laxalt Family at home in Washoe Valley, from left, Joyce, grandchildren Gabriel Urza, Alexandra Urza, Kevin Nomura, Amy Nomura, Robert, and family dog, circa 1994.

In addition, for nearly twenty years, he had suffered increasing neuromuscular spasms that caused his legs to lock up, halting him for a few minutes before he could resume walking. He saw a neurologist in Reno for the progressive weakness in his legs that began to spread to his arms. He also suffered from a "cyst-like structure in his cervical spinal cord" a condition, physicians thought, that was created when one of his youthful boxing opponents at the Stewart Indian School punched him so hard in the back of his neck it caused him to lose control of his legs during a fight. In 1996, he underwent surgery during which a shunt was placed in the upper cervical spine to drain fluids that provided some relief from pain.

Laxalt continued to welcome students to his home where Joyce's experience as a school teacher was put to work helping with lesson plans. Students welcomed her presence as the colleague of her husband that she had been through their years of travel and her own editing, writing, and lifetime of voracious reading. He went to the Royal typewriter every day for what his author daughter Monique called "the pure love of writing."

"He was so sick it was a wonder he could write at all," she told a friend. The books he continued to write "showed so much of his character. He couldn't live without writing. There was no reason for it other than that he was a writer who wrote for the value of writing, not for the prospects of a best seller, but to put things down on paper and to create. I was amazed, it was the pure love of writing."

Laxalt's writing talent and dedication were recognized by Allard, the gifted essayist and photographer for the *National Geographic,* who credited Laxalt for coming up with the idea of the book they jointly produced, *A Time We Knew.* Allard reflected after its publication: "That book would not have existed if Bob hadn't dreamed of putting us together and his warmth as a person and as a writer is greatly evident. . . . Of the books I've published, it's one of my favorites. . . . It has simplicity and cleanliness, I believe, in both pictures and words."

Allard had gone to the Basque Country in 1967 and photographed the people, villages, and landscapes for the *Geographic.* Laxalt developed the idea for the University of Nevada Press to publish the book with Laxalt writing the text. He paid tribute to Allard in a note on an opening page entitled: "About the Book."

> During the decades of the 1960s, the seeds of change began to stir in the homelands of the Basques.

Before that, an old, old way of life had remained virtually unchanged in the villages and on the remote farms, and living there was like being thrust a century backwards in time.

A photographer with rare talent came into the country one day and, understanding what he saw, preserved the vestiges of a peasant way of life before they were lost forever.

This book, then, is a chronicle of that time.

Río analyzed the collaboration of the two publishing veterans. "Throughout *A Time We Knew*, there is a consistent thematic harmony between the photographs in the book and the accompanying texts. . . . Thus, Allard's intimate photographs, which bring the reader close to the faces of the people of the Basque Country and to the colors of the land, are perfectly complemented by the lyrical and evocative tone of Laxalt's prose, which nevertheless does not degenerate into excessive sentimentality. It is quite simply a past time captured in images and presented with an appropriate complementary text."

Laxalt's health problems did not steer him away from continuing his mission of bringing publishing life to others, from the student beginners who came to his home and worked with him as he breathed through an oxygen canister to the highly acclaimed professionals such as Allard whose work he enabled into life on the printed page.

Nor did the health problems keep him from putting his own words to paper. He turned his attention to five more books of his own starting with *Dust Devils* where he shifted his focus from Basques and sheepherders to cowboys and Indians.

As had his other books, *Dust Devils* won appreciation of newspaper reviewers when the University of Nevada Press published the slim but action-packed book in 1997. Lenita Powers wrote in the *Reno Gazette-Journal*, "The idea for Nevada author Robert Laxalt's new book, *Dust Devils,* grew from a true story his father told him many years ago. 'My dad was running sheep and cattle up around (northern California's) Surprise Valley. And rustlers stole his horse. He was 19 or maybe 20 and he tracked those rustlers across the Smoke Creek Desert and the Black Rock Desert all the way to Winnemucca.' The story planted the seed for the 102-page novella, but *Dust Devils* is much more than the tale of a young man's quest to recover a stolen colt. It's about a youth's coming of age, a father and son coming to terms and two races coming together." His knowledge of his boyhood Indian friends helped him tell the story of the protagonist,

Ira Hamilton, a young cowboy whose best friend was a Native American Indian named Cricket from the Paiute tribe. The friendship, literally a brotherhood, created friction between Ira and his Indian-hating father.

Bob at the height of his acclaim about L990, setting aside his typical western wear for formal suit and tie.

Laxalt explained to the reviewer that he had long wanted to write a story about the old West. "I wanted to portray the way things were. I tried to avoid all the clichés. Over the years, I picked up an awful lot of lore through my father and the cowboys around Carson City. My uncle was a bronc rider, so I always had been exposed to that lifestyle."

Laxalt created suspense with the first sentence of the book.

> Riding at an easy walk beside his father's big roan, Ira wondered who was going to give way when white man and Indian reached the point of convergence on the wagon road.
>
> That they would converge at just about the same time and place, there was little doubt. The Indian cavalcade had been climbing the trail from the bottom of the canyon for at least an hour . . .

Black Rock Tom on his pinto stallion would not make a show for hurrying any more than Ira's father would. It was beneath his dignity. Ira reflected on how similar the two men were, though that was a comparison he would never dare make in his father's presence.

Even their faces resembled each other if one forgot about the coloring. Their features might have been sculpted out of the same stone, the only difference being that Black Rock Tom seemed always to be scowling and Ira's father, John D. Hamilton by God, looked and was stubborn.

The University of Nevada Press promoted the book as showing "the last days of the Old West, when cowboys, sheepmen, and Indians still struggled to survive and overcome their long-standing animosities, and violent men rode boldly and unhindered across the harsh landscape."

The American Library Association named *Dust Devils* one of the Best Books for Young Adults for 1999 and the New York Public Library selected it for its Books for the Teen Age.

Publishers Weekly, however, was quite critical of the story, calling it "surprisingly thin and textureless. . . . Although Laxalt's prose is as beautiful as ever, plot rather than character sustains this predictable novella, which might be suitable for YA readers, though even that audience may feel it lacks emotional intricacy."

There was no question of "lack of emotional intricacy" in Laxalt's next book, published one year later, *A Private War: An American Code Officer in the Belgian Congo*. He dedicated the book "for Joyce again and always" to his wife of forty-nine years who was caring for him through his illnesses at their home and assisting him in his teaching.

Laxalt explained in a preface how the book came to be:

> This book, or more precisely memoir, had a curious genesis. My son and I had gone to my father's sheep camp in the Sierra. One night around the campfire, the conversation turned to war and "a man's duty to serve his country." Even as I uttered it, that phrase sounded almost embarrassing in its old fashioned quality. The debacle that Viet Nam turned into had gone a long way toward destroying the credibility of war and patriotism with which my generation had grown up.
>
> Our talk went back to World War II, the war in which I had grown up. That war was probably the last one where words like my country, patriotism, duty and service would flame white hot.

My son knew I had gone to Africa in that war, but not as a member of the armed forces. He did not know why I, being exempt, even went. I tried to explain my own and my generation's attitude toward service to one's country. Again, the words seemed outdated and downright corny.

He was mystified at my fury at not being allowed to carry a gun into battle, my humiliation at being rejected by the armed forces because of a childhood heart murmur, and my desperate desire to go *overseas*.

Laxalt's son, Bruce, who would go on to be a trial lawyer and poet, asked why Laxalt had not written about his wartime experience. Laxalt responded that the subject was too painful and, what's more, "I wasn't the kind of writer who laments about his misunderstood youth." Eventually, however, he thought more about it, found an old journal filled with notes he had taken during his time in the Congo, where he has been stricken with malaria, and decided he could write a valid book about the experiences.

The memoir was filled with emotional intricacy which was noted by reviewer John Trent who wrote:

> The lean, carefully crafted 103-page book . . . takes the reader into the heart of darkest Africa in 1944. Young Laxalt (he was 21), on the run from his conflicted feelings, is tossed into the middle of diplomatic intrigue in Equatorial Africa during World War II's waning months, as agents of the Allies and Axis vie for uranium with which to build a secret bomb. Laxalt's prose, as always, is clear, athletic and enjoyable. . . . He introduces the reader to a variety of almost shadowy figures of questionable origin. . . . The most intriguing character of all is Laxalt. The book, he admits, is a look into one of the darkest periods of his life. . . . Laxalt's rejection by the military, and his furious reaction to desperately right the wrong by joining the overseas diplomatic service . . . was clearly a fecund period of experience in which much of the underpinning for all of the future great writing . . . was developed. Laxalt presents a vivid picture of a young man at a crossroads, where ultimate reward is found not in the netherworld of clandestine diplomatic machinations, but in the knowledge that familiarity and family are the things this preeminent Nevada writer holds nearest and dearest to his heart.

The reviewer knew Laxalt well when he focused on "familiarity and family," which was what Laxalt was addressing in a manuscript with the working title "A Basque Journal" to be published one year later as a new book about an old subject, as *The Land of My Fathers: A Son's Return to the*

Basque Country. Laxalt greeted the reader at the opening of the book with three quotes:

> "The Basque spirit is indefinable."—Laurent Apezteguy
>
> "There is one word which covers all the qualities that go to make up Basque character. That word is insularity."—Rodney Gallop
>
> "It is even doubtful if the Basques understand themselves."—*Anonymous*

He explained in an Author's Note:

> The tiny homeland of the Basques—barely a hundred miles in diameter—straddles the crest of the western Pyrenees Mountains between France and Spain. It is a land of deep oak forests, green mountain valleys, and the rugged seacoasts of the Bay of Biscay.
>
> In these mountains and on these shores dwell an ancient people called the Basques.

The book was met with enthusiasm by scholars, prepublication manuscript readers, and the general public, which included longtime readers of Laxalt books and magazine stories about his roots and seemed to always welcome more of the same because his work always brought new revelations.

"In *The Land of My Fathers,* there are many references to the common scenes of Basque rural life that have already appeared in Laxalt's earlier books, primarily in *In a Hundred Graves* and *A Time We Knew,* but also on occasion in *A Cup of Tea in Pamplona,*" writes Río. He cited activities ranging from farm life to pigeon hunting to smugglers, troubadours, folk dancers, and shepherds. He added that while some might see the book as "repetition or review of the scenes and motifs already common in Laxalt's literary output . . . if we analyze in detail each of the sections . . . it can be seen that Laxalt presents new data quite frequently and introduces variations in the perspective or in the tone he uses in his stories." He cited Laxalt bringing high prominence to Basque women being shrewd in the marketplace, creative in the origins of unique dances, and courageous in the lives of fishing village families.

> Little is heard about the wives who stay behind. Theirs is the task of keeping a household, feeding a family, acting the absent father's role as disciplinarian to children, coping with emergencies and injuries, bargaining with butcher, baker and cobbler, and finally, worrying that their

husbands will survive the storms at sea without being washed overboard with no chance of rescue. Though all attention is focused upon the fishermen . . . it is the wives who are the unsung heroes of a fishing village.

The University of Nevada Press, like most scholarly presses, required independent and unidentified readers to analyze manuscripts submitted by first-time and veteran writers alike. Laxalt's work was no exception even though he founded the press and brought regional, national, and international acclaim to it many times over. Sara Velez Mallea, managing and Basque acquisitions editor, sent one such review to Laxalt with a note. "I am enclosing a blind copy of the reader's report for your review and comments. . . . I would like to receive your reactions to this report in writing by mid-April if possible, so that I can share it with members of the editorial board."

The unidentified reader commented:

> Laxalt's 'Basque Journal' adds notably to his reputation as the premiere imaginative voice of the Amerikanuak. Here are the recognizable markers of his literary artistry: intriguing glimpses of Basque society and culture, provocative historical and biographical vignettes of the *paysans*, revealing descriptions of place and event, and numerous pithy sayings by and about Euskaldunak. Like the numerous brief sections of *In a Thousand Graves*, the abbreviated portraits in this manuscript add up to a mosaic of Basque character and culture.

The reader got the title of *In a Hundred Graves* wrong but went on to outline the strengths in the manuscript. "Any reader acquainted with Laxalt's previous writings will recognize here the terse, minimalistic, stylistic grace notes that characterize his writing. Other readers will be drawn to the familiar subjects Laxalt treats: Basque women and families, farmers and herders, the role of the Church, smuggling, and the powerful, persisting influences of tradition. Still other readers will recognize Laxalt's balance, as seen, for example, in his willingness to deal with darker subjects such as those in the 'Pantasha' and 'Bohemes' sections. So *YES*, this manuscript should obviously be published. It will add to the strong reputations of the author, the Press, and the Basque Book Series."

The text was accompanied by "An Album of Photos from the Basque Country" taken by Joyce Laxalt during their travels captured black-and-white images of Laxalt with an elderly aunt, a cousin poised with an upright rake in a field, fishing boats at moorings in the quaint but working harbor of Donibane Lohitzune, hillside farm houses in Lower Navarre where Theresa's family had lived, handball players smacking tiny balls at high speed toward the outside wall of a church, market day shoppers in the villages, shepherds and their flocks in the hills and sheep shearing and pig slaughtering on the farms.

The Press promoted *The Land of My Fathers* for what it called a "rare insight into the nature of the Basques and the isolated, beautiful mountain world where they have lived for centuries."

As *The Land of My Fathers* was being prepared for publishing, Laxalt was deeply into resurrecting an idea he had for a book over forty years earlier when he and his family were traveling in the Basque Country. It was to be a novel about rabies spreading through the livestock herds of Northern Nevada. The manuscript had been in a locker in the Laxalt vehicle that was broken into by thieves while the family watched a festival of music and dancing in Donibane Lohizune. The theft left Laxalt in despair with no way of putting the creative details of the unfinished story back together from memory. But the idea had lingered in his mind and in the late 1990s he turned to the Royal one more time to try to work the story into prose.

Laxalt began the story with the technique of suspense that he had used so well in other books:

> At the base of the jumble of boulders, there was a black hole that penetrated the hillside. The dozing coyote's attention was caught by a flutter of movement as the bat emerged from the hole.
>
> If the coyote were equipped to wonder about such things, he would have been surprised to see a bat come out into the daylight. Night was the time for bats to emerge from their subterranean chambers.
>
> The coyote watched as the bat fluttered erratically over the tops of the sagebrush that concealed the hole in the boulders. The bat seemed to have no hesitation at all, until it saw the coyote. Then its flight straightened as it clasped its webbed wings together and dived at the coyote. Never having been confronted by such an attack, the coyote raised its head in wonder. The next thing he knew, the bat had fastened itself on his nose, sinking its eyeteeth into the tender flesh.

The story was on its way. A *Salt Lake Tribune* review summed it up almost satirically before moving on to covering the book in more serious depth: "*Time of the Rabies* is short (92 pages) and simple. A rabid bat bites a coyote, the coyote bites a sheep, a dog gets bitten, the dog bites a teenage boy, cowboys shoot a lot of coyotes, sheepherders and cowboys fret, a teen-age girl cries for the teen-age boy, and her father's not too happy about that. The story takes place in the 1920s, when, according to a note at the start of the book, 'an episode of rabies sweeps through the sheep bands of Western Nevada.'"

The review then addressed Laxalt's style. "Laxalt writes in clean, unadorned prose, giving his stories a sense that suggests both large meaning and a young audience. For example, early in his new novella, he writes, "Sometimes a lamb died during birth, and at other times a mother would refuse to accept her lamb. Then the herders would skin a dead lamb, make a jacket out of its hide, and slip it on a motherless lamb. The orphan and a lambless ewe were then confined together in a pen until the lamb had suckled for the first time, so to be accepted by the mother who had lost her lamb in birthing."

The reviewer, noting Laxalt's linkage "to the closest of all relationships," commented that such a "paragraph might be found in a tenth-grade textbook" and added: "The result is a continuing tension underlying the narrative, a force that drove, for example, Steinbeck's *Of Mice and Men* and Hemingway's *The Old Man and the Sea,* two novellas on the American canon of great literature, both of which are widely assigned to high schools."

The *Dallas Morning News* commented:

> *Time of the Rabies,* a slender novella by Nevada writer and historian Robert Laxalt opens like a Disney nature commentary gone wrong. In the Disney manner, Mr. Laxalt's animal characters are described as if they were human; they wake up "out of sorts with the world" and feel pleasure, rage, joy and disgust. Mostly, though, they just feel bad. It's Old Yeller territory as Mr. Laxalt unleashes an apocalyptic vision of plague and terror on the rugged landscapes of the High Sierra, one from which no animal—and soon—no human—is safe. The rabies epidemic comes, hellishly enough from the depths of the earth, carried by a bat that emerges in broad daylight and flies straight into the face of a bemused coyote, drawing blood with its foam-flecked fangs. Joined by diseased lynxes and mountain lions, the coyote passes the virus along the food chain, attacking dogs, sheep and horses. The sheep and horses suffer and die in agony, the dogs turn on their human masters, and the remote ranches of Nevada become a backdrop for a ghastly elemental struggle for survival.

Publishers Weekly noted that when the rabies spread to a mountain lion that chased a ranch hand "it becomes clear that a full-blown epidemic is threatening the surrounding countryside." The review traced the story's growing drama of a young Basque apprentice herder falling into complicated love with the daughter of the principal rancher whose shotgun-armed cowboys battled the epidemic by killing off the stricken coyotes. "Though perhaps more suited to young adult audiences, the simple tale ably dramatizes a historic plague threatening man and beast alike."

In a brief afterword, Laxalt took the reader into the devastation:

> And so the crises passed . . . for . . . the sheep ranchers whose flocks had been ravaged by the disease that had appeared out of nowhere. No one knew where it had come from, but it was done with now. The desert hills were littered with the bones of coyotes, bobcats, wildcats, mountain lions. And even skunks. Many of them had been shot to death, but the greatest killer had been the disease itself. Like the scourges of Europe, the rabies had run its course, and normalcy had returned to the land.

Time of the Rabies would be the last of Laxalt's books published during his lifetime. But it would not be his last book.

The Legacy

Bob Laxalt knew about death. He knew he was close to it as a child when he was stricken by rheumatic fever and restricted to his bedroom and he knew about death when, at twenty-one, he watched others including himself suffer from malaria in his World War II service in the Congo. Each time, he fought back, first becoming a young athlete and boxer against the stern advice of his teachers and his mother who had restricted his physical activities and again as he recovered from the disease of the African jungle in the fresh scents of pine and sagebrush in the breezy air of his father's sheep camp high above Lake Tahoe.

Laxalt knew about death in his journalistic forays to the Nevada State Prison gas chamber to watch murderers who had taken others' lives lose their own at the hand of the state and he knew even more about death through his fiction when he created smugglers who would, through vengeance, kill their own compatriots as the penalty for breaking their honored codes of life.

Laxalt knew sadness in the deaths of his father and mother, Dominique in 1971 at age eighty-four after a long illness brought on by the ailments of strenuous life in the mountains and deserts, Theresa in 1978 at eighty-seven after a rigorous life that prompted a newspaper to hail her as a modern-day pioneer who built a family through love, dedication, and hard work.

Laxalt knew about his own pending death when his health deteriorated and his wife and children and caretakers provided comfort for him in the Washoe Valley home he and Joyce had built and filled with the antique furniture of their own families including the rolltop desk where he wrote in his study on the old Royal typewriter. And, knowing it, he did what he always did. He wrote—about life, his own, in his final book which would be entitled *Travels with My Royal.*

And on March 23, 2001, in Saint Mary's Regional Medical Center in Reno, where he had been treated for lower gastrointestinal bleeding after a long illness, Robert Peter Laxalt met his own death. He was seventy-seven.

The family gathered quickly and began informing his extended family and friends around the country and abroad. Monique Laxalt called me as a close friend. "We lost Pop this morning." The news was jolting. She asked me to join the family along with Monsignor Leo McFadden, a Catholic priest and journalist, at the end of that day to begin planning a memorial. I was so emotionally moved that after we finished our brief conversation and I set the phone down, put my skis on my car rack and drove to the nearby Mount Rose ski area on Slide Mountain, not far from the Laxalt sheep camp site at Marlette Lake, rode a chairlift to the top and took two fast runs down the steep Northwest Passage trails in an almost dazed gesture of respect for Bob. Back in the car, I used my mobile phone to call the AP bureau in Carson City to break the story. The news moved quickly around the world from Nevada's daily newspapers and broadcast stations and beyond to media in England, France, Spain, Argentina, and the Basque Country where editors put together their own obituaries.

Robert at home in Washoe Valley recovering from illness, circa 1999. Photograph by Reed Bingham.

The *Reno Gazette-Journal* published the story on the front page with bold headlines the next morning, Saturday, March 24, 2001.

ROBERT LAXALT: 1923–2001
Nevada author dies at 77
Impact on state extended beyond his books

The story by Gaye Delaplane identified Laxalt as one of Nevada's most renowned authors and summed up his books as notable for their simple yet elegant style that won him international acclaim. The story was accompanied by a color photograph of Laxalt's face showing a dimpled warm smile, his deep brown eyes dancing with genuine empathy, caught by staff photographer Marilyn Newton seven years earlier at a newsworthy moment. The editors selected a quote from an interview to accompany the photo, "I like people. That's why I've become a writer, because I like people"—Robert Laxalt. The caption beneath the photograph called Laxalt, in bold, capital letters, a "SILVER STATE FOLK HERO."

The New York Times, which had published reviews of several Laxalt books, carried a Reno-datelined story. University of Nevada Press marketing director Sandy Crooms, surprised at the pace of the developing news, said, "It's incredible. I'm just amazed at how quickly word has gotten around."

Joe Crowley, the retired university president who had established the Distinguished Author Chair honoring Laxalt, said Laxalt would be remembered along with Walter Van Tilburg Clark as one of Nevada's greatest authors and that as a teacher he made an indelible mark on his students. Through them, he has influenced the literature of the future. One of those students, Verita Black Prothro, remembered Laxalt's gift for getting the best out of the students. A family friend, Alan Abner, described Laxalt as a "strange combination—part rugged Westerner and yet sensitive and introspective." The *Reno Gazette-Journal* coverage dominated almost one third of its front page and continued over two more inside pages in the kind of extensive detail usually given to the deaths of major political or entertainment figures. Opinion page editor Bruce Bledsoe chose his words carefully for an editorial:

> He had drifted away from us of late—hidden away in his home, a rumor more than a reality, heard mainly in the voices of relatives and very close friends who relayed his health to the rest of us. But that is what

you do when the years weigh down like anvils and the days become mountains to climb. Little by little, you go away.

But if you are an artist, you never stop creating. If you are Renoir, you tie brushes to your arthritic hands and broad-brush the canvas. If you are Matisse, you work from your wheelchair or your bed with a long stick. And if you are Robert Laxalt, you pound the typewriter until the fingers will pound no longer, to give existence one more time to the beings who throng so impatiently inside your brain, demanding life.

You do not stop because in your late 70s you cannot always maintain the power and vision that dominated your maturity. You write because you must, because it is like breathing, because it is what you are. So if last year's *Time of the Rabies* seemed to some of us to somehow fray at the edges, to not quite go as far as it might, it demanded to be written nonetheless, and you sent it out into the world with the same hope that accompanied all your other children of ink.

And those of us who have loved your writing . . . turned to it as to a welcoming spring, nourished again by the prose that was still lean, the sagebrush land that was still stark and beautiful, to the men who were still solitary and passionate and proud—to a Nevada fading now, but held forever alive on your indelible pages.

The Associated Press dispatched a story by Sandra Chereb quoting Laxalt's brother Paul: "Someone once said that Bob was the Basque people's literary spokesman in America. But Bob's wonderful books spoke not just to Basques but to all the sons and daughters of immigrants, to those who love the American West and indeed all readers who enjoy simple but eloquent writing. I've always felt that he was Nevada's answer to Ernest Hemingway."

The family and close friends gathered at St. Theresa's Catholic Church for a funeral mass four days after Bob's death and escorted Joyce, Bruce, Monique, and Kristin to the small cemetery where he was laid to rest near the graves of his mother and father in the shadow of the Sierra Nevada. The wooden headstone was carved with the words "Maitatua" in Basque, meaning "Beloved," and in English: "A good father and an honest writer."

The next day, Wednesday, March 28, more than five hundred people filled the university's Nightingale Hall for a memorial service attended by Nevada's leading public officials and figures, writers, editors, painters and sculptors, students, academic leaders and business executives, and seasoned ranch families who traditionally frequented the state's little Basque hotels serving their hearty meals to continuing generations. The drama of the occasion was captured by writer Merlyn Oliver who observed that a most eloquent statement was made without words at the entrance to the auditorium.

"People arriving saw Laxalt's saddle, in the style of the Nevada buckaroo, with his straw hat propped over the horn. Next to it was his Royal Quiet Deluxe typewriter, placed on a small pedestal table with tiny wheels. Above, several framed photos conveyed a sense of this spiritual son of Nevada," she wrote in the Reynolds School of Journalism online magazine *Zephyr*. One photograph showed Laxalt on horseback, another in a tack room amid bits and bridles. The mood was noted by AP reporter Scott Sonner who described how Basque folk dancers, poets and politicians gathered to say goodbye to the author, teacher, and friend.

Laxalt's son Bruce, an attorney, said in a eulogy that his father was shaped by the times and seasons of his life:

> He was born an immigrant kid in the tiny hospital in Alturas, where his mother–two years before the wealthy young wife of a young-buck, up and coming, Basque rancher with a hundred thousand acre spread–was cooking in the camps after the sheep crash of '21.
>
> He grew up tough and scrappy in Carson, where she had moved her family for some semblance of stability—buying a house and forcing her kids to learn English—while her husband, now broke, trudged the mountains in the summer and the high deserts in the winter with the tiny herd he'd been able to save from the bankers.
>
> That's when the family grew tight, turned inward, grew clannish. Bascos weren't fashionable then. They were accented immigrants with old country ways in a Protestant world.

Bruce quoted Senator Pat McCarran's famous statement on the Senate floor favoring Basques when he was outlining immigration legislation that would enable them to enter the country as indentured servants imported as sheepherders. The senator declared, "Basques are not like white people." The implications were that they worked harder. Bruce spoke of Laxalt's bond with his brothers, saying they "grew close in a wordless way that even those in my generation cannot fathom to this day. And that time—that season—shaped him forever. . . ."

> And now is the time and the season for Robert Laxalt—the writer—to live and breathe forever in the lines and pages of his works—to live each day in the mountains and deserts, and in the hearts and souls of his readers. And now is the time and the season for Bob Laxalt—the teacher—

to live and breathe through the written voices of his students—and *their* students as they take the proud duty of passing the torch and continue the lonely work of slowly honing their craft.

Daughters Monique and Kristin read from the last part of the final chapter in *Sweet Promised Land* alternating a few paragraphs at a time as they gave voice to what their father had created. The audience, filled with so many who had revered the book, could almost recite the lines the daughters spoke:

> I saw a band of sheep wending their way down a lonely mountain ravine of sagebrush and pine, and I smelled their dust and heard their muted bleating and the lovely tinkle of their bells. I saw a man in crude garb with a walking stick following after with his dog, and once he paused to mark the way of the land. Then I saw a cragged face that that land had filled with hope and torn with pain, had changed from young to old, and in the end had claimed. And then, I did know it. We walked in silence down the wooded trail, and in a little while the voices died away.

Poet Shaun Griffin, who lived in Virginia City where Laxalt once shyly sought out the advice of Nevada's famed writer Walter Van Tilburg Clark, had spent many hours with Joyce and Bob Laxalt in their Washoe Valley home through the final days of illness. He rose to the podium to comment: "I can think of no writer who calls Nevada home who has not been influenced by Robert Laxalt" and then he read a poem he was inspired to write which he dedicated to Laxalt.

One by one ten speakers rose to the podium. Among them, Governor Kenny Guinn, President Emeritus Crowley, and Rollan Melton, a newspaper executive and *Reno Gazette-Journal* columnist, who said Laxalt was a master teacher who taught by his own incomparable work. Basque celebrations in song and dance brought drama and life to the ceremony's opening and close.

Few among the hundreds attending the memorial were aware that Bob's literary voice would find new life in a final book that would be published within two months of his death.

Only a few family members, close friends, and colleagues knew that Bob had been working on a special manuscript for nearly three years before his death. In it, he told the stories of how he had become a writer. He decided to call the book *Travels with My Royal: A Memoir of the Writing*

Life. He was notified in a letter from the University of Nevada Press September 26, 2000, six months before he died, that the manuscript had been approved for publication in the spring of 2001.

Bob had developed the book in sections, "Growing Up," "Writing Days," "Selected Books" and "How They Came to Be," "Genesis of a Trilogy," and a postscript, "The Library and I," which would be about learning to love books as a child and the gift of story telling that inspired him to become a writer. In the final chapter, "The Writing Life," he disclosed,

> Once having decided back then to become a writer, I hadn't the remotest idea of what was involved in the writing life. As a boy just growing into adulthood, I knew no writers, nor had I ever read anything about the lives they led. I knew nothing about what a writer writes, how a writer lives, how much money he makes, where a writer goes to find things to write about, what makes a story . . . and most important of all, where and to whom a writer goes for enlightenment on these myriad questions.
>
> I was to learn the answers through the years of growing up and the years that followed. They came in a slow and often painful process that never ended. I suspect they will continue to come all of a writer's life, until the day he puts his pen aside for the last time.

Travels with My Royal won immediate acceptance by Laxalt's analytical readers and, like three of his earlier books, was entered in competition for a Pulitzer Prize. Río said the book

> is a somewhat special posthumous work in-as-much as it does not contain the elements typical of such works. On the one hand, it is not an unfinished work, like *Juneteenth* by Ralph Ellison and *Of Time and the River* by Thomas Wolfe. . . . *Travels with My Royal* is not consistent with the model of the classic posthumous novel whose publication is achieved only through the determination of the author's family, in some cases to fulfill the writer's last wishes, as happened with John Kennedy Toole's excellent novel *A Confederacy of Dunces*. . . . We are talking about a manuscript that had already been completely finished by the author . . . and whose publication had been announced.

Río analyzed the varied sections of the book and concluded: "The final section . . . Selected Books . . . constitutes, beyond all doubt, the most noteworthy part of the whole work. Here Laxalt includes interesting observations on the genesis of some of his principal works and on the processes of creation involved, topics on which he had already spoken previously in different interviews . . . but which had not had literary expression until this point."

Travels with My Royal added to Laxalt's legacy that embraced not only his seventeen books but also his creation of the University of Nevada Press, his teaching literary journalism and magazine writing for eighteen years, his local, regional, national, and international awards and tributes. The legacy deepened with the creation of the Robert Laxalt Distinguished Writer Program by the Reynolds School of Journalism that would bring acclaimed journalists and authors annually to the Reno campus to meet with classes and then give a major public lecture and eventually expand to even broader Nevada humanities programs.

They have included William Albert Allard of the *National Geographic* who had worked with Bob in producing the book *A Time We Knew*. Another was veteran journalist and author Lou Cannon. As a young reporter he received encouragement from Laxalt who predicted that Cannon would one day turn his journalism into the authorship of books. He did so, as a Ronald Reagan biographer and in other books as well.

Among the other important figures selected for the lectureship of note is Isabel Wilkerson, who had won the 1994 Pulitzer Prize for feature writing as the Chicago bureau chief for *The New York Times* and, in so doing, became the first African-American woman to win a Pulitzer Prize in Journalism. Her book traced the immigration of African Americans from the Deep South to the northern and western cities of the country between 1914 and 1917 for opportunities to improve their lives. *The Warmth of Other Suns: The Epic Story of America's Great Migration* became a bestseller.

Mark Kurlansky, veteran *Chicago Tribune* correspondent in Spain and Latin America, was a most acclaimed Laxalt Distinguished Lecturer. The choice of the journalist-turned-author Kurlansky could not have been more appropriate, since, among the many other books he has authors is the best-seller *A Basque History of the World*.

Laxalt's legacy was not limited to such seasoned professionals, however. Bob's legacy reached into a younger generation with an honoree who was just the opposite in the 2005 selection of twenty-three-year-old Alicia Parlette who had graduated only a year earlier and taken a beginning copy editing job at the *San Francisco Chronicle*. She had been stricken with a rare form of cancer identified as alveolar soft part sarcoma and her doctors gave her the shocking diagnoses that her life was in jeopardy. She soon would become known to—and inspired by—hundreds of thousands of newspaper and magazine readers and television viewers worldwide who followed the story she would write about her disease. It would be called *Alicia's Story*. Scores of young students gathered at the Laxalt program to pay homage to Alicia who fought the disease for five more years and died surrounded by family and friends in a San Francisco medical center April 22, 2011. She was twenty-eight.

Still another Laxalt Distinguished Lecturer selection turned out to include a funny story. A major part of the legacy of Robert Laxalt had been his appointment by President Reagan to the National Council for the Humanities Endowment where his voice brought attention and focus during his Washington, D.C., meetings to the culture of the American West. During one of those meetings he would meet another author whom he didn't know and who didn't know him.

Rhodes scholar Clay Jenkinson had built a spirited storytelling career that stretched from impersonations of Meriwether Lewis and John Wesley Powell western explorations to White House residencies of Thomas Jefferson and Teddy Roosevelt. Jenkinson met Laxalt in the spring of 1989 when he received the Charles Frankel National Humanities Prize from President George H. W. Bush in the White House. Laxalt was there as a member of the National Council for the Humanities. Jenkinson recalled, in correspondence with me: "My family was there. I was standing in a corner feeling all alone in the universe, and unworthy, when a man I had never met came up to congratulate me and to urge me to relax and enjoy the event. He introduced himself as Robert Laxalt. I had never met him before nor, for that matter, even heard of him. He was dressed in a very handsome suit, white shirt and tie, and really fine cowboy boots. He did not tell me he was a writer or the brother of Paul Laxalt, just that he was on the National Council of the NEH . . . he shook my hand. Then he said, 'If you ever get to Nevada, come look me up.' He reached down and pulled up a pant leg—this was the White House—and took his wallet out of the top of his cowboy boot. He was wearing garish light blue socks with his dark suit. The card was rumpled and a little damp. I was absolutely charmed by his unassuming and generous manner. I immediately ordered a couple of his books."

So Laxalt's legacy of writing about the human spirit continues to be celebrated for new generations of both readers and writers just as his legacy has been commemorated through past acknowledgements of his work. Many honors were bestowed upon him during his lifetime and others posthumously.

Despite his national and international acclaim, his lack of ego throughout his career was noted in an interview I had with long-time friends Bill
Bliss, who first met Bob in their teenage caddying days at Glenbrook on the
Nevada shore of Lake Tahoe, and Gene Empey, who had taken the photograph that appeared on the back cover of *Sweet Promised Land*. Empey had
grown up on a ranch in Eastern Oregon and gone on to become a journalist and prominent Nevada businessman. We knew that Bob would have
chuckled when Gene looked at us and said he was just a cowboy and Bob
was just a sheepherder.

We talked about how Bob didn't regard himself as a famous writer
when we gathered together with our families for dinner at the little Basque
hotel restaurants in Reno and Gardnerville in the Carson Valley. We talked
about what all families talk about: how the weather was up in the mountains and how the rain added a fresh scent to the sagebrush. It came down
to a simple equation that pretty well summed up Bob Laxalt. If you were
a friend, you were a friend. That feeling flowed through his writing and
caused readers to welcome him not only as a storyteller but also as a friend
in their homes where his books are valued by generations.

This value was recognized when Laxalt's essay "The Library and I" was
read aloud to a hushed crowd at the Nevada State Library on Nevada Statehood Day October 31, 2003. It was then that a bronze plaque was dedicated in Bob's honor with the etched words, "In the years of my growing up
in tiny Carson City, the Nevada State Library was my second home." The
writer was, once again and finally, at home where *Sweet Promised Land* had
offered so much promise to so many.

The promise has been fulfilled. Robert Laxalt has taken his proper
place among the celebrated tellers of the often mythical and sometimes
brutally honest stories of the American West, from a long list of writers to
the magical filmmakers of Hollywood culminating with his one-time literary hero Walter Van Tilburg Clark and the forever acclaimed Mark Twain.
Laxalt may well become larger than either Clark or Twain in telling the
stories and perpetuating the literary landscape of the modern Nevada and
its setting in the American West.

Laxalt will always cause the reader to explore his roots as such a
storyteller. Was he forever the reporter of his youthful writing days or
was there an illusive mixture and perhaps even smooth blend as he rose
to literary heights? Did he abandon journalism for literature or build
upon it and carry its instinctive ways with him? Many of his students saw

him as autobiographical as he taught them how literature and journalism melded through the works of Hemingway, Steinbeck, Crane, and so many others who started out as he did and traveled as they did to their literary destiny. For readers who know him only through his literature, the challenge now is to determine how and why he came to be the unique storyteller that he was.

Endnotes

Preface

13   *Thérèse (Theresa)*: Thérèse was the official spelling of Robert Laxalt's mother's name. However, she took the spelling Theresa after her arrival in the United States. Therefore, when referring to her as girl, I have used Thérèse and when referring to her life in the United States I have used Theresa.

Chapter 1

16   *"new worlds opened up for me"*: Laxalt, "The Library and I," (Reno: Black Rock Press, University of Nevada, 1999). Fifth anniversary publication for the Nevada State Library and Archives, May, 27, 1999.

16–17   *what truly mattered to him and why*: Laxalt, *Travels with My Royal*, 138.

17   *warm woolen shirts of the sheepherder*: Laxalt, *Sweet Promised Land*, 23.

18   *write it as it happened*: Laxalt, *Travels with My Royal*, 140.

19   *simply were not coming to him*: Author conversation with Joyce Laxalt, October, 2009.

20   *the mere four chapters he had submitted*: Laxalt, *Travels with My Royal*, 141.

20–21   *"even of making it maudlin"*: Douglass, "Foreword," in *Sweet Promised Land*, xix.

21–22   *"boundaries of the western genre"*: Ronald, "Foreword," in *Sweet Promised Land*, ix–x.

22   *"Robert Laxalt will be there for you"*: Author recollection of Charles Kuralt commentary about Laxalt at Scripps Dinner, Reynolds School of Journalism, University of Nevada, Reno, May, 1984. Readers interested in this connection should consult the University of North Carolina's Southern Historical Collection's Charles Kuralt Collection, 1935–1997 (Collection Number: 04882), box 48, folder 634.

Chapter 2

24   *Liginaga-Astüe (Laguinge-Restoue)*: It is very common that place names in the Basque Country have two names: a French or Spanish and a Basque version. In this book, place names are given in Basque, with the French or Spanish version given in parenthesis at first mention.

23   *birth certificate was changed to Robert Peter Laxalt*: Río, *Robert Laxalt*, 23.

24   *writing about the running of the bulls*: Ibid., 25.

25   *Basque Country from his home in Paris*: "Notes on My Mother's Life and Family," Robert Laxalt papers, 85-09, box 13, Special Collections and Archives, University of Nevada Reno Libraries.

25   *never return her natal country*: Laxalt, *Child of the Holy Ghost*, 41–42.

27–28   *paid the whiskey and wine broker with cash*: Laxalt, *Travels with My Royal*, 7.

28   *"kept the 'Basque door' wide open"*: Paul Laxalt, *Nevada's Paul Laxalt*, 10.

28   *water daily for the silver-mining boomtown*: Cameron, *Above Tahoe and Reno*, 28.

29–30   *"I went to find refuge and solace"*: Laxalt, *Travels with My Royal*, 39.

Chapter 3

31   *"I developed an insatiable appetite for all these treasures," he would one day write:* Laxalt, "The Library and I."

31   *Albert Payson Terhune's* Sunnybrook Farm: This is not to be confused with Kate Douglas Wiggin's 1903 children's book, *Rebecca of Sunnybrook Farm.*

32   *restrictions caused him to fail to meet his goals:* Robert Bini interview with Laxalt's sister, Marie Bini, January 2010, shared with author.

33   *he could love each word:* Río, Robert Laxalt, 27.

33   *write like Mark Twain or Bret Harte:* Laxalt, *Travels with My Royal*, 51–54.

34   *tell of it in a book about the state:* Laxalt, *Nevada*, 8. This is the *Nevada* from the States of the Nation series, not *Nevada: A Bicentennial History*, published in 1977.

34   *the master of this rugged terrain:* Ibid., 10.

35   *"towered aloft three thousand feet higher still!":* Twain, *Roughing It*, vol. 1, 18; Cameron, *Above Tahoe and Reno* with text by Warren Lerude, 6–7.

35   *"it must surely be the fairest picture the whole earth affords":* Ibid.

35   *"tiny as ants grazing in green pastures":* Laxalt, *Nevada*, 10.

35–36   *shape him for the rest of his life:* Ibid., 10–11.

36   *"the only white guy on the Stewart Indian School boxing team":* Feature story, 1974 *Sierra Nevada Boxing Championships Program* magazine, Robert Laxalt papers, 85–09, box 13, Special Collections and Archives, University of Nevada Reno Libraries.

37   *fifteen to twenty amateur fights, John thought:* Author interview with John Laxalt, March, 2010.

38   *"did not demean them a bit":* Laxalt, *Travels with My Royal*, 49.

38   *He was upset that she had offended them:* Robert Bini interview with Marie Bini, January, 2010.

38   *in his first grade schoolyard:* Paul Laxalt, *Nevada's Paul Laxalt*, 14.

Chapter 4

41   *as the Basque of her birth:* Laxalt, *Travels with My Royal*, 30.

41   *"eyes still stuck with sleep":* Laxalt, *Sweet Promised Land*, 101.

41   *"spoke with a brogue":* Laxalt, *Travels with My Royal*, 22.

42   *"I'll talk to Momma":* Paul Laxalt, *Nevada's Paul Laxalt*, 21.

42   *"Mom didn't speak to us for two months":* Robert Bini interview with Laxalt sister Marie Bini, January 2010.

44   *"Yes, Sir!":* Laxalt, *A Private War*, 6.

46   *the personally devastating rejection:* Ibid., 10.

45   *"I just can't pass you":* Ibid., 11

45–46   *"Smells like draft-dodger to me":* Ibid., 12

46   *"helping my country in time of war":* Ibid., 13.

46   *"I hope I never see you again":* Ibid., 4.

Chapter 5

47   *different from his combat-bound shipmates:* Trent, *Silver & Blue*, University of Nevada Alumni Magazine, Reno, January 1999.

47   *saved the survivors:* Osborne, *World War II In Colonial Africa*, 193.

47–48   *sank 597 ships:* Churchill, *Closing the Ring*, 5, 673.

48   *"Now, you pass muster":* Laxalt, *A Private War*, 14–44 includes Laxalt description on ship, in code office assignment.

50   *white sandy beaches:* Citations for this paragraph, ibid., 27–29.

51   *"you'll be straddling the equator":* Ibid., 30.

51–52   *"it'd better that you don't know"*: Citations here from ibid., 41–42.
52   *guerrilla operatives fighting allied enemies*: "Office of Strategic Services," *Britannica Concise Encyclopedia*.
52   *"uranium is Belgian Congo"*: Einstein letter cited in Osborne, *World War II in Colonial Africa*, 31.
53   *the Pacific war four years later*: Ibid., 10.
53   *"Anger against my country was waning"*: Laxalt, *A Private War*, 66
53–54   *"Jumbo and Barbo will kill them pretty quick"*: Ibid., 69.
54   *"happier group we'll be"*: Ibid., 71–72.
54   *"I could not bear it I lose you two, too"*: Ibid., 75.
54   *"Your sister in Christ"*: Ibid., 76–77.
54   *"foolish things one does in an outrage!"*: Ibid., 78.

Chapter 6

55   *she rented a furnished apartment*: Robert Bini and author interviews with Marie Bini, January, February, April, 2010.
56   *"since you're a Basco, too"*: Laxalt, *Travels with My Royal*, 57.
56   *family could never hurt anyone*: Author interview with Theresa Supera, April 8, 2010.
57   *malaria attacks had stripped from him*: Ibid., 58.
59   *separated the campus from the little city*: Author interview with Joyce Laxalt, April, 2010.
59   *smitten at first sight of her*: Laxalt, *Travels with My Royal*, 71.

Chapter 7

65   *went to bed, shaken*: Author interview with Joyce Laxalt, April, 2010.
67   *"graduated last week from the University of Nevada" et al.*: Citations from newspaper stories in Robert Laxalt papers, 85–09, box 13, Special Collections and Archives, University of Nevada Reno Libraries.

Chapter 8

81   *"grace under pressure"*: Quoted by Dorothy Parker November 30, 1929 in *The New Yorker* as "Guts" and later popularized as "Courage."
81   *"Something very deliberate and calculated"*: Interview with Earl Biederman, *Nevada State Journal*, January 18, 1977, Robert Laxalt papers, 85–09, box 25, Special Collections and Archives, University of Nevada Reno Libraries.
82   *"It just took too long to die"*: Ibid.
84   *gunned down by Detroit mobsters*: Laxalt newspaper clippings, Robert Laxalt papers, box 25, Special Collections and Archives, University of Nevada Reno Libraries.
84   *senatorial hearings to explore Nevada mob activity*: *Reno Gazette-Journal*, April 19, 1981, Robert Laxalt papers, box 25, Special Collections and Archives, University of Nevada Reno Libraries.
84   *"Nevada's 20th Century pioneers"*: Ibid.
86   *"Two house-to-house soap salesmen"*: The AP in the *Tri City* (Washington) *Herald* March 13, 1952, Robert Laxalt papers, box 25, Special Collections and Archives, University of Nevada Reno Libraries; Harpster, "The Extraordinary Life and Lasting Legacy of Eccentric Nevada Millionaire La Vere Redfield," chapter 10.
87   *earning the trust of the millionaire*: Letter to *The American Weekly*, March 6, 1952, Robert Laxalt papers, 85–09, Box 9, Special Collections and Archives, University of Nevada Reno Libraries.
89   *"showgirls and tales of murder and suspense"*: American Weekly page, JVJ Publishing website. See www.bpib.com/illustra2/various2.htm (last accessed April 15, 2013).

89   *history of Nevada*: Referring to Laxalt, *Nevada*.

90   *"the carmine of her lips"*: Feature story, *The American Weekly*, May 1, 1949. Can be found in Robert Laxalt papers, 85–09, box 26, Special Collections and Archives, University of Nevada Reno Libraries.

91   *a rather banal killing*: Davis, "Lawless Elements," 246. Here is the story as told by Davis:

Farmer Peel was a singular character . . . When sober he was as mild and agreeable a gentleman as one could wish to meet, but when in liquor he was a demon. But, drunk or sober, his instinct was to kill . . . he bore the invidious title of "Chief," and had to be always ready to defend it; and he was careful that no one should ever get the drop on him. Thus when El Dorado Johnny, a silly little Irishman and fresh-comer, with pretensions as a bad man, walked into Pat Lynch's saloon one morning and casually asked if there were any Chiefs about . . .

"You probably intend that remark for me," said Farmer Peel, who was standing at the bar.

"Anyone can take it up that likes," replied Johnny.

"Very well; we'll settle it right now," rejoined Peel, "Come, out into the street."

Poor, guileless Johnny went out into the street as proposed, but Peel stopped at the doorway, and, as Johnny turned to look at him, fired a shot that dropped him dead. Peel was never punished for any of his Virginia City killings . . . the police did not appear anxious to meddle with him.

91   *factual accuracy in his UP journalism*: Author conversations with retired Nevada archivist Guy Rocha; social anthropologist William Douglass at the University of Nevada, Reno; and attorney Thomas R. C. Wilson II, February 2011.

Chapter 9

93   *as he turned to literary writing*: Laxalt, *A Lean Year and Other Stories*, author's note, xiii.

93   *the comments offered by the highly respected editor, Frederic Birmingham*: Ibid., xii.

95   *"and Old West types to Virginia City"*: Ibid., xiii.

96   *"the magic kingdom I knew nothing about"*: Laxalt, "Foreword," *The City of Trembling Leaves*, xiii.

96   *visit with him and his wife Barbara*: Ibid.

96   *firmly in the realistic tradition*: Benson, *The Ox-Bow Man*, 73.

97   *"did not look too forbidding"*: Laxalt, "Foreword," *The City of Trembling Leaves*, xiii.

97   *"dead tones of Mafia executioners"*: Ibid.

97   *alcoholic and religious hatred*: User "B. Berthold 'brad13,'" Amazon.com customer review, "High Sierra Drama," June 2, 2009. Available at www.amazon.com/The-Track-Walter-Tilburg-Clark/product-reviews/0884113892 (last accessed February 26, 2013).

97   *"reading* The Track of the Cat": User "Michael Barb," Amazon.com customer review, "Uneven but at times powerful evocation of Sierra Nevada," July 6, 2000. Available at www.amazon.com/The-Track-Walter-Tilburg-Clark/product-reviews/0884113892 (last accessed February 26, 2013).

98   *"flowed like a physical force"*: Laxalt, "Foreword," *The City of Trembling Leaves*, xiv.

101   *who had matriculated to book authorship*: Río, *Robert Laxalt*, 38–39.

Chapter 10

105   *create a news service and publications office*: Laxalt, *Travels with My Royal*, 93.

106–107 "*but I guess it must be*": Ibid., 21–22.

108   *"an old man"*: Laxalt, *Sweet Promised Land*, 25–26.

109   *both geographically and vocationally*: Author conversations with various Laxalt family members, March–May, 2011.

109   *Basque province of Zuberoa (Soule)*: The Basque Country has a long and complex history of naming places, with the same places generally having at least two names: a Basque name and a Spanish or French name. It is the policy of the Center for Basque Studies to use Basque place names, giving the French or Spanish version in parenthesis at the first mention.

109–110   *"will forget he ever lived in this country!"*: Río, *Robert Laxalt*, 24; Laxalt, *Sweet Promised Land*, 29–30.

110   *then shifted to the potential trip*: Ibid., 32–33.

112   *"that close to losing your job"*: Ibid., 62–63.

112   *forty-three theaters in thirty-four cities*: PaperPast Yearbook, www.paperpast.com/html/1953_boxing.html (last accessed April 15, 2013).

112–113   *in Paris on his way to the New World*: Laxalt, *Sweet Promised Land*, 82–84.

114   *"May you always be together!"*: Ibid., 120.

Chapter 11

117   *Reno campus full of turmoil*: Río, *Robert Laxalt*, 36; Laxalt, *Travels with My Royal*, 93–94.

117   *views on shared governance with the administration*: Kille, *Academic Freedom Imperiled*, 4–5.

117   *Stout said to the faculty when he first addressed*: Ibid., 7.

118   *"participation in university decisions and governance"*: Ibid., 10.

118   *"So it's back to burning the midnight oil"*: Laxalt, letter to Naomi Burton, January 15, 1954, Robert Laxalt papers, 85–09, box 1, folder "Writing Correspondence (mainly with Curtis Brown)," University of Nevada Special Collections and Archives, University of Nevada Reno Libraries.

119   *"even his interoffice memos were good reading"*: Río, *Robert Laxalt*, 36.

119   *"I was not about to bring it up"*: Laxalt, *Travels with My Royal*, 93–94.

119–120   *lower admissions standards for high school graduates*: Hulse, *The University of Nevada*, 52–59.

120   *"deal with the situation"*: Ibid., 54.

121   *"half judicial, half-theatrical" hearing*: Ibid., 54–55.

121   *"so polarized the academic community"*: Ibid., 55.

121   *"punished for attempting to exercise it"*: Ibid.

122   *burn Stout in effigy from the world famous Reno Arch*: Observations by author who participated in the march as an eighteen-year-old freshman student; Hulse, *A Centennial History*, 57; Kille, *Academic Freedom Imperiled*, 83–85.

123   *"I'll be swinging from the chandeliers"*: Laxalt, letter to Naomi Burton, April 1, 1957, Robert Laxalt papers, 85–09, box 1, folder "Correspondence and Notes: Sweet Promised Land," Special Collections and Archives, University of Nevada Reno Libraries.

123–124   *"common goals in mutual confidence and respect"*: Hulse, *A Centennial History*, 59–60.

124   *elected from academic colleges and professional units*: Ibid., 60–61.

Chapter 12

125–126   *"father's reactions to the trip"*: Burton, letter to Robert Laxalt, August 28, 1953, Robert Laxalt papers, 85–09, box 1, folder "Correspondence and Notes: Sweet Promised Land," Special Collections and Archives, University of Nevada Reno Libraries.

125–126   *"jarring experience to see him in a closed room"*: Laxalt, letter to Naomi Burton, August 31, 1953, Robert Laxalt papers, 85–09, box 1, folder "Correspondence and Notes:

Sweet Promised Land," University of Nevada Special Collections and Archives, University of Nevada Reno Libraries. See the story of the runaway priest on pages 68–71; the story of Dominique's bankruptcy and the death of his sheep on pages 147–51; compare the final two sentences of this letter to the eventual opening of *Sweet Promised Land*, "My father was a sheepherder, and his home was the hills."

127   *did not know which way to go*: Laxalt, *Travels with My Royal*, 140.

127   "*It wasn't invented*": Ibid.

127   "*home was the hills*": Ibid.

127   "*The story found itself*": Ibid., 141.

127–128 "*never have known in America*": Ibid., 142.

128   "*Don't you know that?*" and "*the voices died away*": Laxalt, *Sweet Promised Land*, 157–58.

128–129 "*The sweet promised land of Nevada*": Clark, *The City of Trembling Leaves*, 452.

131   *incorporated into the University of Nevada in 1972*: Río, *Robert Laxalt*, 45.

131   "*there never were*": Ibid., 45–46.

131   "*live in Sodom and Gomorrah*": Douglass, "Foreword," in Robert Laxalt, *Sweet Promised Land*, xiv.

131   "*writers who can still do that*": Correspondence regarding movie production of *Sweet Promised Land* see letters dated July 6, 1977 and October 11, 1979 from Los Angeles literary agent Marjel De Lauer; April 21, 1978 from Playboy Productions associate Betsy Cramer; letter dated January 21, 1980 and undated letter from De Lauer, Laxalt notes for inclusion in *Travels with My Royal*, 117–19, Robert Laxalt papers, 85–09, box 13, Special Collections and Archives, University of Nevada Reno Libraries; this section is also based on author conversations with Robert and Joyce Laxalt over several years.

132   *the voyage to Le Havre*: Author conversation with Monique Laxalt, July 2011.

Chapter 13

133   "La vie est chere": Literally, "life is dear." Notes for inclusion in *Travels with My Royal*, 117–19, Robert Laxalt papers, 85–09, box 13, Special Collections and Archives, University of Nevada Libraries.

133–134 "*errant French drivers*," "*when it comes to the French*," and "*slow-moving teachers*": All ibid.

136–138 "*not even Christ*," "*without making it attractive?*," "*and finally me?*," "*musty dungeons of corridors*," "*a magic wand*," and "*thank them for me?*": Laxalt, "From a Balcony in Paris," in Griffin, *The River Underground*, 3, 4, 4–5, 5, and 15, respectively. Attribution to the original publication in *Cosmopolitan* is made in the acknowledgments, xvii.

138   *the echo of Joyce's voice*: Author conversations with Shaun Griffin, Monique Laxalt, and Kristin Laxalt, July 2011.

139   "*left in a state of despair*": Laxalt, *Travels with My Royal*, 146–47; Río, *Robert Laxalt*, 48; memo to author from Monique Laxalt, July 2011.

139   *isolated, inward-looking culture*: Taken from Laxalt, *The Land of My Fathers*, xiii. The literature on Basque culture is vast and I am no specialist, interested readers may want to see for a general introduction Xamar, *Orhipean: The Country of Basque*; Douglass and Zulaika, *Basque Culture*.

139–140 *wondered if the snake story might be told as a book*: Laxalt, *Travels with My Royal*, 145

140   "*a death-dry rattle*" and "*curled lazily and sensuously about him*": Laxalt, "The Snake Pen," in *A Lean Year and Other Stories*, 174.

141   *the characters' fears*: Laxalt, *Travels with My Royal*, 150.

141   "*people deal with fear and prejudice*": Ibid., 148–49.

141–142   *"deceptively straight forward story"*: Press clippings from Robert Laxalt collection, Robert Laxalt papers, 85–09, Special Collections and Archives, University of Nevada Reno Libraries.

Chapter 14

144   *"That's all we need, another university press"*: Laxalt, *Travels with My Royal*, general discussion 94–97, quote, 95.

145   *"period of meteoric growth"* and *"university is to become distinguished"*: University of Nevada Press report to Nevada Legislature with outline of purpose, Robert Laxalt papers, 85–09, box 10, Special Collections and Archives, University of Nevada Libraries.

145   *edited by Laxalt and his limited staff*: Hulse, *The University of Nevada*, 95.

145   *Reifschneider's botany book and Hulse's history fit the startup plan*: Author interview with James Hulse, May 2010.

145–146   *won a five hundred thousand dollar grant*: University of Nevada Press outline of purpose, Robert Laxalt papers, 85–09, box 10, Special Collections and Archives, University of Nevada Reno Libraries.

146   *the special series was born*: Oiarzabal, *A Candle in the Night*, 4–7.

146   *"Mexico, Argentina and Venezuela"*: University of Nevada Press outline of purpose, Robert Laxalt papers, 85–09, box 10, Special Collections and Archives, University of Nevada Reno Libraries.

146–147   *claimed Laxalt was "juggling funds"*: "Mello Conflict," *Reno Evening Gazette Journal* editorial May 5, 1979, August 12, 1979, These and the newspaper articles cited below can be found in the Robert Laxalt papers, 85–09, box 10, Special Collections and Archives, University of Nevada Reno Libraries.

147   *"increase of salary to my wife"*: "Nevada press director calls Mello claims 'Absurd,'" *Reno Evening Gazette*, August 2, 1979.

147   *"additional money they could receive"*: "Mello seeks investigation: wife turns down promotion," *Reno Evening Gazette*, July 31, 1979.

147–148   *"10 years of outside editing."*: "Press Director Defends Funds," *Las Vegas Sun*, August 3, 1979.

148   *Mello's committee approved*: "Mello Defends Press Budget," *Las Vegas Sun*, August 2, 1979.

148   *"I never threatened Mr. Laxalt"*: "Laxalt letter claims Mello threats," *Nevada State Journal*, August 4, 1979.

148–149   *"a cum laude graduate"*: "Mello considers lawsuit in Laxalt flap," *Reno Evening Gazette*, August 4, 1979.

149   *"why we shouldn't all be fired"*: *Nevada State Journal*, August 4, 1979.

149   *extra $7,500 for both editing and advertising*: Ibid.

149   *"appears that those charges are without foundation"*: "University Press: Early Audit Study Clears Office of Juggling Funds," *Nevada State Journal*, August 12, 1979.

149   *"the aura of a witch-hunt"*: "Mello Conflict," *Reno Evening Gazette, Nevada State Journal*, August 12, 1979.

150   *"No victory here for the chairman of Ways and Means"*: Author interview with President Emeritus Joe Crowley of University of Nevada, April 2012.

150–151   *"however, they may be classified"*: Forum, *Reno Evening Gazette*, August 15, 1979,

151   *"the heritage of our state for future generations"*: Discussion here above and below from report to legislature, Laxalt papers, 85–09, Special Collections and Archives, University of Nevada Libraries

152   *faculty members and representatives*: Ibid., membership list of UNR deans of the College of Engineering, Charles R. Breese, and the College of Arts and Sciences, Rebecca

S. Stafford; faculty from English, Dr. Thomas L. Clark and Dr. Mark A. Weinstein, both of the University of Nevada, Las Vegas; Basque Studies, Dr. William A. Douglass, UNR; libraries, Mr. Harold H. J. Erickson, UNLV; oral history, Mrs. Mary Ellen Glass, UNR; social sciences, Dr. George F. Isham, Clark County Community College; history, Dr. Ralph J. Roske, UNLV, and Dr. Wilbur S. Shepperson, UNR, and George M. Herman, UNR faculty emeritus.

152   *critical attention from thrift-minded legislators*: Author interview with Nick Cady, March 2012.

152–153 *scathingly critical book about the state*: James Hulse interview, May 2010.

153   *membership looked like a Who's Who of Nevada*: Author collection, Friends of the University of Nevada Press booklet listing membership from Carson City and Washington, D.C., executive branch leadership including George Abbott, George Dickerson, Leslie Gray, Peter Laxalt, Thomas R.C. (Spike) Wilson, Clifton Young and Frankie Sue Del Papa, physicians Dr. Fred Anderson and Dr. Louis Lombardi, rancher Molly Knudtsen as regents, businessmen Preston Hale and Gene Empey, rancher Ted Bacon, scion of Tahoe pioneer family William W. Bliss, community leaders Nancy Cashell, Francis Crumley, Gloria Mapes and Lilly Fong, marketing expert Mark Curtis, author and Fleischmann Foundation trustee Sessions (Buck) Wheeler, newspaper publishing executives E. W. (Ted) Scripps, Rollan Melton and Warren Lerude. Chancellor of the University of Nevada System Dr. Robert Bersi served as finance advisor and *ex-officio* member.

153   *"friendly attitude of many Nevada politicians"*: Author correspondence with Cameron Sutherland, March 2012.

153–154 *"sensed his fine hand and encouragement"*: Author interview with Bill Bliss, February 16, 2012.

154   *his concentration on Basque topical books*: Author conversations with many Laxalt colleagues and family members through the years.

154–155 *novel Wheatfield as his most important work*: Author interview with William A. Douglass. April 2012; Douglass email February 11, 2012 to author about his English translation of the Spanish language biography, *William A. Douglass: Mr. Basque* by Miel Elustondo, published in 2011 in Pamplona, Spain by Pamiela.

155   *"I am just a Basque who writes"*: David Río, "Robert Laxalt: A Basque Who Writes," *EuskoNews & Media*, July 20–27, 2001. Available at www.euskonews.com/0132zbk/elkar13201en.html (last accessed April 16, 2013).

Chapter 15

159   *"how to write a 5,000-word story"*: Notes for class on writing for *National Geographic*, Robert Laxalt papers, 85–09, box 23, Special Collections and Archives, University of Nevada Libraries.

160   *"he feels should be incorporated"*: Notes for undated talk, Robert Laxalt papers, 85–09, box 23, Special Collections and Archives, University of Nevada Reno Libraries.

160–161 *"doesn't know what he's talking about"*: Laxalt, *Travels with My Royal*, 102.

160–161 *"50 million readers around the globe"*: Notes for undated talk, Robert Laxalt papers, 85–09, box 23, Special Collections and Archives, University of Nevada Reno Libraries.

161   *Everyone was five years older*: Author conversation with Monique Laxalt, July 2011; Jackie Leonard story, "Page One," *Reno Evening Gazette*, August 13, 1966; Laxalt, *Travels with My Royal*, 125–31; Río, *Robert Laxalt*, 66–75.

164   *Douglass as editor*: Author conversation with William A. Douglass, August 2011.

165   *could not learn enough to do a novel in an authentic way*: Laxalt, *Travels with My Royal*, 157–63; Río, *Robert Laxalt*, 67; Laxalt, *In a Hundred Graves*, 1–11.

165   *"am filled with amazement"*: Laxalt, *In a Hundred Graves*, 3.

166   *He created a "Grand House"*: Citations in this paragraph, respectively, ibid., "Our Grand House," 4; "School in a Fortress," 5; "The House of No Name," 6–8; Dominika in "A Lesson of the Eyes," 8–9; "Perpetual Spring," 10–11; and "Our Town Crier," 12–13.

166   *the American accepted as ritual*: Laxalt, *Travels with My Royal*, 160; *In a Hundred Graves*, "Eyes of the Dove," 160.

166   *"and an embroidered covering,"* and *graphic realities of Basque farm life*: Ibid., "Basque Kitchen," 160–61; "Acceptance," 29–32.

167   *"pumped out in a jet"* and *"we drank wine over the smoldering heap"*: Ibid., 31, 32.

167   bertzolari *(singular) or* bertsolariak *(plural)*: Laxalt provides two spellings, "Bertzolari" in *In a Hundred Graves*, 33, "bertsolariak" in *Travels with My Royal*, 162.

167   *"at least a diversion on a rainy night"*: Laxalt, *In a Hundred Graves*, "The Basque Troubador," 32–40, quote 40.

167–168   *"The healer is the seventh son of seven sons"*: Quotes in this extract a collage from ibid., quotes: "The healer," in "The Healer," 43; "There was a funeral," in "Homecoming," 53; "Today was market day," in "A Newborn Lamb," 63; "Last night while the valley," in "April," 65; "There was an auction of horses," in "Victor's Horses," 79; "He had always wanted," in "The Monk," 81; "Ramon is my cousin's, " in "Ramon," 138.

167–168   *"flaxen braids fly in the wind"*: Ibid., "Peace," 132–33.

168–169   *"sing or their ability to dance"*: Río, *Robert Laxalt*, 68.

169   *"William Carlos Williams and Hemingway"*: Reviews, Robert Laxalt papers, 85–09, box 31, Special Collections and Archives, University of Nevada Reno Libraries.

Chapter 16

171   *"The time has come to say goodbye"*: A Basque journal manuscript with edits (photocopy), Robert Laxalt papers, 85–09, box 30, Special Collections and Archives, University of Nevada Reno Libraries. Comparing this to the published version of *The Land of My Fathers* is illustrative of how the editing process changed this piece.

Chapter 17

175   *"word isn't good 24 hours"*: Río, *Robert Laxalt*, 41.

175   *Bob's journalistic eye made him a keen political observer*: Author conversations with Basque Studies Program and literary colleague William Douglass, long-time Paul Laxalt aide, press secretary, and chief of staff Ed Allison, August, 2011.

176   *"the children of immigrants all know"*: Laxalt, *Sweet Promised Land*, special edition, 181.

176   *"the final trigger"* and *"the end of our privacy as a family"*: Ibid., 182.

177   *Paul phoned him the next day with his decision to run*: Paul Laxalt, *Nevada's Paul Laxalt*, 82–83.

177   *Bell had been stricken with a heart attack and died*: Ibid., 84.

178   *"costing the taxpayers millions of dollars"*: Ibid., 94.

178   *The race was down to the wire*: Ibid., 49.

179   *"an awful nothing in between"*: Laxalt, *Sweet Promised Land*, special edition, 182.

179   *Pearson did so curiously*: Paul Laxalt, *Nevada's Paul Laxalt*, 100.

179   *"the son of a Basque sheepherder could one day be governor?"*: Ibid., 101.

181   *"skimming in certain casinos"*: Ibid., 124; See also Governor's race 1966 news release, Robert Laxalt papers, 85–09, box 11, Special Collections and Archives, University of Nevada Libraries.

181   *"we'll find out in a hurry"*: Paul Laxalt, *Nevada's Paul Laxalt*, 124.

181   *"the rumors of skimming were hard to combat*: Farmer, *Gaming Regulation in Nevada*, 2006.

181   *"this childish war with the FBI"*: Governor's race 1966 news release, Robert Laxalt papers, 85–09, box 11, Special Collections and Archives, University of Nevada Libraries.

182   *"put an end to the hearings"*: Farmer, *Gaming Regulation in Nevada*, 2006.

183   *it had become, in effect, the property of the Basque people*: Author conversation with William A. Douglass, August 2011.

184   *"his duty lay in his own lifetime"*: Laxalt, *Sweet Promised Land*, special edition, 186.

185   *"it was as if both had"*: Urza (Laxalt), *The Deep Blue Memory*, 85–86.

185   *"and usually both"*: Ibid., 90.

185   *"murder in his eyes"*: Ibid., 92.

186   *black-and-white judgmental thinking*: Author conversation with Monique Laxalt, August 2011.

186–187 *"a place of protection," "corner by the window, silent," "put the opponent in his place," "the eyes of the voters," "the top of the table," "in Reno, filling it,"* and *"the background rhythm of their home"*: Urza (Laxalt), *Deep Blue Memory*, 92–94; *"the background rhythm of their home"*: Ibid., 13.

187   *sister Suzanne was a Catholic nun*: Paul Laxalt, *Nevada's Paul Laxalt*, 198–200

187   *"We used it well"*: Author interview with Jerry Dondero, September 2012.

188   *"pull the plug"*: Conversations with Laxalt aides Ed Allison and Greg Ferraro, November 2012.

Chapter 18

189   *"and on old card tables"*: Laxalt, "The Other Nevada," *National Geographic* 145 (June 1974), 733.

189   *"Las Vegas was salted into the middle"*: Teaching notes, Robert Laxalt papers, 85–09, box 23, Special Collections and Archives, University of Nevada Reno Libraries.

191   *"that is the other Nevada"*: Laxalt, "The Other Nevada," 760.

196   *"traversing forty peaks exceeding 10,000 feet"*: Laxalt, *Travels with My Royal*, 107–8.

Chapter 19

197   *"more formalized histories"*: Robert Laxalt, *Nevada*, preface, n.p.

198   *"the said and unsaid"*: Ibid.

198   *"past of the state"*: Río, *Robert Laxalt*, 130.

198   *"interpretive monograph on Nevada's history"*: Rocha, *Idaho Yesterdays*, Spring Edition, 30–31.

201   *"And what's going to happen now?"*: Author interview with Rocha, February, 2011.

202   *"on a first-name basis"*: Chan, *Pacific Historical Review*, 145.

203   *"and occasional talk," "what was to become Nevada," "Help yourself, but don't be a hog," "the founder of Las Vegas,"* and *"enduring essence of land and seasons"*: Laxalt, *Nevada*, 21, 40, 89, 102, 127, respectively.

204   *"combined with delightful anecdotes"*: University of Nevada Press promotional copy, author's files.

Chapter 20

205   *Sangre de Cristo Mountains of New Mexico*: Laxalt, "New Mexico's Mountains of Mystery," *National Geographic*, vol. 154, no. 3, September 1978, 416–36. All following quotations are from the article.

209   *"I got up in the first light"*: Laxalt, "Last of a Breed: The Gauchos," *National Geographic*, vol. 158, no. 4, October 1980, 478. The following quotes are from the same article, pages 482, 490.

213   *"For days on end the fearsome tempests"*: Laxalt, "The Indomitable Basques," *National Geographic,* vol. 168, no. 1, July 1985, 69–71.

Chapter 21

216   *"independent minded spirit"*: Author correspondence with E. W. (Ed) Scripps III, August 2011.
217   *"three of my five undergraduate years"*: Author correspondence with John Evan Frook, August 2011.
218–219 *"especially his modesty"*: Río, *Robert Laxalt,* 19–20.
219   *developed an outline with topical headlines*: Teaching notes, Robert Laxalt papers, 85–09, box 23, Special Collections and Archives, University of Nevada Reno Libraries.
220–221 *"Bob was the obvious choice"*: DeChick, "Teaching Is a Pleasure for UNR's Distinguished Author Laxalt," *Reno Gazette-Journal,* November 27, 1988, 5.
221   *"I was one of the wheedlers"*: Author conversations with John Metzker, March 2010, correspondence, August 2011.
222   *"epitomized the greatness of Northern Nevada"*: Author conversation with Metzker, March 2010, Metzker letter to Joyce Laxalt, January 9, 2002.
223   *Black that she surely had stories, including books, to write*: Author conversations with Verita Black Prothro, August, September 2011.
224   *"Porched Suitcases"*: Griffin, ed., *The River Underground,* 323–38.
224   *"woke from the dream and walked to our cars"*: Author correspondence with Shaun Griffin, September 2011.
225   *bronchodilator medications to his lungs*: Author correspondence with Laxalt daughter Dr. Kristin Laxalt, M.D., August 2011.
225–226 *a special student-produced book*: Barker, ed., *Nevada Sampler,* 10.
226   *"submitted a sample of my work to Robert Laxalt"*: Author correspondence with Chuck Alvey, August 2011.
227   *in a Pulitzer Prize entry*: Author introduction text, author files.
227   *"Reno bureau of the United Press"*: Laxalt text, Scripps dinner, author files.
228   *"Robert Laxalt will be there for you"*: Author recollection, Scripps Howard Dinner, University of Nevada, Reno, Nevada, 1984.

Chapter 22

229   *"what I was trying to accomplish"*: Teaching notes, Robert Laxalt papers, 85–09, box 23, Special Collections and Archives, University of Nevada Libraries. Ellipses are in original and follow style of reporting notes.
230   *black-and-white drawings were hauntingly poetic*: Sullivan, *The New York Times Book Review,* May 18, 1986, 15.
230   *"gain in money they lose in conscience"*: Banegas, *Reno Gazette-Journal,* November 4, 1985, 1D.
232   *"the welfare of his family"*: Laxalt, *Travels with My Royal,* quote here and below from pages 177–84.
234   *"deserves a place on the same shelf with those works"*: Author's personal files.

Chapter 23

235   *"claim his reward at the throne"*: Urza, *Solitude,* vii.
237   *cast him into a Franco jail*: Author conversation with Laxalt during a monument project fund-raising trip to the Basque Country, May 1988.
237–238 "this tribute to our heritage": Urza, *Solitude,* 9.
238   *immediately set off a controversy among potential donors*: Ibid., 17–18, 20.

238   *rose to prominence as a sculptor*: Author's collection, Basque government booklet
       Basque Country, Navy Pier, May 1984, 7; Urza, *Solitude*, 18.

239   *"herder symbol would be expressed,"* and *"put in that position,"*: Urza, *Solitude*, 20–21.

239   *Laxalt advised that Basques*: Ibid., 16.

240   *"human character for peoples of all nations"*: Ibid., 29–30.

242   *the pilots repeatedly flew back to German bases*: Author recollection of the mayor's and
       Laxalt's conversation in Gernika.

242   *rallied for democracy over fascism from fifty-two countries*: Author research for my
       previous book *American Commander in Spain*, conversations with Oiarbide in Spain,
       Urza in Reno.

243   *Americans sent letters of support*: Urza, *Solitude*, letters here and below from pages
       33–38.

244   *"economic and political achievements"*: Reno Gazette Journal, August 28, 1989.

246–247 *"we dedicate to our herders"*: Urza, *Solitude*, 26–28.

247   *"feel very much like the American people"*: Reno Gazette-Journal, February 28, 1989.

Chapter 24

249   *"My approach was wrong"*: Land, *Reno Gazette-Journal*, September 1, 1989, 1D; Land,
       University of Nevada *Silver & Blue*, June, 1992, 21. Author conversation with Barbara
       Land, July 2011. All reviews footnoted in this chapter are from Robert Laxalt papers,
       85-09, box 31, Special Collections and Archives, University of Nevada Reno Librar-
       ies.

250   *"authenticity of the trilogy is founded"*: Laxalt, *Travels with My Royal*, 185–86.

251   "the greatest Nevada writer": Evans, *Las Vegas Review*, November 12, 1989.

253–254 *"with authentic charm"*: Allen, *The New York Times Book Review*, September 24,
       1989.

254   *"sense of growth and a sense of change"*: Western American Literature, vol. 25, no. 3,
       November 1990, 289–90.

254   *"the resolution of her life"*: Laxalt, *Travels with My Royal*, 189.

254–255 *"prayers every morning and night"*: Laxalt, *Child of a Holy Ghost*, 9.

255   *"the cruelty of village life"*: Río, *Robert Laxalt*, 103.

256   *"for literary collections"*: Rome, *Literary Journal*, November 15, 1992, 101.

256–257 *"It is a fiction book"*: Akinaga, *Reno Gazette-Journal* story, and Trissell, *Nevada Appeal*
       story, without publishing dates.

257   *"I'll give you a report"*: Letter from Emilie Jacobsen, March 5, 1993, Robert Laxalt
       papers, 85-09, box 31, Special Collections and Archives, University of Nevada Reno
       Libraries.

257   *"best to Joyce and God Bless"*: Letter from Mike Horan, February 9, 1993, Robert Laxalt
       papers, 85-09, box 31, Special Collections and Archives, University of Nevada Reno
       Libraries.

258   *"is related in the book"*: Laxalt, *Travels with My Royal*, 196.

258   *"living in a dream world"*: Laxalt, *The Governor's Mansion*, 18.

259   *"love have missed very much"*: Ibid., 8–9.

260   *"slick packaging of candidates"*: Publishers Weekly, September 12, 1994.

260   *Río believed well-founded, "politics on the protagonist's family,"* and *"first steps in the
       world of politics"*: Río, *Robert Laxalt*, 110–11, 113.

260–261 *"Laxalts have become prominent Americans"*: Davies, *The Maverick Spirit*, 128 in chap-
       ter 8, essay by Cheryll Glotfelty.

Chapter 25

264   *a shunt was placed*: Author correspondence with Laxalt daughter Kristin Laxalt, M.D., October and August 2011.

264   *"the pure love of writing"*: Author conversation with Laxalt daughter Monique Laxalt, October 2011.

264   *"in both pictures and words"*: Author correspondence with William Albert Allard, August 2011.

264–265 *"a chronicle of that time"*: Allard and Laxalt, *A Time We Knew*, n.p.

265   *"an appropriate complementary text"*: Río, *Robert Laxalt*, 85.

266–267 *"looked and was stubborn"*: Laxalt, *Dust Devils*, 2.

267   *"it lacks emotional intricacy"*: *Publishers Weekly*, September 22, 1997.

267–268 *"my desperate desire to go overseas"*: Laxalt, *A Private War*, ix.

268   *"holds nearest and dearest to his heart"*: Trent, *Silver & Blue*, January/February, 1999.

268   *a manuscript with the working title "A Basque Journal"*: Author conversation with Margaret Dalrymple of the University of Nevada Press, October 2011.

269   *"ancient people called the Basques"*: Laxalt, *The Land of My Fathers*, xiii.

269   *"occasion in* A Cup of Tea in Pamplona*"* and *"tone he uses in his stories"*: Río, *Robert Laxalt*, 88.

269–270 *"the unsung heroes of a fishing village"*: Laxalt, *The Land of My Fathers*, 18–19.

270   *"mosaic of Basque character and culture"*: Sara Velez Mallea letter February 19, 1998 attaching unidentified reader review, Robert Laxalt papers, 85–09. box 13, Special Collections and Archives, University of Nevada Reno Libraries.

271   *"eyeteeth into the tender flesh"*: Laxalt, *Time of the Rabies*, 1–2.

271–272 *"sheep bands of Western Nevada"*: Naparsteck, *Salt Lake Tribune*, September 3, 2000.

272   *"elemental struggle for survival"*: McNamee, *Dallas Morning News*, February 11, 2001.

273   *"threatening man and beast alike"*: *Publishers Weekly*, August 28, 2000.

273   *"normalcy had returned to the land"*: Laxalt, *The Time of the Rabies*, afterword, n.p.

Chapter 26

275–276 *lower gastrointestinal bleeding after a long illness*: Author conversation with Laxalt's daughter Kristin Laxalt, M.D., October, August 2011.

277   *"SILVER STATE FOLK HERO"*: *Reno Gazette-Journal*, March 25, 2001.

277   *"amazed at how quickly word has gotten around"*: *Reno Gazette-Journal*, March 24, 2001.

278   *"Nevada's answer to Ernest Hemingway"*: *The Associated Press*, March 23, 2001.

279   *"immigrants with old country ways in a Protestant world"*: Bruce Laxalt Memorial Service Speech, March 28, 2001, provided to author by Pam Sutton, December 2011.

280   *"little while the voices died away"*: Laxalt, *Sweet Promised Land*, 176.

281   *"pen aside for the last time"*: Laxalt, *Travels with My Royal*, 216.

281   *entered in competition for a Pulitzer Prize*: *Reno Gazette-Journal*, September 29, 2001 story about nomination.

281   *"publication had been announced"* and *"expression until this point"*: Río, *Robert Laxalt*, 139.

282   *They have included*: Paige Williams, *The New York Time*; Alicia Parlette, *San Francisco Chronicle*; Lou Cannon, *The Washington Post* and Reagan biographer; Clay Jenkinson, National Humanities Scholar and author; James D. Houston, novelist; Isabel Wilkerson, *The New York Times* and author; Stephen G. Bloom, journalist and author; Rebecca Solnit, journalist and author; Mark Kurlansky, journalist and author.

282   *turn his journalism into the authorship of books*: *Reno Gazette-Journal*, November 4, 2006; Cannon text, author files.

283   *Many honors were bestowed upon him*: In 1978, The Nevada State Council of the Arts presented Laxalt with the Decade Award. That same year, Governor Mike O'Callaghan presented him a citation for "exemplary service to the state." In 1982, The Friends of the Library named Laxalt a Distinguished Nevada Author. In 1984, the Board of Regents honored him as a Distinguished Nevadan. In 1986, the City of San Sebastian in Spain presented Laxalt with the prestigious "Tambor de Oro" (Golden Drum) Award for his contributions to the Basque Country through his writing. In 1988, The Friends of the Library inaugurated the Nevada Writer's Hall of Fame with Laxalt and Walter Van Tilburg Clark as its first laureates. In 1988, the Alumni Association named Laxalt Alumnus of the Year. In 1998, Texas Christian University included Laxalt's work in The Literary Chronology of the American West. In 1999, the *San Francisco Chronicle* listed *Sweet Promised Land* among the 100 Best Nonfiction Books of the Twentieth Century by an Author from the Western United States. In 2003, Nevada Statehood Day, Nevada Humanities and the Nevada Center for the Book—as part of the Literary Landmarks Register of the Friends of Libraries USA—held a special ceremony to unveil Laxalt's own Literary Landmark, a bronze plaque on the wall of the Nevada State Library.

Bibliography

Robert Laxalt Books

The Violent Land: Tales the Old Timers Tell. Reno: Nevada Publishing Co., 1953.

Sweet Promised Land. New York: Harper & Brothers, 1957.

A Man in the Wheatfield. New York: Harper & Row, 1964.

Nevada. New York: Coward-McCann, Inc., 1970.

In a Hundred Graves. Reno: University of Nevada Press, 1972.

Nevada. States of the Nation Series. New York: Coward-McCann, 1970.

Nevada: A Bicentennial History. New York: W. W. Norton & Company, 1977.

A Cup of Tea in Pamplona. Reno: University of Nevada Press, 1985.

The Basque Hotel. Reno: University of Nevada Press, 1989.

A Time We Knew: Images of Yesterday in the Basque Homeland. Photographs by William Albert Allard. Reno: University of Nevada Press, 1989.

Child of the Holy Ghost. Reno: University of Nevada Press, 1992.

The Governor's Mansion. Reno: University of Nevada Press, 1994.

A Lean Year and Other Stories. Reno: University of Nevada Press, 1994.

Dust Devils. Reno: University of Nevada Press, 1997.

A Private War: An American Code Officer in the Belgian Congo. Reno: University of Nevada Press, 1998.

The Land of My Fathers: A Son's Return to the Basque Country (With photography by Joyce Laxalt). Reno: University of Nevada Press, 2000.

Time of the Rabies. Reno: University of Nevada Press, 2000.

Travels with My Royal: A Memoir of the Writing Life. Reno: University of Nevada Press, 2001.

Robert Laxalt Magazine Articles

"The Challenge of El Dorado Johnny." *The American Weekly.* Hearst Newspapers Sunday Magazine Supplement, May 1, 1949.

"Down to His Last Million: LaVere Redfield Wasn't Greatly Upset when Burglars robbed him of $2,500,000." *The American Weekly.* Hearst Newspapers Sunday Magazine Supplement, April 13, 1952.

"What Has Wide-Open Gambling Done to Nevada." *Saturday Evening Post* Vol. 225 No. 12, September 20, 1952.

"From a Balcony in Paris." *Cosmopolitan,* August, 1964. (Reprinted by Shaun T. Griffin, *The River Underground: An Anthology of Nevada Fiction.* Reno: University of Nevada Press, 2001.)

"Basque Sheepherders, Lonely Sentinels of the American West." *National Geographic* Vol. 129 No. 6, June 1966.

"New Mexico: The Golden Land." *National Geographic* Vol. 138 No. 3, September, 1970.

"Golden Ghosts of the Lost Sierra." *National Geographic* Vol. 144 No 3, September, 1973.

"The Other Nevada." *National Geographic* Vol. 145 No. 6, June, 1974.

"Life in the Enduring Pyrenees." *National Geographic* Vol. 146 No. 6, December, 1974.

"New Mexico's Mountains of Mystery." *National Geographic* Vol. 154 No. 3, September, 1978.

"Gauchos: Last of a Breed." *National Geographic* Vol. 158 No. 4, October, 1980.

"16th Century Basque Whaling in America." *National Geographic* Vol. 168 No.1, July, 1985.

"Unconquerable Chasm: Exploring the Grand Canyon." *National Geographic Traveler* Vol. 1 No. 1, Spring, 1984.

General Bibliography References

Barker, Cristi, ed. *Nevada Sampler: Introducing Eleven Nevada Writers.* Reno: Mountain Shadow Press, 1995.

Basterrechea, Nestor. *Basque Country.* Vitoria, Arada, Spain: Eusko Jaurlaritza Basque Government, 1984.

———. *Bastepretxea Antologica*. Madrid: Museo Espanol De Arte Contemporaneo, 1987.

Benson, Jackson J. *The Ox-Bow Man: A Biography of Walter Van Tilburg Clark*. Reno: University of Nevada Press, 2004.

Clark, Walter van Tillburg. *The City of Trembling Leaves*. New York: Random House, 1945. Reprinted by the University of Nevada Press, 1991.

Davis, Sam P. "Lawless Elements." In *The History of Nevada*, Volume 1, edited by Sam P. Davis. Reno: The Elms Publishing Co., 1913.

Douglass, William A. "Foreword." In *Sweet Promised Land*, Robert Laxalt, ix–xiix. Reno: University of Nevada Press, 1986.

Douglass, William and Joseba Zulaika. *Basque Culture: Anthropological Perspectives*. Reno: Center for Basque Studies, 2007.

Elustondo, Miel. *William A. Douglass: Mr. Basque*. Pamplona: Pamiela, 2011.

Farmer, Guy. *Gaming Regulation in Nevada: The First Sawyer Administration*. Reno: University of Nevada Oral History Program, 2006.

Glotfelty, Cheryll. "Creating Culture in the Desert." In *The Maverick Spirit: Building the New Nevada*, edited by Richard O. Davies, 114–132. Reno: University of Nevada Press, 1999.

———. "Foreword." In *Travels with My Royal*, Robert Laxalt, xiii–xxi. Reno: University of Nevada Press, 2001.

Griffin, Shaun. *The River Underground: An Anthology of Nevada Fiction*. Reno: University of Nevada Press, 2001. See also entry under "A Balcony in Paris" in Laxalt articles.

Houston, James D. *Snow Mountain Passage: A Novel of the Donner Party*. San Diego: A Harvest Book, Harcourt, 2001.

Hulse, James W. *The Nevada Adventure: A History*. Reno: University of Nevada Press, 1966.

———. *The University of Nevada: A Centennial History*. Reno: University of Nevada Press, 1974.

———. *Forty Years in the Wilderness: Impressions of Nevada 1940–1980*. Reno: University of Nevada Press, 1986.

Hulse, James W., Leonard F. Goodall, and Jackie Allen. *Reinventing the System: Higher Education in Nevada, 1969–2000*. Reno: University of Nevada Press, 2002.

Kille, J. Dee. *Academic Freedom Imperiled: The McCarthy Era at the University of Nevada.* Reno: University of Nevada Press, 2004.

Laxalt, Paul. *Nevada's Paul Laxalt: A Memoir.* Reno: Jack Bacon & Company, 2000.

Laxalt, Robert. An Inventory of the Robert Laxalt Papers Collection No. 85–09, box 25. Special Collections and Archives, University of Nevada Libraries.

———. "Epilogue." In *Special Edition: Sweet Promised Land* 177–186. Reno: Paul Laxalt U.S. Senate Campaign, 1974.

Lerude, Warren. *American Commander in Spain: Robert Hale Merriman and the Abraham Lincoln Brigade.* Reno: University of Nevada Press, 1986.

Melton, Rollan. *Sonny's Story: A Journalist's Memoir.* Reno: University of Nevada Oral History Program, 1999.

Oiarzabal, Pedro. *A Candle in the Night: Basque Studies at the University of Nevada.* Reno: University of Nevada Oral History Program, 2007.

Osborne, Richard. *World War II in Colonial Africa: The Death Knell of Colonialism.* Indianapolis: Riebel-Roque Publishing Company, 2001.

Parlette, Alicia. *Alicia's Story, Cancer, Despair, Hope, Faith.* San Francisco: San Francisco Chronicle Press, 2005.

Río, David. *Robert Laxalt: The Voice of the Basques in American Literature.* Reno: Center for Basque Studies, 2007.

Ronald, Ann. "Foreword." In *Sweet Promised Land.* Robert Laxalt, ix–xx. Reno: University of Nevada Press, 2007.

Urza, Carmelo. *Solitude, Art and Symbolism in the National Basque Monument.* Reno: University of Nevada Press, 1993.

Urza, Monique. *The Deep Blue Memory.* Reno: University of Nevada Press, 1993.

Wheeler, Sessions and William W. Bliss. *Tahoe Heritage: The Bliss Family of Glenbrook, Nevada.* Reno: University of Nevada Press, 1992.

Wilson, Thomas, ed. *Nevada, Portfolio of Paintings: The First Hundred Years.* Reno: Harolds Club, 1964.

Xamar. *Orhipean: The Country of the Basques.* Iruña-Pamplona: Pamiela, 2006.

Index

Warren Lerude is co-author of a best seller, *American Commander in Spain: Robert Hale Merriman and the Abraham Lincoln Brigade*, and author of the text of another best seller, *Robert Cameron's Above Tahoe and Reno.* He is a former editor and publisher of the *Reno Evening Gazette* and *Nevada State Journal* newspapers at which he led a team of three journalists to win the Pulitzer Prize in Journalism for Editorial Writing in 1977. He has served as professor of media law, management, and professional internships for three decades at his alma mater, the Reynolds School of Journalism, University of Nevada, Reno. He and his wife Janet live in Reno and San Francisco.